The RHS Encyclopedia of Practical Gardening

GARDENING

TECHNIQUES

ALAN TITCHMARSH

Editor-in-chief Christopher Brickell
Technical Editor Kenneth A. Beckett
Editor of the revised edition David Joyce

MITCHELL BEAZLEY

The Royal Horticultural Society's Encyclopedia of Practical Gardening © Reed International Books Limited 1981

The Royal Horticultural Society's Encyclopedia of Practical Gardening: Gardening Techniques © Reed International Books Limited 1981, 1993

First published 1981
Reprinted 1982, 1984, 1986, 1988, 1989, 1990
Revised edition published 1993, reprinted 1993

ISBN 1 85732 976 7

Edited and designed by Mitchell Beazley, an imprint of
Reed Consumer Books Limited
Michelin House, 81 Fulham Road, London SW3 6RB
and Auckland, Melbourne, Singapore and Toronto

Contents

Introduction

The craft of gardening remains fresh and fascinating because there is always something to learn; but what all gardeners need is a knowledge of principles and basic techniques. This volume of *The Royal Horticultural Society's Encyclopedia of Practical Gardening* provides the essential information to allow anyone to garden with "green fingers". The techniques that are explained here can be utilized in the fruit and vegetable garden and the greenhouse as well as where hardy ornamental plants are grown. Many have been tried, tested and improved over the years but modern advances and short cuts have also been included. Accompanying the text are step-by-step line drawings that provide clear guidance on how to tackle a task.

How the book is organized

The book is arranged to be of particular help to the gardener who is tackling a new plot or one which is overgrown or neglected, so the first pages deal with the soil types likely to be found and their inherent problems. Advice and clear instruction are given on drainage, soil cultivation, modification and enrichment so that the ground can be brought into a fertile and workable state before planting and basic construction begins.

The section on Cultivation Techniques provides instruction on the techniques that a gardener will need to master, from simple propagation (covered in detail in a companion volume) to the cultivation of crops. Weather and climate and their effects on the garden are discussed in detail, as are the complexities of plant names and plant breeding.

A major section on Garden Design and Construction provides an outline of basic design and the positioning of plants. The section goes on to cover construction tasks such as building a rock garden and a pool, the role of fences and screens, and plant supports. This is followed by an exhaustive account of the Tools and Machines needed by the gardener. The methods of using the major basic and specialist tools are illustrated, as are the tools themselves. Tools are for use and this section ensures that the gardener has full knowledge of the best way to put his equipment to work.

The section on Special Techniques covers areas such as raising and planting bedding plants, constructing miniature gardens, planting up and caring for window boxes, and renovating neglected borders, lawns, trees and shrubs and roses.

Finally, the use of the garden for leisure is covered in the section on Living in the Garden. Construction of barbecues, sandpits and swings is linked with the laying out of pitches for games and the precautions necessary when children and pets use the garden.

The glossary at the beginning of the book, and the section on The Year in the Garden at the end, are designed to be used both individually as reference aids and in conjunction with the main text. The glossary (pages 4-9) lists 300 gardening terms from all areas of horticultural specialization. Its aim is to allow the gardener, novice or expert to look up a concise definition of a term or process with which he is unfamiliar.

Safety

One theme that runs throughout the book is the need for gardeners to be safety conscious. Power tools, electrical equipment and chemicals, for example in the form of pesticides, are valuable aids to gardening, but careless handling or storage can lead to serious accidents. A few simple measures will minimize risks: always wear appropriate clothing, especially stout footwear when digging, using cultivating equipment or power tools; use only equipment that meets recognized safety standards; check and service equipment regularly; protect any outdoor electrical circuit with a Residual Current Circuit Breaker; wear rubber gloves when mixing and applying chemicals; and store all chemicals securely out of the reach of children and animals.

3

Glossary 1

Abort Failure to develop properly; usually refers to flowers or their parts.

Acid Describes soil with a pH of below 7.

Adventitious buds Growth buds that arise without any direct relation to the leaves, usually in response to a wound.

Adventitious roots Roots that develop from stems.

Aeration The process of spiking a lawn in order to allow air into the soil and relieve compaction.

Alkaline Describes soil with a pH over 7.

Annual A plant that completes its life-cycle within one growing season.

Anthers The pollen-producing structures at the apices of the stamens of a flower.

Anti-desiccant Chemical used as a spray to reduce water loss when transplanting trees and shrubs in the dormant season. Especially useful with evergreens and conifers.

Apex The tip of a stem, hence apical bud, the uppermost bud on the stem, and apical shoot, the uppermost stem on a system of branches.

Apical bud The bud at the shoot tip.

Apical dominance Used of a terminal or apical bud which inhibits the growth of lateral buds and grows more rapidly than they do.

Axil The upper angle between a leaf, or leaf-stalk, and the stem from which it grows.

Bacteria Parasitic or saprophytic single-celled micro-organisms. Many are beneficial but some cause diseases.

Bare-root plant A plant lifted from the open ground (as opposed to a container-grown plant).

Bare rootstock Rootstock lifted from the open ground to be used for bench grafting.

Bark-ringing The removal of a ring of bark from the trunk of an unfruitful tree to check shoot growth.

Base dressing Fertilizer applied immediately before sowing or planting.

Bedding plant A plant used for temporary garden display, usually in spring or summer.

Bench grafting Grafting on to a rootstock that is movable – that is, a pot-grown or a bare rootstock.

Biennial A plant that completes its life-cycle over two growing seasons.

Blanching The exclusion of light from an edible vegetable to whiten the shoots.

Blindness A condition in which a shoot or bud fails to develop fully and aborts.

Bloom Either a blossom, or a natural white powdery or waxy sheen on many fruits and leaves, or an abnormal white powdery coating of fungus on galled leaves.

Bolting Producing flowers and seed prematurely.

Bonemeal Bones ground to a powder and used as a fertilizer.

Bottom heat The warmth, normally provided artificially, from under the compost in, for example, a propagator.

Bract A modified, usually reduced, leaf that grows just below the flowerhead.

Branched head A branch system on a tree in which there is no central leader shoot.

Brassica The cabbage, cauliflower and turnip genus of the family Cruciferae.

Break The development of lateral shoots as a result of pruning a shoot to an axillary bud.

Broadcast To distribute seed evenly over the entire seedbed, as opposed to sowing in rows.

Bud The embryo shoot, flower or flower cluster, hence growth bud, flower bud.

Bud burst The period at the end of the dormant season when new buds begin to swell and produce leaves or flowers.

Budding A method of grafting using a single growth bud rather than part of a stem with several buds.

Bulb An underground storage organ that consists of layers of swollen fleshy leaves or leaf bases, which enclose the following year's growth buds.

Bulbil A small bulb, formed in the leaf axil on a stem or in the inflorescence.

Bulblet Very small bulbs that develop below ground on some bulbs.

Cap A hard crust on the soil surface.

Capillarity The process by which water will rise above its normal level.

Carpeting plant A plant whose stems take root as they spread; also known as a carpeter.

Catch crop A rapidly maturing crop grown between harvesting one vegetable and sowing or planting the next on the same ground.

Central leader The central, vertical, dominant stem of a tree.

Chard The young stems of salsify, seakale, beet or globe artichokes.

Chelated Describes a special formulation of plant nutrients, which will remain available in alkaline soils.

Chitting The germination of seeds or sprouting of potatoes prior to sowing/planting.

Chlorophyll The green pigment present in most plants, by means of which they manufacture carbohydrates.

Chlorosis The abnormal yellowing or whitening of foliage when a plant fails to develop normal amounts of chlorophyll.

Climber A plant that climbs by clinging to objects by means of twining stems with hooks or tendrils, or more generally, any long-stemmed plant trained upwards.

Clone A plant propagated vegetatively, with identical characteristics to its parent.

Compost, garden Rotted organic matter used as an addition to or substitute for manure.

Compost, seed and potting Mixtures of organic and inorganic materials, such as peat, coir, sand, and loam, used for growing seeds, cuttings and pot plants.

Conifer A tree or shrub that bears its seeds in cones.

Contact insecticide An insecticide that kills pests by direct contact.

Contractile roots Roots of bulbs and corms that contract in length, thereby pulling the organ deeper into the soil.

Copper naphthenate A liquid timber preservative which is harmless to plants once it is dry, unlike creosote.

Cordon A normally branched tree or shrub restricted by spur pruning to a single stem.

Corm A solid, swollen stem-base, resembling a bulb, that acts as a storage organ.

Cotyledon A seed leaf; usually the first to emerge above ground on germination.

Crocking The use of small pieces of clay flower pot placed concave-side down in a pot or container over the drainage hole to facilitate drainage.

Crown Either the basal part of an herbaceous perennial plant from which roots and shoots grow, or the main branch system of a tree.

Cultivator A tool used to break up the soil surface to improve its texture. A rotary cultivator, or rotavator, has revolving tines or blades and is power-driven.

Current year's growth/wood The shoots which have grown from buds during the present growing season.

Cutting A detached piece of stem, root, or leaf taken in order to propagate a new plant.

Deciduous Describes a plant that loses all its leaves at the end of the growing season.

Dead-head To remove the spent flowers or the unripe seedpods from a plant.

Dibber A tool that is pushed into the soil to make a planting hole.

Dicotyledon A flowering plant that produces two seed leaves at germination.

Die-back The death of branches or shoots, beginning at their tips and spreading back towards the trunk or stem.

Disbudding The removal of surplus buds or shoots that are just beginning growth.

Dot plant Bedding plant used to give height or contrast to carpet plant arrangements.

Double leader Two shoots competing as leaders on a tree, each trying to assert apical dominance.

Dressing A material such as organic matter, fertilizer, sand or lime that is incorporated into the soil. A top dressing is applied to the surface only, without being dug in.

Dribble bar A sealed, perforated tube attached to a watering can spout that enables weedkiller or other liquid to be dribbled on to plants or soil.

Drills Straight furrows, narrow and shallow, in which seeds are sown.

Dwarf pyramid A tree pruned to form a pyramid-shaped central-leader tree about 7ft (2.1m) high.

Earth up Mounding earth around the base and stems of a plant, e.g. potato.

Espalier A tree trained against a support with a vertical main stem and tiers of horizontal branches.

Etiolation The blanching of foliage and lengthening of stems caused in green plants by insufficient light.

Evergreen A plant that retains its foliage for more than one year.

Eye Used to describe a growth bud, particularly of roses, vines and potato tubers.

Fallowing Allowing land to remain uncropped for a period.

Family A group of related genera. For example, the genera *Poa* (meadow grass), *Festuca* (fescue) and *Agrostis* (bent) all belong to the family of grasses, Gramineae.

Fan A shrub or tree in which the main branches are trained like the ribs of a fan against a wall, fence or other support system.

Glossary 2

Fertilizer Material that provides plant food. It can be organic, i.e. derived from decayed plant or animal matter, or inorganic, i.e. made from chemicals.

Flowers of sulphur Pure yellow sulphur in finely powdered form, used to reduce the pH of some soils.

Flushes Irregular successive crops of flowers and fruit, as on perpetual strawberries.

Foliar feed A liquid fertilizer sprayed on to, and partially absorbed through, the leaves.

Foot The base of the main stem of an herbaceous plant.

Forcing The hastening of growth by providing warmth and/or excluding light.

Friable Describes a fine, crumbly soil with no hard or wet lumps.

Fritted trace elements A special formulation of plant nutrients, which will remain available to plants in alkaline soils.

Frost-lifting The loosening and lifting of plants in the soil after hard frost.

Fungicide A substance used for controlling diseases caused by fungi and some bacteria.

Gall An abnormal outgrowth of plant tissue.

Genus (plural genera) A group of allied species in botanical and zoological classification.

Germination The development of a seed into a seedling.

Grafting Propagation by uniting a shoot or single bud of one plant – the scion – with the root system and stem of another – the stock or rootstock.

Growing point The extreme tip of roots or shoots.

Growth bud A bud that gives rise to a shoot.

Habit The natural mode of growth of a plant.

Half-hardy A plant unable to survive the winter unprotected but not needing all-year-round greenhouse protection.

Half-standard A tree grown with 3-4ft (90-120cm) of clear stem.

Harden off To acclimatize plants raised in warm conditions to colder conditions.

Hardy Describes a plant capable of surviving the winter in the open without protection.

Heeling in The storing of plant material, upright or inclined, in a trench which is then filled in with soil and firmed.

Herbaceous perennial See Perennial.

Herbicide Synonym for weedkiller.

Hormone weedkiller Chemicals which, when applied to weeds, affect their growth, often causing the stems to extend rapidly before the plant collapses and dies.

Host A plant that harbours, or is capable of harbouring, a parasite.

Humidity The amount of water vapour in the atmosphere. Relative humidity is the amount of water in the atmosphere, relative to it being saturated, at a particular temperature. (Warm air will hold more water than cool air.)

Humus Fertile, organic matter that is in an advanced stage of decay.

Hybrid A plant produced by the cross fertilization of two species or variants of a species.

Incipient roots Roots that develop from stems; they frequently abort.

Inflorescence The part of a plant that bears the flower or flowers.

Insecticide A substance used to kill injurious insects and some other pests.

Lanceolate Describes a leaf that is much longer than it is wide, and is shaped like the head of a lance.

Lava The active immature stage of some insects. The larva of a butterfly, moth or sawfly is known as a caterpillar, a beetle or weevil larva as a grub, and a fly larva as a maggot.

Lateral A side growth that develops at an angle from the main stem of a plant.

Layering Propagating by inducing shoots to form roots while they are still attached to the parent plant.

Leaching The removal of soluble minerals from the soil by water draining through it.

Leader shoot The shoot that is dominating growth in a stem system, and is usually uppermost.

Leaf axil See Axil.

Leaf-fall The period when deciduous plants begin to shed their leaves.

Light The glass or plastic covering of a cold frame.

Lime A compound that contains calcium or calcium with magnesium, added to the soil to reduce acidity.

Line out To plant out young plants or cuttings in temporary positions.

Loam A fertile soil with balanced proportions of clay, sand and humus.

Long Tom A pot about half as deep again as a normal pot.

Maiden A one-year-old tree or shrub.

Manure Bulky material of animal origin added to soil to improve its structure and fertility.

Mature A plant that can produce flowers and, hence, reproduce sexually.

Mechanical digger *See* Cultivator.

Micro-organisms A microscopic animal or plant organism that can cause plant disease. Micro-organisms are beneficial when decomposing plant and animal residue to form humus.

Mole plough A plough pulled through the soil to form a drainage tunnel.

Monocotyledon A flowering plant that produces only one seed leaf.

Mosaic A patchy variation of normal green colour; usually a symptom of virus disease.

Mound layering An alternative term for the technique of stooling.

Mulch A top dressing of organic or inorganic matter, applied to the soil around a plant.

Mutant or Sport A plant that differs genetically from the typical growth of the plant that produced it.

Naturalized Describes plants grown in natural surroundings where they increase of their own accord and need little maintenance. Also plants established in an area, although they are not native to it.

Nitrate A fertilizer containing nitrogen that can be natural, such as potassium or sodium nitrate, or synthetic, such as calcium nitrate.

Nymph The active, immature stage of some insects and mites.

Offsets Small bulbs produced at the base of the parent bulb; also a young plant developing laterally on the stem close to the parent.

Organic matter Matter consisting of, or derived from, living organisms. Examples include farmyard manure and leaf-mould.

Ornamental A plant grown for its decorative qualities.

Over-winter Refers to the means by which an organism survives winter conditions.

Pan A hard layer of soil beneath the surface.

Parasite An organism that lives on, and takes part or all of its food from, a host plant; usually to the detriment of the latter.

Perennial A plant that lives for more than three seasons and usually much longer.

Perlite A neutral, sterile, granular medium derived from volcanic rock. Used as a rooting medium and in potting, cutting and seed composts.

Pesticide A chemical used to kill pests or to control pests and diseases.

Petiole The stalk of a leaf.

pH The degree of acidity or alkalinity. Below 7 on the pH scale is acid, above it is alkaline.

Phosphatic fertilizer Fertilizer with a high proportion of phosphorus.

Photosynthesis The process by which a green plant is able to make carbohydrates from water and carbon dioxide, using light as an energy source and chlorophyll as the catalyst.

Pinching (or Stopping) The removal of the growing tip of a shoot.

Planting mark The slight change in colour on the stem of a bare-root plant, indicating the depth at which it was formerly planted.

Plunge outside To bury container plants up to the pot rims in ash, peat or sand beds to protect the roots from frost in winter.

Pollination The transference of pollen from the male to the female parts of a flower.

Polymer A natural or synthetic material added to a growing medium to increase its water-holding capacity.

Potash (K_2O) A component of all balanced fertilizers, supplying the mineral potassium, which is essential for plant growth.

Pot-bound The condition reached by a pot plant when its roots have filled the pot and exhausted the available nutrients.

Presser board A piece of flat wood with a handle used to firm and level compost.

Pricking out The transplanting and spacing out of seedlings.

Propagation The production of a new plant from an existing one, either sexually by seeds or asexually, for example by cuttings.

Proteins Organic nitrogenous compounds synthesized by plants from simple substances. An essential component of living cells.

Quicklime Chalk or limestone which has been burnt in a kiln. It is caustic and will burn foliage and skin, so the milder hydrated lime is usually employed in reducing soil acidity.

Rambler Roses producing long, flexible basal canes, trained on walls, fences and screens.

RCCB (Residual Current Circuit Breaker) A safety device that cuts off power to electrical

Glossary 3

equipment if there is any leakage of current to earth.

Recurrent flowering The production of several crops during one season more or less in succession.

Regulatory pruning Pruning to remove crossing, crowded and weak shoots and branches.

Relative humidity See Humidity.

Renewal pruning Pruning to maintain a constant supply of young shoots.

Resistant Describes a plant that is able to overcome completely or partially the effect of a parasitic organism or disorder. It also describes a pest or disease that is no longer controllable by a particular chemical.

Rhizome A creeping horizontal underground stem that acts as a storage organ.

Rhizomorph A root-like mass of fungal threads, by means of which certain fungi spread through the soil, e.g. honey fungus.

Riddle To sieve soil, compost or leaf-mould.

Rod The main, woody stem of a vine.

Rootball The soil or compost ball formed among and around the roots of a plant.

Root cutting A piece of the root of a plant used for propagation.

Rootstock See Grafting.

Rose (spray head) The watering can or hose attachment producing a fine spray.

Rosette A small cluster of overlapping leaves, often close to ground level.

Rotavator See Cultivator.

Runner A rooting stem that grows along the surface of the soil, as in strawberries.

Run-off When spraying, the point at which a plant becomes saturated, and further liquid runs off on to the surrounding area.

Sap The fluid in living plants that transports nutrients to various parts of the plant.

Scab A roughened, crust-like, diseased area.

Scarifying The process of vigorously raking a lawn in order to remove thatch.

Scion See Grafting.

Scramblers Climbing plants that do not twine or bear tendrils, clambering up by pushing through surrounding trees and shrubs, e.g. the so-called climbing roses.

Seedcoat The tough, protective layer around a seed.

Seed dressing A fine powder applied to seeds before sowing to protect them from pests or diseases.

Seed drill A machine for sowing at regular intervals in rows.

Seedheads Faded flowerheads that have been successfully fertilized and contain seeds.

Seed leaf (syn. cotyledon) The first leaf or leaves produced by a germinated seed.

Self-sterile Describes a plant whose pollen cannot fertilize its own female parts.

Semi-evergreen Describes a plant intermediate between evergreen and deciduous. It bears foliage throughout the year, but loses some leaves during the winter.

Sepal The outermost, leaf-like structures of a flower.

Shrub A perennial plant with persistent woody stems branching from the base. If only the lower parts of the branches are woody and the upper shoots are soft and usually die in winter, it is known as a sub-shrub.

Silt Very fine soil formed from clay.

Snag A short stump of a branch left after incorrect pruning.

Soakaway A pit into which water drains.

Soil profile Used to describe a cross-section of soil from surface to bed-rock, showing layers such as sub-soil, top-soil.

Species A group of closely related organisms within a genus. Abbreviations: sp. (singular) or spp. (plural).

Spit The depth of a normal digging spade, roughly equal to 10 in (25cm).

Spore A reproductive body of a fungus or fern.

Sport See Mutant.

Spot-treat To treat a small defined area or a particular plant, usually with weedkiller, fungicide or pesticide.

Spp. See Species.

Spreader A substance added to a spray to assist its even distribution over the target.

Spur A slow-growing short branch system that usually carries clusters of flower buds.

Ssp. Abbreviation for sub-species.

Stamen The male reproductive organ of a flower, comprising a stalk with an anther.

Standard A tree or shrub grown with 5-7ft (1.5-2m) of clear stem.

Station sowing The individual sowing of seeds at a predetermined spacing in the site in which they will grow until pricking out or harvesting.

Stock See Grafting.

Stool The base of a plant, such as a cane fruit, that produces new shoots.

Stopping *See* Pinching.

Strain A distinct group within a species of fungus or eelworm.

Strike To take root, usually of cuttings.

Strike off To remove excess compost above the rim of a pot or seed tray.

Sub-lateral A side-shoot growing from a lateral shoot.

Sub-shrub *See* Shrub.

Sub-soil *See* Top-soil.

Sub-species A category intermediate between a variety and a species.

Succulent A condition in certain plants that has developed as a response to a lack of readily available fresh water. A succulent plant is capable of storing relatively large quantities of water.

Sucker A shoot growing from a stem or root at or below ground level.

Suckering plant A plant that spreads by means of underground shoots, suckers or stolons.

Sump Syn. for soakaway.

Syn. Abbreviation for synonym.

Tap root The primary vertical root of a plant; also any strong-growing vertical root.

Terminal bud, shoot, flower The uppermost, usually central, growth on a stem. (*See* Apex.)

Thatch On a lawn, a layer of dead or living organic matter, along with debris, found between the roots and foliage of the grass.

Tilth A fine crumbly surface layer of soil. It is produced by weathering or careful cultivation.

Tine The prong of a fork, rake or other tool.

Tolerant Describes either a plant that can live despite infection by a parasitic organism, or a fungus that is unaffected by applications of a certain fungicide.

Top dressing *See* Dressing.

Top-soil The upper layer of dark fertile soil in which plants grow. Below this lies the sub-soil, which is lighter in colour, lacks organic matter and is often low in nutrients.

Transpiration The continual loss of water vapour from leaves and stems.

Trace elements Food materials required by plants only in very small amounts.

True leaves Leaves typical of the mature plant as opposed to simpler seed leaves.

Truss A cluster of flowers or fruit.

Tuber A swollen underground stem or root that acts as a storage organ and from which new plants or tubers may develop.

Turgid Plant material that contains its full complement of water and is not therefore limp or under stress.

Union The junction between rootstock and scion or between two scions grafted together.

Var. Abbreviation for the botanical classification *varietas* (variety); it refers only to naturally occurring varieties.

Variety A distinct variant of a species; it may be a cultivated form (a cultivar) or occur naturally (varietas).

Vegetative growth Leaf and stem growth as opposed to flowers or fruit.

Vermiculite A sterile medium made from expanded mica. It is light, clean and moisture retentive and is used in seed, cutting and potting composts.

Virus Disease-causing organism, not visible to the naked eye, that may live in plants and less often in the soil.

Watering-in To water around the stem of a newly transplanted plant to settle soil around the roots.

Water shoot A vigorous, sappy shoot growing from an adventitious or dormant bud on the trunk or older branches of a tree.

Water stress A variable condition of wilting in which plant material is losing water faster than it can take it up.

Water table The level in the soil below which the soil is saturated by ground water.

Weedkiller, contact action A weedkiller that kills only those green parts of plants with which it comes into contact.

Weedkiller, residual A weedkiller that acts through the soil and remains effective for a period ranging from a few weeks (short-term residual weedkillers) to several months (long-term residual weedkillers).

Weedkiller, translocated or systemic A weedkiller that is absorbed through the leaves and stems and is carried via the sap-stream to kill the whole plant.

Wetting agent A substance added to composts and included in sprays that allow greater contact with water.

Wind-rock The loosening of a plant's root system by strong winds.

Soil 1

Soil is the result of organic forces working on the inorganic rock. In a ceaseless process rocks are broken down and living creatures colonize the resulting debris. The nature of the parent rock decides much of the character of the resulting soil.

Soil formation
Several factors are responsible for the development of soil; the most important of these is climate. Rainwater passing over and through the parent rock breaks it down, and repeated freezing and thawing shatters the rock into smaller particles. Organic matter, such as leaves and dead animals, lodges in this rock waste, allowing bacteria and fungi to go into action. Seeds germinate in the resulting mixture. Once plants are established they will contribute organic matter to the soil, so making it capable of supporting other life in the form of more bacteria and fungi, insects, worms and other animals.

Soil profile
A cross-section of the soil (known as a soil profile) can often be seen in the side of a ditch or trench. In most temperate climates there will be five layers or "horizons" (see diagram right). The shallow, topmost layer (a) will consist of humus unless the ground has recently been cultivated, in which case this layer will have been incorporated in the top-soil. The most important layer as far as the gardener is concerned is the top-soil (b). Ideally this should be 2-3ft (60-90cm) deep to sustain a wide range of crops. It should contain adequate supplies of plant nutrients and organic matter, and should be well-drained and aerated. Below the top-soil is the sub-soil layer (c), consisting of partially broken-down rock. It is infertile but can contain useful nutrients. A layer of fragmented rock (d) may occur between the sub-soil and the solid parent rock or bedrock (e). Soil profiles will tend to vary from area to area depending upon the geology, the climate, the history of cultivation and the vegetation cover.

Types of soil
From the gardener's point of view soils are classified according to the amount of sand or clay particles they contain, and according to their acidity or alkalinity.

Clay Clay particles are very small and tend to adhere to one another, making drainage and air penetration slow and cultivation difficult. Clay soils are sticky when wet, hard when dry, slow to warm up in spring and described by the gardener as heavy. They are usually rich in nutrients and, unlike sands, chemically active. To test a soil for clay, squeeze a moist sample between finger and thumb. If the particles slide readily and the soil looks shiny it has a high clay content. A squeezed handful will readily bind together.

The addition of organic matter greatly improves clay soils, for it causes the particles to climb together in larger groups, so allowing water and air to pass between them. Lime, when added to clay soils, also causes particles to bind together by the process of flocculation (forming into compound masses or clumps).

Sand Sandy soils consist of large particles surrounded by air spaces. Water drains through them rapidly and there is ample air for plant roots. They are easy to cultivate and quick to warm up in spring, but they dry out very easily and, due to their rapid drainage, nutrients are quickly washed away. To test a soil for sand, squeeze the particles between finger and thumb. If the sand content is high the particles will both look and feel rough. A squeezed handful will not bind together well. Improve

Soil profile

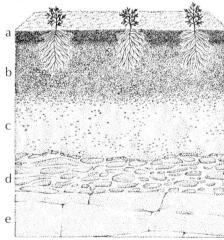

SOIL TESTING

Simple soil-testing kits can be bought which allow a rough check to be made on the soil's pH level. Take small random samples of soil from different parts of the garden and shake them up in the solution included with the kit. Allow soil to settle then check the colour of the liquid against the range of colours on the chart in the kit. The pH value is indicated by the depth of the colour of the solution in the tube.

Testing kits are also available which measure mineral levels in the soil and allow deficiencies to be corrected. Alternatively, send a soil sample to one of the educational or commercial laboratories that offer a testing service.

Check the pH level regularly, especially if attempts are being made to modify the soil's pH level.

sandy soils by adding organic matter such as garden compost.

Silt Silty soils have particles intermediate in size between sand and clay. They are sticky and fairly heavy, and can be difficult to cultivate because they are not flocculated and liming is of little help. Improve the texture of silt soils by applying large amounts of humus-producing material.

Loam This is the ideal soil, containing a mixture of clay, sand and silt particles, plus an adequate supply of organic matter and plant nutrients. It is easy to cultivate, retains moisture and nutrients, yet is well drained. Loam varies and may be classified as light, medium or heavy, depending on the clay-to-sand ratio.

Peat Made up of partially decomposed organic matter, peaty soils are inclined to be acid and poorly drained. The addition of lime, nutrients, coarse sand, grit or weathered ashes, and the construction of artificial drainage systems improves their quality.

Acidity and alkalinity

The amount of lime a soil contains governs its acidity. A soil rich in lime or chalk is said to be alkaline. One which lacks lime is described as acid or sour. The degree of acidity or alka-

linity is measured on the pH scale which runs from 0 to 14. A soil with a pH of 7.0 is termed neutral; higher readings are alkaline, lower acid. Soils with pH readings above 8.5 and below 4.5 are rare. Most plants can be grown satisfactorily in a soil with a pH in the range 6.0 to 7.0.

Humus

The dark brown crumbly organic matter within the soil is humus. It consists of plant and animal remains in various stages of decay and ensures the continued survival of bacteria which are essential if a soil is to be fertile. Humus also retains moisture, keeps the soil well aerated and is a source of plant nutrients. On cultivated ground humus breaks down more quickly than it would if left undisturbed, so it is important that the soil is amply replenished with well-rotted manure, compost, leaf-mould or other humus-forming material whenever possible.

Soil life

Earthworms, insects, burrowing animals, slugs, snails, bacteria and many other forms of life all contribute to the organic content of the soil and, unless their presence is a severe nuisance, they should be encouraged.

Soil 2

Plant nutrients

A good soil will contain all the nutrient elements necessary for plant growth. The major ones, required in relatively large quantities, are nitrogen, potassium and phosphorus plus lesser amounts of magnesium, calcium, sulphur, carbon, hydrogen and oxygen. The minor or trace elements are iron, manganese, boron, molybdenum, zinc and copper.

A plant lacking any of these elements shows certain symptoms. The more common ones are: nitrogen deficiency – slow, stunted growth and pale leaves; phosphate deficiency – stunted growth with red or purple leaves; potassium deficiency – pale yellow or brown leaves; magnesium deficiency – yellowing of older leaves; and iron deficiency – yellowing of young leaves. For further details see the companion volume *Garden Pests and Diseases*.

Drainage

Both water and air are necessary in the soil if plants and soil organisms are to thrive. In poorly drained soils, the roots of plants are restricted to the top few inches of ground where they cannot anchor the plant firmly or search very far for nutrients. Lack of air inhibits the uptake of minerals from the soil.

Causes of bad drainage The structure of the soil may be responsible for poor drainage. Small tightly packed particles of clay or silt may make the escape of water difficult, or problems may be produced by a sub-soil pan (see Box right) or a high water table. The water table is the level in the soil below which the ground is saturated with water. The level is higher in winter than in summer. In bogs and marshes the water table may be level with the surface of the ground; but normally it is to be found within 6-8ft (1.8-2.4m) of the surface. In soils where a high water table inhibits cultivation, some artificial means of drainage must be constructed to move water to a lower level (see pages 14-17).

Natural drainage Under natural conditions, rainwater which lands on the soil is distributed in several ways. Some of it runs off the surface; some is taken up by plant roots and later transpired by the foliage; some evaporates, and the rest drains down through the soil.

Artificial drainage This is vital where the incorporation of organic matter, coarse sand and grit fails to improve the natural drainage sufficiently. Very heavy clay soils, ground where the water table is inconveniently high and land with impenetrable sub-soil all have to be provided with artificial drainage to make healthy plant growth possible. See pages 14-17 for details of drainage systems.

Water retention If all rainwater were carried too rapidly down to the level of free drainage in the soil, plant roots would have little time to absorb water. In most soils, however, the humus content acts like a sponge, absorbing moisture for the plant's needs and allowing excess water to drain away naturally.

Light soils lacking in humus, such as those with a high sand or chalk content, dry out quickly. Frequent applications of well-rotted organic matter – leaf-mould, peat and compost – improve moisture retention by creating sponge-like humus.

Adding organics

Dig in organic material to improve soil condition, especially on clay, where organics will encourage particles to stick together.

PANNING

Soil particles rich in elements such as iron and aluminium sometimes form a hard layer, or pan, often only 12-18in (30-45cm) below the surface. This impairs drainage, makes digging difficult, prevents root penetration and inhibits plant growth.

Continuous ploughing or rotavating at the same level and compaction caused by vehicles can also form pans. On small plots, use a club hammer and a heavy steel bar to break up the pan. Deep digging will also help to break up pans formed by cultivation. Over large areas, traverse the land with a tractor fitted with a mole plough. This will break the pan and leave a gully below it into which water can drain. After dealing with a pan, take care to cultivate at different levels to avoid a recurrence of the problem.

The water cycle

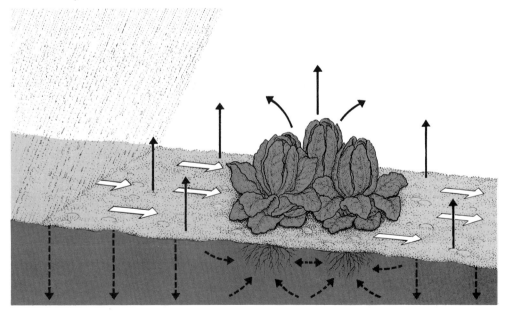

Water in the form of rain or melted snow percolates through the soil and runs off into streams and ditches, is retained in the soil, sinks down to the water table, or is lost through evaporation into the atmosphere. Plants tap the water retained in the soil. This can be up to two-thirds of the rain that falls.

Drainage 1

If a piece of land must be provided with a drainage system, the gardener can choose from a number of alternatives.

Ditches The cheapest way of draining land is to dig ditches to carry the excess water from the cultivated soil to a soakaway, stream or river. Ditches are of particular value on flat, low-lying land where the necessary slope or "fall" needed for tile drains is difficult to obtain. A system of ditches will allow drainage of the water from the soil. Once in the ditches, it will disperse by evaporation or by flowing into a watercourse.

On slightly sloping ground, dig a cut-off ditch at the top of the plot to intercept water from higher ground before it has a chance to saturate the soil further down. Dig another ditch parallel to the first at the foot of the slope to disperse the water received by the slope itself. The top ditch should be connected to the bottom one either by another ditch or by a system of tile drains. The water discharges from the bottom ditch into a soakaway or stream.

Open ditches must be excavated properly at the outset, either by mechanical digger or with a spade. Make them 3-4ft (90-120cm) deep and slope the sides outwards at a 20-30 degree angle to make them stable. The banks of ditches in clay soils will be more stable than those in sand, so they can be steeper.

Clear all ditches of weeds and undergrowth at least once a year and check that there are no blockages which will restrict the flow of water. For safety and efficiency it is a good idea to erect a fence along the ditchside.

Land drains Land or tile drains are short sections of earthenware or longer sections of plastic pipe which are laid end to end, usually in a herringbone system of filled trenches, to collect drainage water and discharge it at a chosen point. The plastic pipes are perforated, flexible and can be bent to avoid obstacles. Concrete drains are a relatively inexpensive alternative.

Dig trenches 2-3ft (60-90cm) deep and about 1ft (30cm) wide, taking care to keep top-soil and sub-soil separate. Give the trenches an overall slope of about 1 in 40 to ensure that they can take away water

Laying a tile drain system

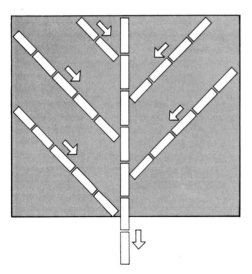

1 Plan ditches in a herringbone pattern, the main pipe leading to a soakaway. Space ditches 15ft (4.5m) apart on clay, 25ft (7.5m) on loam and 40ft (12m) on sandy soils.

2 Dig trenches 2-3ft (30-90cm) deep with an overall slope of at least 1 in 40. The side trenches should meet the main drain at an angle of 60 degrees.

efficiently. The spacing of the side drains (which run into the central main drain) will depend on the nature of the soil – on heavy clay they will need to be closer together than on lighter soils. As a rough guide, space them 15ft (4.5m) apart on clay, 25ft (7.5m) apart on loam, and 40ft (12m) apart on sandy soil.

The central drain should consist of 4in (10cm) pipes and the subsidiary or side drains of 3in (8cm) pipes. Lay the pipes at the bottom of the trench on a 2in (5cm) layer of coarse gravel or pebbles and cover them with more rubble or gravel before replacing the top-soil. Discard the sub-soil. The pipes are simply butted together to allow water to percolate between them and the side drains should meet the main drain at an angle of 60 degrees. Cover these junctions with a piece of flat tile to prevent blockages.

Rubble drains On small sites where ditches and tile drains would be impractical, use rubble drains. Take out a single trench across the plot and lead it to a soakaway in an out-of-the-way corner. Make the trench the same dimensions as a tile drain trench and give it a similar fall. Fill it with rubble to half its depth, cap this layer with gravel, then with turf placed upside down and replace the top-soil. Such a system will drain a modest-sized plot adequately and unobtrusively.

Soakaways Tile drains, rubble drains and ditches can all be connected to a soakaway if there is no convenient watercourse into which their water can be discharged.

Dig a hole approximately 6ft (1.8m) in diameter and at least 6ft (1.8m) deep (the overall size of the soakaway will be governed by the size of the plot being drained). For best results line the sides with bricks to support the wall of soil and to prevent silting, yet allow the water to seep through. Fill the soakaway with brick rubble or coarse clinker and top with turf, again, to prevent silting.

Mole drains These are constructed by a tractor attachment which pulls a torpedo-shaped steel head through the sub-soil at a chosen depth. The "mole" makes a continuous drain in the sub-soil which allows excess water to disperse. This system of drainage is really effective only when used on land which has

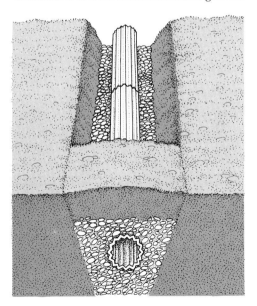

3 Lay the plastic or clay pipes on a 2in (5cm) layer of gravel and add more gravel before replacing the soil. The pipe sections are butted together, not joined.

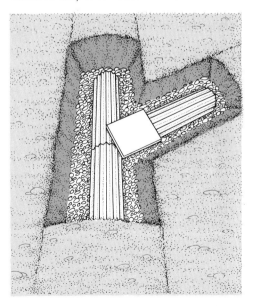

4 Cover pipe junctions with a piece of flat tile to prevent blockages before replacing first sub-soil, then top-soil.

Drainage 2

clay sub-soil, where it will last for several years. Mole drains should be excavated to the same pattern, depth and fall as tile drains.

Cultivation It is important to keep a careful check on the depth of soil cultivation where underground drains have been constructed. Deep digging or ploughing may break them and create boggy patches.

Draining hard surfaces

Patios and paths can be made impassable by every shower of rain if they are constructed so that they shed water. When making a paved or concrete area, build in a slight slope so that water is shed and does not stand about in pools. A fall of about 1 in 40 will move water quite quickly either on to border soil (where it can be used by plants), or into a shallow gully which can be led to a soakaway or drain. Construct the gully from half-round ceramic pipes bedded in cement, or from cement which has been trowelled into a similar shape.

If a hidden gully is desirable on a patio or path, lay half-round ceramic pipes down the centre of the area and slope the paving or concrete very gently towards the gully, overlapping the edges. A ½in (1.25cm) gap in the centre will let water run into the channel.

Retaining walls

A reservoir of water will often build up behind a retaining wall if no provision is made for drainage. Not only does the water make the soil inhospitable to plants but it also causes the brick or stonework to become discoloured. To overcome this problem, lay a single row of tile drains, with a suitable fall, immediately behind the wall at its base. Surround the tiles with coarse gravel and lead them to a soakaway or drain. "Weep-holes" are made in the front of the wall to allow more water to escape. Leave one vertical joint unmortared every 5-6ft (1.5-1.8m) along the wall in every second or third course of bricks or stones. Alternatively, insert short lengths of pipe, sloping forwards, at similar intervals to do the same job. Lay a gully of half-round pipes at the foot of the wall if the soil is likely to shed large amounts of water.

Ditches

If the land slopes, dig a cut-off ditch across the top of the plot to intercept water from higher ground. Connect it to another at the bottom of the slope by ditches or tile drains.

Rubble drains

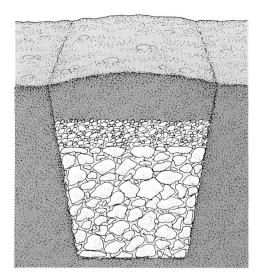

Half fill a 2-3ft (60-90cm) trench, dug at the same spacings as tile drain ditches, with broken bricks or rubble. Cap with a layer of gravel then replace the top-soil.

SOAKAWAY

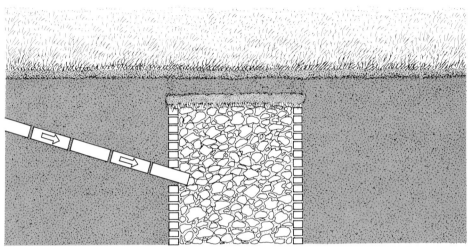

A soakaway must be constructed if there is no suitable watercourse for a drainage system to run to. Dig a hole up to 6ft (1.8m) deep and across. Line it with unmortared bricks then fill the soakaway with rubble or coarse clinker. Top with turf.

Mole drains

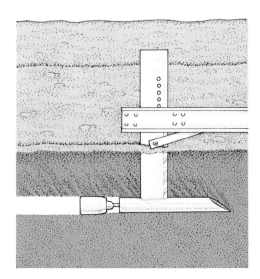

Mole drains are effective in clay soils. They are made by an attachment fitted to a tractor, and can thus only be used on large open plots.

Retaining walls

Lay a row of tile drains in gravel at the base of the wall. Leave vertical joints unmortared in every third course, 6ft (1.8m) apart, to allow water to pass through.

Improving the soil 1

As soon as a piece of land is tilled or dug, the process of humus breakdown is speeded up. Added to this, the gardener may discover that the soil is not ideally suited to the crop he wants to grow. This means the soil structure and the organic and chemical content may have to be altered to provide a more satisfactory medium. There are many materials, bulky or granular, organic or inorganic, that can be used to improve soil and turn it into the best possible growing medium for a wide range of plants.

Organic enrichment

Humus is essential in the soil. It helps to retain water and hence nutrients dissolved in it, while at the same time improving drainage (especially in clay). It also helps keep the soil well aerated, maintains soil structure, and it supports the bacteria which break down organic matter into humus. A soil may be rich in chemical fertilizers but if no organic matter is present, most bacteria will not be able to survive. In such impoverished soils plant growth is poor. Humus-rich soils are dark in colour and thus absorb heat more readily than pale soils.

Bulky organic manures have other advantages over fertilizers than the obvious one of improving soil texture and structure by virtue of their consistency. They are often rich in trace elements which may be lacking in fertilizers, and they release their nutrients relatively slowly.

Although each plant has its own particular preferences, it is usually possible to compromise and provide a soil which will suit a number of crops. (See rotation, pages 68-69.)

Most plants thrive in soil that has been dressed with well-rotted manure or compost in the autumn before planting. Fresh manure should not be added to the soil before it has had a chance to decay, because in its fresh state it gives off harmful ammonia. Also, until bacterial decay occurs, nitrogen in the soil is not available to plants.

The nitrogen cycle The nitrogen cycle, by which nitrogen passes from the air to soil to plants and animals and back to the air, involves five basic processes: fixation of nitrogen from the air by micro-organisms and by lightning to form nitrates in the soil; use by plants of these nitrates to make proteins; conversion of proteins into ammonia compounds in decaying plant and animal matter; and finally the recycling of ammonia compounds either into nitrates or into nitrogen gas, which is released into the atmosphere.

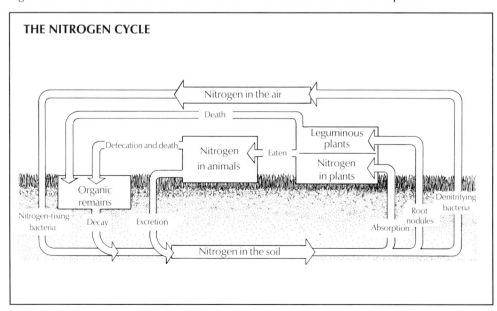

THE NITROGEN CYCLE

Nitrogen in the air

Death

Defecation and death

Nitrogen in animals

Eaten

Leguminous plants

Nitrogen in plants

Organic remains

Denitrifying bacteria

Nitrogen-fixing bacteria

Decay

Excretion

Root nodules

Absorption

Nitrogen in the soil

Organic materials

A wide variety of organic materials can be used to improve soil. The choice is often governed by what is available, but some substances, such as pulverized bark, are easier to store and apply than are manure and garden compost.

Leaf-mould The leaves of deciduous trees, collected in autumn and stacked (in an open position) can be returned to the soil the next year, after they have broken down to a crumbly dark brown mould. Leaf-mould is valued more for its ability to improve soil texture and structure than for the small amounts of plant food it contains. It has the disadvantages of breaking down rather quickly in the soil and may contain weed seeds. Leaves of the plane, poplar, sycamore and horse chestnut take longest to decompose while those of the oak take a relatively short time. Leaf-mould can be dug into the soil or applied as a mulch. Application rate: 5lb (2.3kg) per square yard (metre).

Animal manures Manure consists of animal droppings, urine and variable amounts of litter such as straw, peat, sawdust, or wood shavings. It must always be stacked before being used so that the litter can be allowed to decompose. Animal manures contain a good proportion of nutrients and many trace elements and are among the best soil conditioners. Horses produce the richest manure, followed by pigs, cows and poultry. Horse manure is quick-acting; pig and cow manure break down more slowly. Pig and chicken manure are caustic to roots and should not be applied fresh. All are best dug into the soil in autumn or applied as a mulch in spring, where decomposition has occurred during stacking. Application rate: 10-15lb (4.5-6.8kg) per square yard (metre).

Peat Peat consists of partially decayed plant remains in which decomposition has been slowed down by the presence of water. Sedge peat comes from lowland marshes in which sedges and reeds predominate. Sphagnum peat (moss peat or peat moss) is from peat bogs in moorland and its main ingredient is sphagnum moss. Peat was once widely used as a soil improver but because of the environmental damage done by peat extraction other materials are often being substituted for it.

Coir or coconut fibre This material has properties close to those of peat and is increasingly used as a peat alternative in potting composts and as a soil improver. It can be variable in consistency.

Cocoa shell This by-product of cocoa manufacture is a loose light material that becomes more compacted as it begins to decompose under moist conditions.

Garden compost Garden compost is a valuable alternative to animal manures, which may be difficult to obtain. It may consist of a wide variety of garden and kitchen waste which has been rotted down over a period of several months. (See pages 22-25.) Garden compost is relatively rich in nutrients and a good soil conditioner. It may be applied as a mulch or dug into the soil. Application rate: 10kg (4.5kg) per square yard (metre).

Spent hops A by-product of the brewing industry, spent hops may be available in certain areas. They contain relatively few nutrients but are a good soil conditioner and can be dug in during autumn and winter. Spent hops make a useful mulch. Application rate: 10lb (4.5kg) per square yard (metre).

Hop manure Spent hops with the addition of fertilizers from hop manure. Because it includes artificial fertilizers, it should be used more sparingly than other manures. It can be used as a mulch. Application rate: 1lb (500g) per square yard (metre).

Spent mushroom compost Although they vary considerably in their nutrient value, the spent composts sold off by mushroom growers are well worth using to boost the organic content of soils. They usually contain animal manure, loam and chalk in varying quantities and can be used in all soils except those being used to grow rhododendrons and other lime-hating plants. Application rate: 5-10lb (2.3-4.5kg) per square yard (metre).

Seaweed Gardeners in coastal areas may have the opportunity of using seaweed as an organic manure. Spring tides and storms often deposit large amounts of it on beaches. Seaweed contains reasonable amounts of plant nutrients, particularly potash, and it decomposes quickly. It may be dug straight into the ground while wet, or else composted with garden waste and applied when partially broken down. Dried seaweed meal can be

Improving the soil 2

bought from garden suppliers. Application rate of wet seaweed: 10-12lb (4.5-5.5kg) per square yard (metre).

Pulverized bark This product is now widely available with or without the addition of fertilizers. The ordinary kind, which does not contain fertilizers, needs nitrogen to break down the bark so it is mainly used as a mulch. Pulverized bark is slow to break down. Use it as a 2-3in (5-8cm) thick mulch.

Shoddy Wool waste or shoddy is a by-product of the textile industry and can sometimes be obtained in industrial areas. It contains a good supply of nitrogen and rots down fairly quickly in the soil. It is best dug in during autumn and winter. Application rate: 11lb (5kg) per square yard (metre).

Sewage sludge Dried sludges described as "digested" or "activated" are the safest way to use sewage. Raw sludge may transmit human diseases if applied to ground where salad ("raw") crops are being grown. Sludge-treated land should not be used for "raw" crops for 12 months. Sewage sludge is not particularly high in organic matter, but contains a good supply of nitrogen and some phosphates. It is best dug into the ground in autumn and winter. Application rate: 1½-2½ lb (0.7-1kg) per square yard (metre).

Green manure This is a method of improving soil with organic material by sowing certain crops and then digging them into the ground to enrich the soil. (See page 24.)

Other materials

On heavy soils the incorporation of materials such as coarse sand, grit, sawdust, wood shavings and pine needles may be of considerable help in making cultivation easier. These materials will open up the soil to some degree, allowing in air. However, their value on their own is limited and they are best used in combination with one or more of the organic materials listed above.

Modifying pH

Although ground limestone will improve the structure of a clay soil by encouraging the soil particles to combine into larger groups, so allowing water to drain away more freely, it is as a means of adjusting the acidity, or sourness, of a soil that it is of greatest value. This is

especially so on light, sandy soils which drain freely and lose lime rapidly by leaching. Some bacteria also will not increase or thrive in acid soils and liming improves the breaking down of organic material.

Some plants find it easier to extract nutrients from an acid soil, others prefer to grow on chalk. While it is generally advisable to grow plants which are suitable to the soil, sometimes this is neither desirable nor practicable. Then the pH, or acid/alkali balance, of the soil has to be adjusted.

A soil with a pH of between 6.0 and 7.0 will grow a wide range of crops, and 6.5 is a figure one can aim for when correcting acidity. Soil with a pH balance below 6.0 affects the uptake of some major and minor plant nutrients. Hydrated lime (calcium hydroxide) is the most effective type to use for pH adjustment as relatively small amounts of it will be needed. Another possibility is to use ordinary ground limestone or chalk (calcium carbonate), which is often cheaper. An advantage is that it can be used before planting or sowing without damage to the crop.

More lime will have to be applied to acid clay soils, and those containing large quantities of organic matter, than to acid sandy soils. See the instructions on the packet for recommended application rates. Acid soil should be tested every one or two years and suitable amounts of lime added to replace that lost.

Applications of lime are usually made in autumn or early winter. Lime should not be allowed to come into contact with manure or it will react with it, releasing valuable nitrogen into the air. Apply lime and manure in different years, or allow several weeks to elapse between the digging in of the manure and the dusting of the lime. Left on the surface of the soil the lime will gradually be washed in. If necessary, a vegetable plot may be limed in autumn and manured in winter with no ill effects.

Alkaline soils

It is much more difficult to alter the pH of an alkaline soil than that of an acid one and impractical if the soil is chalky or strongly alkaline. Start by enriching the soil with well-rotted organic matter. Then sulphur at the rate of 4oz (110g) per square yard (metre) on sandy soils and 8oz (220g) per square yard (metre) on heavy soils. Test the soil at intervals during the summer to monitor the pH. As soil acidity increases the availability of nitrogen, phosphorus, potassium and molybdenum decreases while that of iron and manganese increases. On soils with a high pH calcium decreases the uptake of potassium. If the soil is very alkaline, the only sensible course is to make a virtue of necessity and to grow plants that will tolerate some degree of alkalinity. An efficient drainage system will help to leach some of the chalk out of the soil.

Where iron deficiency is a problem on chalky soils, iron chelates or fritted iron can be watered on to make this nutrient more readily available. Three or four applications a year at the manufacturer's recommended rate should be sufficient.

Fertilizers such as sulphate of ammonia and hoof and horn are acid-reacting and should be used on chalky ground in preference to nitro-chalk, bonemeal and other fertilizers of an alkaline nature.

Types of fertilizer
There are two basic kinds of fertilizer: organic and inorganic, and both are equally valuable in the garden.

All organic fertilizers contain carbon and have been derived from living organisms. Before organic fertilizers can be absorbed by the plant they must be broken down in the soil by bacteria and fungi into inorganic chemicals. It will be seen from this that organic fertilizers actually encourage soil bacteria and so increase fertility. They are released for plant use relatively slowly.

Inorganic fertilizers do not contain carbon. They cannot improve soil texture and do not add any humus, but they are often very quick-acting and, pound for pound, richer in nutrients and cheaper than organic fertilizers.

The conscientious gardener will use a combination of organic and inorganic fertilizers together with bulky organic soil conditioners to improve the land and keep it in good heart.

All fertilizers are labelled to show their nutrient content in terms of nitrogen (N), phosphoric acid (P_2O_5) and potash (K_2O). Some fertilizers are described as "straight", meaning that they supply just one of these nutrients; others are called "compound" and supply varying quantities of all three nutrients.

Application
Fertilizers may be applied to the ground before sowing or planting (in which case they are known as base dressings) or while the crop is growing, as top dressings.

Apply base dressings to the soil a few days before sowing crops or at the time of planting, working the fertilizer into the top few inches of soil with a fork or rake.

Dust top dressings of fertilizers around growing plants or crops while the soil is moist and hoe them lightly into the top few inches. Where large areas are being fertilized, wheeled fertilizer distributors may be used. These can be adjusted to spread a given quantity of fertilizer evenly over the surface of the soil.

Certain fertilizers are sold in soluble powder or liquid form and can be watered on to the soil or sprayed over plant foliage. These foliar feeds are generally quick-acting and should be applied when the soil is moist. Foliar feeds are best given in dull weather rather than in bright sunshine.

Assessing plant needs
Most plants will be adequately supplied with nutrients if given a base dressing of a compound fertilizer before being sown or planted and one or two top dressings of a similar material during the growing season. Fertilizers containing a large amount of nitrogen can be used to induce rapid leaf and shoot growth where this is lacking. Those containing phosphates will encourage root activity where trees and shrubs are being planted; and fertilizers rich in potash will improve the fruiting ability for a range of crops from tomatoes and beans to apples and pears. The most important requirement, however, is to balance the soil with a mixture of nutrients necessary for a particular crop. Over-application of one nutrient may cancel the effect of others.

Garden compost 1

Animal manure may be difficult to obtain, and proprietary organic soil conditioners are expensive. An alternative source of bulky organic matter is garden compost. A compost heap will cheaply and quickly turn garden and kitchen waste into valuable soil-enriching material.

Principles of compost making

To make good, crumbly compost the heap must be properly constructed so that the organic material can decompose rapidly and not turn into a pile of stagnant vegetation.

Air, moisture and nitrogen are all necessary if bacteria and fungi are to break down the raw material efficiently. Air is allowed in through the base and sides of the heap. Water should be applied with a can or hose if the heap shows signs of drying out, and moisture can be kept in by covering the heap with sacking, old carpet or polythene sheeting. Nitrogen must be provided in the form of manure, com-

post activator or a nitrogenous fertilizer. It will aid in the breaking-down process.

The heap will be able to function best if it is sited in a sheltered and shady place but not under trees or where tree roots may move into the compost. It must be protected from becoming dried out by the sun and wind. Allow ample time for decomposition.

Compost bins

It is possible to rot down compost satisfactorily by simply stacking it in a spare corner of the garden, but in this way the heap may become untidy and the material on the outside will dry out. Decomposition will take place more rapidly in a home-made or proprietary compost bin which allows air in and retains moisture. For best results, compost bins should not be more than 4ft (1.2m) high. They can be much longer than wide, for example, 4 × 4 × 8-10ft (1.2 × 1.2 × 2.4-3m) is a useful size.

Building a compost heap

1 Choose a suitable site for the heap, and, if preferred, erect a wire or rigid-sided bin.

2 Scatter sulphate of ammonia at ½oz (15g) per square yard over a 6-9in (15-23cm) layer of compostable material.

There are many ways of making a compost bin. One of the simplest is to erect a square cage of wire netting, supported by four stout posts driven into the ground. Make the front removable to allow the rotted compost to be easily extracted. For large bins, make a false floor by placing a layer of twiggy branches or brushwood in the base, or support a few short planks on bricks. This will allow air to permeate the compost. Line the inside of the cage with newspaper to prevent excessive drying out. A piece of sacking or polythene can be weighted down with bricks on the top of the heap to keep the moisture in.

A more solid structure can be made from angle-iron posts and wooden boards which are fashioned with gaps to allow in a certain amount of air. The internal structure of the heap is the same as with a wire cage. Brick or breeze-block structures may be used provided that occasional vertical joints are left unmortared to allow in air. The front of such

bays can be equipped with removable wooden slats.

A series of two or three compost bins is very useful, particularly in large gardens. When one bin is full the compost can be left to decompose and another bin brought into use. In this way a cycle of compost production can be kept going.

There are many proprietary compost bins available. Some are equipped with sliding sides to allow the compost to be shovelled out, and with lids to keep in moisture. Check that the bin is robust and large enough for the garden's compost needs, bearing in mind the length of time it takes to decompose.

Compostable materials
Garden and kitchen waste in great variety can be turned into good compost if it is properly mixed. One of the secrets of ensuring rapid and effective decomposition is not to allow large quantities of one particular

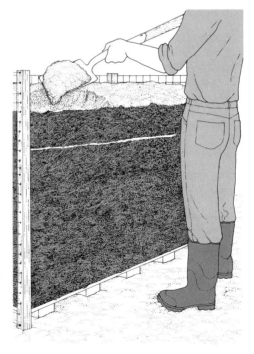

3 Water the heap then add more compost material and sulphate of ammonia. Keep covered.

4 Continue until the bin is full or the heap is 4ft (1.2m) tall. Cover finally with a 2in (5cm) layer of soil.

Garden compost 2

material to build up in the heap. All the following materials may be composted if properly mixed together and then kept well aerated and moist: annual weeds, lawn mowings, potato peelings, tea leaves, crushed egg-shells, animal manure and urine, torn-up newspapers (but not glossy magazines), soft hedge clippings, dead flower-heads, pea pods, vegetable leaves and stems, tree and shrub leaves. Do not use woody material or any vegetation, such as lawn mowings, which has previously been sprayed with herbicides or is affected by diseases and pests.

Constructing the heap

When the bin has been erected the composting can start in earnest. On top of the false floor, if used, place a 6-9in (15-23cm) layer of compost material and lightly firm it down with the head of a rake or the back of a fork. Scatter sulphate of ammonia over this layer at the rate of ½oz (15g) to the square yard

Leaf-mould

Fill perforated polythene sacks with dead leaves. Tie the tops and allow the sacks to stand until the leaf-mould is formed.

(metre) and then add another layer of compost material. Continue in this fashion until the bin is full. Keep a cover over the top of the heap at all times, and if the compost becomes dry, remove the cover and water it to encourage the rotting process.

The layer of sulphate of ammonia may be alternated with one of lime to counteract acidity encouraged by sulphate of ammonia. Never add lime and sulphate of ammonia at the same time. Alternatively, a proprietary compost activator may be used between each layer. Animal manure may also be added between the layers of vegetation but it should not come into contact with the fertilizer or lime. If it does, a chemical reaction will be triggered which will result in valuable nitrogen being given off into the atmosphere. When the bin is full a 2in (5cm) layer of soil may be spread over the top instead of sacking or polythene. Leave the bin and if possible start to construct a second bin.

GREEN MANURE

Seed	Sowing time	Rate/sq yd
Rape	March-June	1/12oz (2g)
Mustard	March-August	⅛oz (3.5g)
Vetches	March-May	¾oz (20g)
Annual lupin	March-July	½oz (15g)

The practice of sowing certain crops and digging the resulting plants into the ground to enrich the soil, provide a source of nitrogen and improve texture is known as green manuring. Rape, annual lupins, vetches, mustard and perennial rye grass may all be used. Broadcast the seed quite thickly over the ground in spring or early summer and then rake it in. The plants will grow quickly; dig them in just before they flower. Apply a dusting of sulphate of ammonia at the rate of 2oz per square yard when the crop is dug in to prevent any temporary deficit of nitrogen. If there are no plants in the area, the sulphate of ammonia will assist bacteria in the breakdown process by providing nitrogen. Green manure plants are also often sown after a crop has just been cleared from the ground, for example in early spring or early autumn.

Using the compost

In a well-made bin which has been sensibly filled the compost will not need turning, for virtually all the material will decompose sufficiently. Decomposition will be more rapid in spring and summer than in autumn and winter, but a good heap should be ready to use within six months of being completed, sooner in warm weather. Check the heap at intervals and, if possible, shovel out the usable compost from the bottom. The compost should be brown and crumbly, though some of the material may still be recognizable. Unrotted material may be left behind as the basis of the new heap.

Use only very well-rotted compost as a mulch, for partially decomposed material may contain weed seeds that will soon germinate and become a nuisance. Alternatively, dig in the compost during soil cultivations in autumn and winter at the rate of 10lb (4.5kg) per square yard (metre).

Leaf-mould The leaves of deciduous trees and shrubs may be rotted down on their own to make soil-enriching leaf-mould. A wire bin (similar to that made for compost) makes a suitable container, and 6-9in (15-23cm) layers of leaves can be sprinkled with sulphate of ammonia. A fast space-saving alternative is to pack the layers of leaves and fertilizer in black polythene sacks that have been perforated to allow in air. Filled, tied at the top and stood in an out-of-the-way corner, the sacks of leaves will form good leaf-mould which can be used in the spring following autumn collection. Leaves in outdoor bins may take rather longer to decay. All leaves of deciduous trees and shrubs can be composted, but plane, poplar and sycamore take longer to decompose than oak and beech. Leaves of evergreens are not suitable for leaf-mould production. Leaf-mould can be dug into the soil or used as a mulch. See page 19.

TYPES OF COMPOST BIN

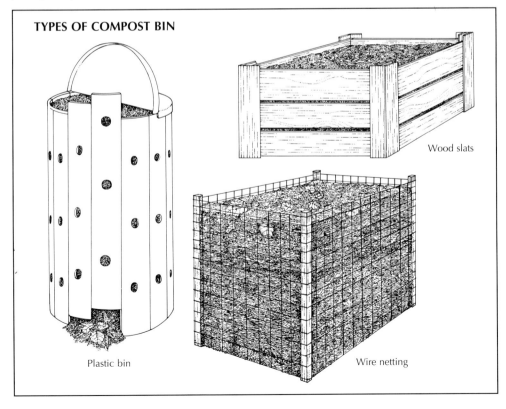

Plastic bin

Wood slats

Wire netting

Digging 1

Single digging

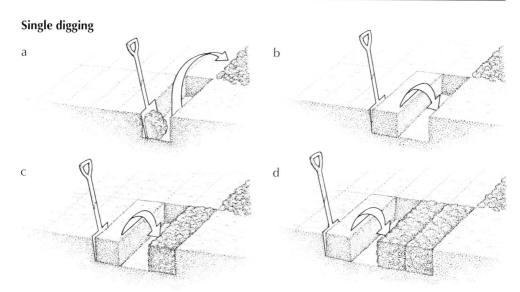

Although in nature the soil is seldom disturbed, except by worms and other underground life, man usually finds it necessary to cultivate the ground in which he grows plants for several reasons. These are: to control the growth of weeds; to incorporate manures, composts and fertilizers; to relieve compaction and improve soil texture, so allowing seeds to germinate and young roots to penetrate the soil; and to allow in air, so speeding up the process of humus decomposition and making nutrients available.

Digging

Digging is the most thorough of all soil cultivations because it disturbs the ground to the greatest depth. It is usually carried out annually on the vegetable plot, or on any ground being brought under cultivation for the first time.

As a general rule, digging is best done in the autumn and winter to allow the frost, wind, snow and rain to work on the rough-turned clods of earth and gradually break them down. This action is particularly valuable on heavy soils containing a high proportion of clay. However, never work on any soil when it is frozen or very wet. Digging is difficult in such circumstances and the soil's structure may become temporarily damaged through compaction by feet and tools.

On lighter soils, exposure to frost is not essential, for the clods will be naturally friable. For this reason, light soils can be cultivated at any time during winter and early spring, provided that they are allowed to settle for two or three weeks before the crop is sown or planted.

There are three main methods of digging, which involve cultivating the soil to different depths. See the illustrations above.

Single digging This is the most widely practised form of digging. It is adequate for most ordinary soils of reasonable depth which do not overlay an intractable sub-soil. During single digging the soil is cultivated to the depth of one spade blade or "spit".

Begin single digging by taking out a trench one spit deep and about 12-15in (30-40cm) wide across one end of the plot to be dug (a). Pile the soil removed from this trench at the opposite end of the plot (it will eventually be used to fill the final trench). If the soil is to be manured as it is dug, throw the organic matter into the bottom of the trench at this point and mix it well in. Now take up the spade, starting behind the trench, lift up a comfortable spadeful of soil and throw it forward into the trench, turning it upside down as you do so (b). This action will ensure that any annual weeds are buried. Perennial weeds such as couch grass, dandelions, dock, bindweed

Double digging

a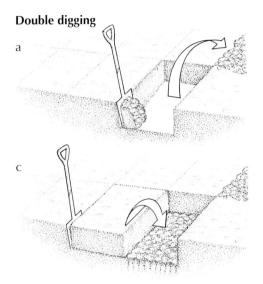

b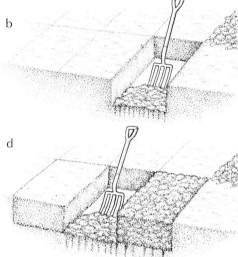

c

d

and ground elder should be painstakingly removed by hand. If a portion of root is left, the weed will multiply. If grassland is being dug, the mat of grass can be skimmed off with the spade and thrown into the trench where it should be chopped up.

Work along the first trench throwing the soil over and forwards until another trench has been created (c). More manure may then be added and the operation repeated (d). When the end of the plot is reached, the soil from the first trench is used to fill the last.

If the plot is very wide, divide it in two lengthways and take out the first trench on one half of the plot, depositing the soil at the same end of the other half. Now work down the first strip of land and back up the second, throwing the soil from the first trench into the last one. By dividing the plot into two the chore of barrowing all the soil from one end to the other is avoided.

Double digging or bastard trenching With double digging the soil is cultivated to a depth of two spits. The technique is especially useful on land which has not been cultivated before or where a hard sub-soil layer is impeding drainage and the penetration of plant roots.

To double-dig a piece of land, take out a trench 2ft (60cm) wide and one spit deep at one end of the plot (a). The soil removed is again positioned alongside the spot to be occupied by the final trench. The plot may be divided in two, as for single digging, if it is very large.

When all the soil has been removed from the first trench, fork over the base to the full depth of the garden fork's tines (b). Compost or manure may be forked into the lower layer of soil or scattered on top of it after cultivation.

When the base of the trench has been cultivated, start to dig and throw forward the soil adjacent to it in the same way as for single digging (c). Make sure that the soil is turned over and perennial weeds are removed. When 2ft (30cm) of soil has been thrown forward into the first trench, the second trench will have been created and the base is forked over (d). The cycle continues until the entire plot has been dug to a depth of about 20in (50cm). This method of digging improves the friability of the sub-soil without bringing it nearer the surface, so the rich layer of top-soil is always closest to the young roots of cultivated plants.

Trenching By far the most labour-intensive way of cultivating soil, trenching should only be practised where a deep sub-soil pan is causing problems. During trenching the ground is cultivated to a depth of about 30in (75cm) – three spits deep – and manure can be forked into the broken-up sub-soil.

Digging 2

Trenching

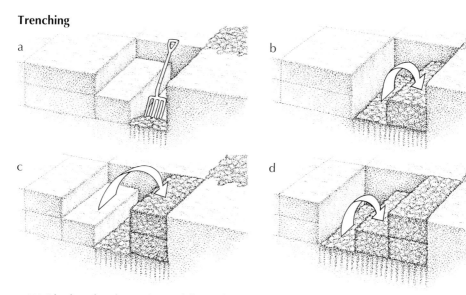

Divide the plot down the middle and dig down one side and back up the other. Dig a trench one spit deep and 3ft (90cm) wide halfway across the plot and place the soil next to the final trench. Deposit this soil at the far end of the plot alongside the top-soil but do not mix the two. The trench will now be "stepped". Fork over the base of the lower half of the trench to the full depth of the fork tines (a), then dig and throw forward the soil from the other half so that it rests on top of the forked strip (b). Fork over the strip of ground just exposed.

Mark out the next 18in (45cm) wide strip of top-soil on the plot using a garden line, and throw this soil forward on to the step of second-spit soil in the front of the first trench, inverting it and removing perennial weeds (c). Now transfer the second spit of newly exposed soil to the forked strip alongside it (d), and cultivate the base of the newly created trench with a fork. This cycle of cultivation continues right down the plot – the two piles of soil taken from the first trench being used to fill the second-spit and first-spit trenches that are left.

Ridging On very heavy soils the type of digging known as ridging may be beneficial, for it exposes a greater surface area of soil to the elements. Divide the plot in two as described from Trenching above. Then mark out a 3ft (90cm) wide strip at one end of the plot to be dug and remove a 1ft (30cm) wide trench at one end of this strip. Pile the soil by the final trench (a). Now work backwards along the marked-out strip, throwing the central spadeful of soil forwards and turning it upside down (b). The spadefuls of soil at either side of this are also inverted, but are turned inwards so that they lie against the first spadeful (c). In this way a ridge will be built up. Repeat the process (d), working along the first strip, then mark out a second and work backwards along that and so on until the plot is ridged.

Digging sensibly The craft of digging is something that can only be learned by practice, but there are some rules that will prevent it from becoming a back-breaking chore. Firstly, remember to keep the spade vertical; a slanting cut achieves less depth. Drive the spade in at right angles across the trench to free the clod of earth and allow it to be lifted away cleanly. Lift up small spadefuls of soil that are easy to handle. It is possible to dig land faster by taking a greater number of small spadefuls rather than a lesser number of very heavy spadefuls which will tire the gardener rapidly.

Secondly, dig a little ground at a time on a regular basis. Cultivate a yard strip every

Ridging

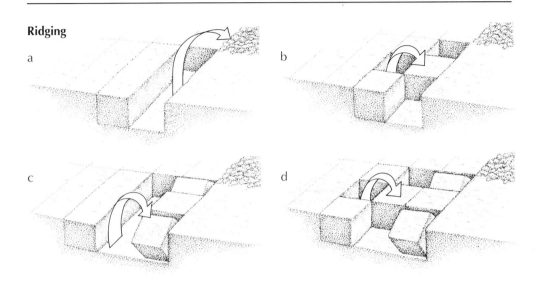

a

b

c

d

day rather than attempting to dig the entire plot at once.

Finally, only dig the soil when it is easily workable, not when it is snow-covered, frozen or very wet.

Forking On very stony or heavy ground which is difficult to penetrate with a spade, a fork may be used instead, and for cultivating the bottom of trenches during double digging and trenching, it is an invaluable tool. The disadvantages of using the fork for the entire digging operation are that it is unable to slice cleanly through surface weed growth, and that light soils may fall through its tines. However, the fork may be used to good effect as a cultivating tool between established plants, and in spring to break down rough-dug land that has been weathered through the winter.

Raking This is an important task but one which is often overdone. The main reason for raking should be to level a piece of ground, either for seed sowing, planting or laying paving materials. Certainly the rake is also used to break down clods of soil to a reasonably fine tilth, but if used to excess it will create a dusty surface that will pan in the first shower of rain. Over-raking will also expose an abundance of stones. As a general rule, it is best to break down the clods of soil with the back of a fork. Then trample the ground to firm it and level it with the rake when the particles are reasonably dry. Use long, steady movements of the arms, drawing the rake to and fro and supporting it so that its teeth sweep over the surface and do not dig in. The rake can also be used lightly to cover seeds after broadcast sowing, to replace the soil in drills, and to collect leaves and other garden debris.

No-dig gardening

Some gardeners believe that digging is harmful to the soil as it disturbs the activity of bacteria and earthworms and so upsets the natural balance. Non-diggers prefer to apply thick mulches of well-rotted compost, manure or peat to the surface of the soil and let earthworms and other organisms incorporate this enrichment. Seeds are sown in the compost and subsequent mulches are applied while the plants are growing.

There is no doubt that this technique works and saves labour, but it does require very large quantities of compost or manure so that organic matter may have to be brought in. Digging may be more laborious but it is certainly cheaper and the yield and quality of some crops has been shown in experiments to be markedly improved in land dug to 3ft (90cm). To dig or not to dig is thus more a philosophical than a horticultural question.

Potting compost

Plants growing in open ground usually have an ample supply of soil in which to sink their roots, but plants in containers have a restricted root run and, therefore, must be supplied with a richer growing medium or compost. Cleanliness, adequate moisture retention, good drainage and a supply of nutrients are the prime requirements of a compost in which plants are potted.

John Innes composts
At one time it was considered that each plant should have its own particular compost, but research at the John Innes Horticultural Institution in the 1930s showed that one or two well-formulated mixtures would grow a wide range of plants to a high standard. Composts mixed according to the John Innes formulae are still widely used today. They can be bought ready-mixed (in which case the seal of the John Innes Manufacturers' Association should be looked for as a mark of authenticity). They can deteriorate if stored for long periods, so make sure that the shop from which the compost is bought has not been storing it for too long. Compost can also be made up at home to the formulae shown below. The main ingredients are loam, peat and sand.

Loam Strictly speaking loam is derived from rotted-down top-spit turves, but good garden soil may be substituted, although it lacks the

---

COMPOST MIXTURES

John Innes potting compost
7 parts by loose bulk sterilized loam
 (passed through 1/2in (1.25cm) sieve)
3 parts by loose bulk granulated peat
 (passed through 1/4-1/2in (0.5-1.25cm) sieve)

2 parts by loose bulk lime-free sharp
 sand or grit 1/16-1/8in (0.15-0.25cm) diameter.
Plus the following amounts of fertilizer
per bushel to make required compost:

John Innes potting No. 1
4oz (110g) John Innes base fertilizer
3/4oz (20g) ground limestone or chalk
Use for rooted cuttings, seedlings

John Innes potting No. 2
8oz (220g) John Innes base fertilizer
1 1/2oz (40g) ground limestone or chalk
Use for most pot plants

John Innes potting No. 3
12oz (340g) John Innes base fertilizer
2 1/4oz (60g) ground limestone or chalk
Use for large and vigorous plants
(such as chrysanthemums and
tomatoes at final potting)

John Innes ericaceous compost
Loam-based but does not include
limestone or chalk

John Innes base fertilizer
2 parts by weight hoof and horn
 (1/8in (0.25cm) grist)
2 parts by weight superphosphate of lime
1 part by weight sulphate of potash
If hoof and horn is not available,

nitroform, a urea derivative, can be
substituted at one-third the weight
for hoof and horn

John Innes seed sowing compost
2 parts by loose bulk sterilized loam
 (1/2in (1.25cm) sieved)
1 part by loose bulk granulated peat
 (1/2in (1.25cm) sieved)
1 part by loose bulk sharp sand
1 1/2oz (40g) superphosphate of lime per bushel
3/4oz (20g) ground limestone or chalk per bushel
Used for sowing most seeds

Cutting compost
1 part granulated peat or substitute
1 part sharp sand

Soilless potting composts
Various formulations, for example:
3 parts granulated peat or substitute
1 part sharp sand
base fertilizer with ground limestone,
Dolomite limestone and fritted trace elements

fibre of traditional loam. It should have a pH range of 5.5-6.5

Peat Granulated peat sold in bales must be broken down to a fine texture by passing it through a 1/4in (0.5cm) sieve before being incorporated. Make sure it is moist at the time of mixing, as it can be hard to re-wet.

Sand Coarse or sharp lime-free sand of 1/16-1/8 (0.15-0.25cm) grist should be used. Do not use silver sand or bright yellow builders' sand.

Mixing compost

Layer all the ingredients evenly on a concrete floor, sprinkling lime and fertilizer at the correct rate (see table) into each layer. Turn this with a clean shovel until it is of an even colouring. John Innes composts deteriorate if left in store after three weeks. If at all possible they should be used as soon as mixed. Plastic sacks or dustbins make good storage containers, if it is necessary to keep the compost for a short time. Compost keeps better dry than damp.

Sterilization

Peat and sand are both naturally sterile but the loam fraction of John Innes composts must be partially sterilized to kill harmful fungi and weed seeds. If a proprietary electric sterilizer is used, the soil should be put in while moist and heated to a temperature of 80°C (180°F) for 10 minutes.

If no specialized equipment is available the soil can be sterilized in a broad, flat container, such as a meat tin, put in the oven at 80°C (180°F) for 30 minutes. Cover the tin with foil and the steam generated will serve to encourage the sterilizing effect. Allow the loam to cool and riddle it before mixing it with the other ingredients.

Soilless composts

Composts with no loam have become popular because of difficulties in obtaining loam of a consistent standard and sterilizing it effectively. In the past peat has been widely used as a component of these, generally in combination with other inert ingredients such as vermiculite, perlite, expanded polystyrene granules and sand. However, increasing concern at the environmental consequences of large-scale peat extraction for horticulture has led to the development and use of various peat substitutes in composts. Coir, a material produced from waste coconut fibres and husks, is one of the most widely used.

There is considerable variation in the formulation of soilless composts. Ground limestone and fritted trace elements are generally added with the base fertilizer.

Soilless composts have several advantages. They are light, clean, naturally sterile and easy to handle. Furthermore, the containers in which they are used do not have to be crocked. However, they do have certain disadvantages. The nutrients they contain are exhausted relatively quickly so that plants need a regular feeding programme, which should commence six weeks after potting. Because they are so light these composts may not provide adequate support for top-heavy plants. Heavy firming at planting will have the effect of destroying the open texture of the compost. Many of these composts now contain a wetting agent to improve water absorption; otherwise they tend to be very difficult to re-wet if they dry out.

Yet another disadvantage is that plants grown in pots in soilless composts are often difficult to establish in the garden. To help wean roots from peat dependency, dig peat or a peat substitute into the soil outside the planting hole.

Cuttings and seed composts

A compost for rooting cuttings must be more or less sterile, chemically inactive and well aerated but sufficiently moisture retentive to help prevent the desiccation of cuttings. A mixture of equal parts sieved peat and sharp sand has been widely used as a cutting compost but various materials, including perlite and vermiculite, are now being used as satisfactory substitutes.

Seed composts, loam-based and soilless, are formulated to provide optimum conditions for germination but they are low in nutrients. Unless seedlings are transplanted at an early stage into a richer compost they will starve.

Multi-purpose composts, that are suitable for seeds, cuttings and general use, are also available.

Special beds

Soil beds for special purposes require varying cultivation techniques, though all benefit from thorough initial digging.

Seedbeds
Many seeds will germinate quite satisfactorily out of doors, and there is no point in sowing them in a greenhouse or garden frame unless such protection is really necessary. An outdoor seedbed has several advantages. It is cheap to construct, the seedlings have a large amount of rooting medium in which to grow, so development is not restricted, the soil will dry out more slowly than compost in a tray or pot, and many plants can be raised in a small area.

Choose a site which receives plenty of sun but which is sheltered from winds by distant trees and shrubs. Take care not to sow next to a hedge where uneven germination or growth of seedlings could result. If drainage is not exceptionally good, raise the level of the seedbed by enclosing it in 9in (23cm) high wooden boards. It is much easier to sow and cultivate narrow seedbeds, so construct 3ft (90cm) wide strips rather than one large area.

Whether the seedbed is to be used to raise vegetable or ornamental plant seedlings, it should be prepared during autumn and winter to allow the soil to be weathered.

Single dig the soil in the seedbed, adding light organic material such as leaf-mould and, where necessary, grit. Do not add manure or compost, which may induce unwanted sappy growth. In spring, a few weeks before sowing, break down the clods of soil with a fork, and then leave the soil alone for a fortnight. During this time weed seeds will germinate and the resulting seedlings can be hoed off or sprayed with the contact weed-killer parquat with diquat a few days before sowing.

Final preparations should be carried out on the day of sowing when the surface of the soil is relatively dry. Level the bed and then apply a base dressing of bonemeal at the rate of 4oz (110g) per square yard (metre). Alternatively use any other phosphatic fertilizer that will encourage root growth. Then rake the soil to a fairly fine tilth. Sow the seeds in drills or broadcast (see page 49) and label.

At no time should the soil in the seedbed be allowed to dry out, and all weeds must be removed by hand or hoe before they have a

Seedbed

Choose a sunny level site. Raise the bed by enclosing it in 9in (23cm) wooden boards secured with pegs. Make the seedbed 3ft (90cm) wide to allow easy access.

Rake the prepared soil to a fine tilth before sowing. Apply bonemeal at 4oz (110g) per square yard. Provide wind protection with screens if necessary.

Some acid-loving plants
Andromeda, Calluna, Cassiope,
Corydalis, Cypripedium, Epimedium,
Erica, Erythronium, Gaultheria,
Gentiana, Incarvillea, Kalmia,
Leucothoë, Lilium, Meconopsis,
Nomocharis, Phyllodoce, Pieris,
Primula, Rhododendron, Sanguinaria,
Tricyrtis, Trillium, Vaccinium.

chance to compete with the rightful occupants of the bed. Extra wind protection may be provided by screens of plastic netting erected around the seedbed.

Beds for dwarf acid-loving plants
Many very attractive plants are difficult to grow in gardens because of their unusual environmental requirements. A large number of dwarf plants that are lime-hating but shade- and moisture-loving can be grown satisfactorily in special beds of acid soil. These are often referred to as 'peat beds', peat having been widely used to condition and acidify the soil. Peat in the form of hard blocks has also been used to build the low retaining walls, the blocks being well soaked before construction and sprayed subsequently whenever they show signs of drying out.

A suitable raised bed can be constructed on all but the most alkaline soils. On neutral or slightly acid ground the bed will retain its acid nature but beds will eventually become contaminated if they sit on chalky soil. This problem can be avoided by laying plastic sheeting as a membrane between the soil, slightly mounded to allow drainage, and the bed.

When constructing a raised bed for acid-loving plants choose a shady site – against a north-facing wall or in the shade cast by trees and shrubs (but not too close). Avoid frost pockets. At the outset remove all weeds.

The addition of peat remains the most effective way of creating suitably acid conditions. Enrich the soil to a depth of one spit with 50 per cent of its own bulk of medium- or coarse-grade peat, adding a light dusting of a lime-free general fertilizer such as blood, bone and fish meal. The peat content of the bed can be minimized by using logs or stone to form the walls and by applying a 2-3in (5-8cm) mulch of pulverized bark. To avoid the bed being walked on, which will cause compaction, place stepping stones as required.

Planting may be carried out in autumn or spring after the bed has been lightly firmed with the feet. Keep beds free of weeds, fallen leaves and garden debris. Do not let beds dry out during the summer months but avoid the use of hard water. Some plants will need thinning out from time to time. In spring replenish the bark mulch and apply a general fertilizer.

Peat bed

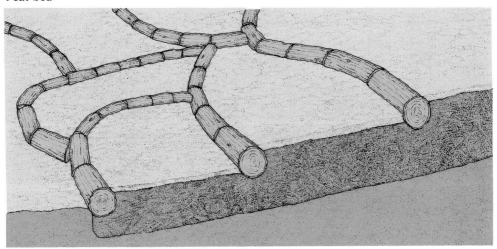

Choose a shady site, avoiding frost pockets. Use hard peat blocks, logs or stones to form the edges of the bed. The soil should be enriched down to one foot deep with 50 per cent of its own bulk of moist peat. Add a light dusting of lime-free general fertilizer such as blood, bone and fish meal.

Watering 1

If plants are to grow healthily without check, they must have access to a constant supply of water (see water cycle, page 13). For most of the year in temperate climates, the soil contains sufficient moisture to satisfy the plants' needs. But during very dry spells in spring and summer the plants may find it impossible to extract sufficient water to keep them turgid; they will wilt and growth is temporarily halted. If water is not made available to them soon after wilting, they will die. For this reason the gardener must be able to provide "artificial" supplies of water, or irrigate, before the plants wilt. Restrictions on mains supplies may make it necessary to conserve water and store it for irrigation (see p.101).

Timing of applications

The timing of irrigation is particularly important with vegetable crops if they are to develop steadily and produce the maximum yield. Care must also be taken to give plants sufficient water, enough to reach the roots, not just to wet the soil surface.

As a general rule, an inch (2.5cm) of water will travel to a depth of 9in (23cm) in the soil. To water an acre (0.4 hectare) of land to this depth, a total of 22,650 gallons (100,000 litres) must be applied. Continuous light applications of water during periods of prolonged drought are not to the plants' best advantage. They will not reach the majority of roots; they will pan the surface of the soil, and will encourage plants to produce surface roots, which will suffer in future droughts.

Sandy soils will dry out much more quickly than those containing clay, and will have to be watered sooner during spells of drought. The surface is seldom a good guide as to the state of the rest of the soil, so dig down for 9-12in (23-30cm) with a trowel to see if the soil is moist. If it is dry or only just moist, water.

With vegetable crops in particular the water can be best utilized while the plants are growing rapidly – usually during late spring and early to mid-summer. Shortages of water at this time cause the greatest check and may even result in some crops bolting (prematurely running to seed).

Food crops Later in summer excessive quantities of water may do real harm to certain vegetables. Melons, for instance, should be kept on the dry side once their fruits are beginning to ripen, otherwise the fruits will split. Late summer rains can impair the storage quality of onions, just when they should be drying off prior to being strung. Beans and peas should be watered at 1-2 gallons per square yard (4.5-9 litres per square metre) per week when the flowers and pods appear. Too much water during early growth encourages leaves at the expense of flowers and crops.

For most green crops such as lettuces and brassicas, good supplies of water will keep them cropping, prolonging and increasing yields. A rate of 2-4 gallons per square yard (9-13.5 litres per square metre) per week is adequate.

Ornamentals Less research has been done on the water needs of ornamental plants. However, ornamental plants have much the same water needs as food crops. Pot-grown flowers and shrubs are at greater risk than those in the open ground. Do not let them dry out.

Planting

Most applications of water to growing plants will be given in spring and summer, rather than in autumn and winter. But this is the

Irrigation and root systems

1 If water is applied in small amounts, the soil surface will harden, and plants will develop surface roots in an effort to reach the moist top layer of soil.

prime planting season for deciduous trees and shrubs, and it is a good idea to water them in well unless the ground is extremely moist at planting time. Such watering-in is not necessary so much to keep the plant growing, as to settle the soil particles around the roots in readiness for spring growth.

Susceptible sites

Plants growing in open ground may certainly dry out due to exposure to sun in summer, but they will also receive their full quota of winter rains. Other sites in the garden may not be so well catered for and the gardener should see that they are given extra attention. Beds and borders against walls are particularly prone to drying out and should be enriched with organic matter to make them absorbent. This means that they can readily soak up any rainfall they receive, and also supplies of irrigation water given during dry spells. Soil close to walls is often poor and low in organic matter and can be very difficult to wet once it is dry. The same goes for soil under trees and alongside hedges.

Plants in tubs, pots and particularly hanging baskets will need regular applications of water through the summer because they can dry out very quickly. When filling the container with compost, leave a gap between the surface of the soil and the rim of the container to allow a sufficient amount of water to be applied. Water when the top inch of the container compost dries out. Aim to keep the top inch damp but not sodden. Both over- and under-watering can harm container-grown plants.

Techniques of watering

Water may be applied to the soil or to plants in containers by several different means.

Watering can The simplest method of transporting water to plants is by the use of a watering can. There are several designs and sizes, but a two-gallon can will be found the most useful for general garden needs. Cans larger than this are heavy and difficult to lift when full, and smaller ones involve too many journeys to and from the tap. Choose a can with a long spout, good balance when full and a long reach. Steel and plastic cans are available and both have their good and bad points. Steel cans have a tendency to develop leaks after a while, but they can usually be repaired. If handled carefully, plastic cans last many years, but once they start to leak they

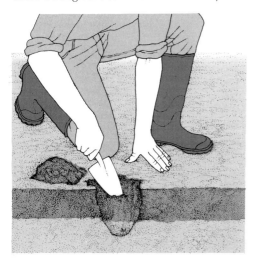

2 Check the moisture content of the soil by digging a hole with a trowel. The state of the soil 9-12in (23-30cm) down is the best guide to watering needs.

3 If the soil is dry, water well to make sure that the moisture reaches the roots of the plants.

Watering 2

are useless. Spray heads or "roses" are supplied with most watering cans. These vary from fine to coarse. A fine rose should be used on seeds and seedlings.

When using a can fitted with a rose to water trays of seedlings, begin pouring to one side of the plant then pass the can over them, maintaining a steady flow. Move the can away from the plants before stopping the flow of water. This technique avoids sudden surges of water which can damage tender plants and displace compost.

Hose pipes If a tap is situated in or near the garden, a hose pipe will avoid tiresome journeys with the watering can. It may be left running on a patch of soil and moved around at intervals, or it may be held over a particular plant or group of plants if the gardener has the patience and time to spare. Take care not to allow strong flows of water to wash away soil and expose the roots of plants. On the vegetable garden water can be allowed to run from the hose pipe along furrows made between crop rows. Water applied in this way will quickly get to the roots. Buy a strong hose pipe which will not kink when bent and which will retain its suppleness over the years. Cheap hose pipes will crack and leak,

especially if used in cold weather. Hose pipes reinforced with nylon threads are especially strong. A wide range of clip-on connectors and nozzles is available for use with hoses.

Perforated hoses Large expanses of ground are time-consuming to irrigate unless some kind of semi-automatic system is used. Sprinklers are useful because they can be turned on and left to apply large quantities of water to the ground in a fine spray which is easily absorbed. This type of application is to be preferred to flooding because it ensures that the water is more evenly distributed in the soil. The perforated lay-flat hose type of sprinkler is attached to a tap and laid across the land to be irrigated. When the water is turned on, it is discharged at many different angles from the pin-prick holes in the hose. Move the pipe from time to time to provide an even distribution of water.

Sprinklers There are two main types of sprinkler, both of which can be attached to a hose pipe. The oscillating type consists of a perforated tube which rocks backwards and forwards, distributing its water over a square or rectangular area. It can usually be adjusted to cover a chosen part of the garden. The rotating sprinkler ejects water from one or

Planting

After planting trees and shrubs, water them in well to settle the soil around the roots. This speeds growth.

Containers

When planting in containers, leave a gap between the compost and the rim of the pot to allow for watering. When watering, carefully fill this space.

more nozzles which are forced around by the water pressure. This type of sprinkler covers a circular area. Both sprinklers may be controlled to a certain extent by the water pressure – the higher the pressure the larger the area they will cover.

Pop-up sprinklers which oscillate or rotate can be laid in lawns or vegetable gardens and supplied with water by underground pipes. The nozzles sit just below the surface of the soil when out of action (useful on the lawn where mowers can then be used safely) and spring up when the water is turned on.

The evenness of distribution of any sprinkler can be tested by placing jam jars at intervals over the soil being watered. The quantities the jars contain after an hour or so can be compared. The jars will also give an approximate indication of when an inch of water has been applied.

Sprinklers may be less effective on ornamental plants than on vegetables, especially in summer. The foliage of some ornamentals will deflect much of the spray, and heavy blooms and foliage can be weighed down and damaged by the water. Sprinklers are best used on ornamentals not in bloom.

Drip irrigation Lengths of pipe fitted with short drip nozzles, or with longer "spaghetti" tubes that can be directed to individual plants, are particularly useful where water has to be kept off plant foliage. In flower beds, borders and garden frames, and among pots and hanging baskets, such pipes can be fitted to dispense water slowly when the tap is turned on. They keep soil disturbance to a minimum and supply the water slowly enough to ensure instant absorption into the soil and fast take-up by plants.

Use of natural water sources
The diversion of streams and ditches is practised infrequently in temperate climates, but it can be used to advantage, particularly at the start of the growing season. If a stream runs through or past the garden, it is a simple task to pump water from it at any time and apply it to crops. Gravity-fed pumps can be obtained which move a small but continuous amount of water from a spring or stream along a contour line. Power-driven pumps can be used to move water from streams or ponds. Most areas have regulations on the abstraction of water which are enforced by the river authorities. Check the regulations before using water.

Watering seedlings

1 Begin pouring to one side of the tray or pot to allow the water to flow steadily.

2 Pass the can across the seedlings, keeping the angle constant, moving it clear of the pot or tray before halting the flow of water.

Weather and climate 1

Weather is what happens day by day, climate is the set of conditions prevailing at a given spot over a period. The climate of a garden depends firstly upon major factors such as latitude, distance from the sea and prevailing winds, and secondly on the local topography. The local climate, which can vary quite widely from the norm of the district, is called the microclimate.

Hardiness

Plants which will grow in a given climate are said to be hardy in that area. Hardiness depends upon resistance to frost and upon adaptation to the cycle of seasons prevailing. Thus plants hardy in sub-tropical areas are not hardy, and must be given protection, in more northern zones. Conversely, sub-Arctic plants used to short growing seasons and long periods of dormancy may not thrive in temperate places.

Zones of hardiness The map, right, divides Europe into zones according to the length of the growing season. The growing season is defined as the number of days in the year when the temperature rises above 6°C (43°F), the temperature at which grass begins to grow. The zones vary from 2, which has only 150 growing days a year, to 10, where growth is continuous.

In the lower zones, speed of growth is the key factor in hardiness. Plants must be able to complete their cycle of growth within the number of days when growing temperatures prevail. Thus in low zones fast-maturing, late-flowering and early-cropping varieties of fruit and vegetables are grown.

Some plants, such as deciduous fruits, require a period of dormancy during winter. In higher zones they are provoked into year-long growth, with consequent loss of quality.

Major climate factors

As can be seen from the map, proximity to the coast is a major factor in moderating climate. Coastal areas are warmer in winter, and cooler in summer, than those in land. Western Europe further benefits from the warmth of the water in the North Atlantic, which allows zone 9 conditions to prevail in the Western Isles of Scotland, which is on the same latitude as the predominantly zone 4

area of Finland. Mountainous areas experience lower temperatures and heavier rainfall. There is usually an area of low rainfall in the lee, or rain shadow, of high ground. This lee is usually to the east of high ground, reflecting the prevailing westerly winds.

Microclimate

As well as being affected by the area climate, each garden has its own microclimate which is governed by more local factors. The secret of coping successfully with a particular microclimate is either to modify it or to grow plants capable of surviving in the conditions it provides.

Sun and shade The aspect of a garden will influence greatly the types of plant that can be grown. A south-facing slope will receive the maximum amount of light and heat, for the ground is presented to the sun at a direct angle. Growth will start earlier in the spring and continue until later in the autumn. Flat ground, or land sloping in directions other than south, is presented to the sun at a more acute angle and therefore the light and heat it receives are less intense and spread over a

Types of windbreak

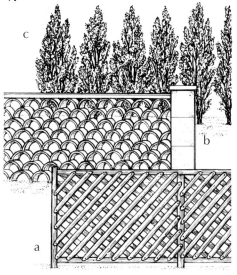

The best windbreaks allow some wind to filter through. They can be of wood (a), concrete blocks (b) or screens of trees (c).

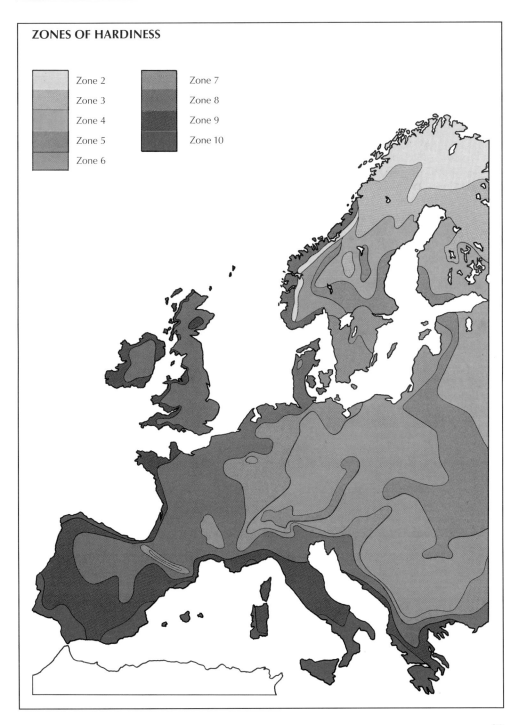

ZONES OF HARDINESS

Zone 2
Zone 3
Zone 4
Zone 5
Zone 6
Zone 7
Zone 8
Zone 9
Zone 10

Weather and climate 2

SUN ANGLES

	Latitude	Summer	Winter
Penzance	50°N	63°	17°
Harrogate	54°N	59°	13°
Shetlands	60°N	53°	7°

The table above shows the noon angle of the sun to the horizon at various latitudes and in representative places. The sun is at its lowest on December 21, and at its highest on June 21. Simple scales, similar to a slide rule, are available, allowing the sun angle at a given date and place to be calculated. When the angle has been calculated, draw a sectional plan of the garden and house, showing shade trees, windows and walls. Using the angle, it will be possible to draw in shady areas. It is thus easy to calculate the areas of sun blinds, to work out which areas will be in shade and which in sun, and otherwise to plan the garden to make best use of the sun. Take care that fences, screens and evergreen hedges do not cut out too much sun, especially in winter.

shorter part of the year. Light is naturally less intense during the winter when the sun is lower in the sky, and sites which are reasonably well lit in the summer may be shady right through the winter. The table in the box above lists the angles of the sun at various latitudes. Ground overshadowed by trees and buildings will be cooler and less hospitable to plants requiring good light, but it will provide an ideal situation for plants native to woodlands. Walls facing north receive less light than south-facing walls, while east- and west-facing walls get full sun for about half the day.

Soil During the day the soil absorbs sun heat and then, under normal conditions, gives off this heat at night when the air above it cools. In this way the soil acts as a heat store, and the heat it radiates protects the plants above it from frost. However, if the soil is mulched it cannot absorb heat so effectively during the day and therefore has less to give off at night. For this reason mulches are laid on the soil in spring and dug in during autumn to allow the soil to absorb more heat in winter. Weeds prevent the absorption of heat in the same way as a mulch and so should be kept under control at all times.

Soils vary in the rate they give off heat absorbed during the day. Clay soils are slow to warm up, and also store heat for longer. Sandy soils absorb and give off heat quickly. Compacted ground is a more effective radiator of heat than soil which has a finely tilled surface that acts as a blanket, keeping in the heat and allowing the plants above to become frosted. Walls absorb and give off heat in the same way as soil, which is one reason why tender plants thrive grown against them. Plants listed as tender in a given zone can be grown in the shelter a wall provides.

Frost Cold air, like water, seeks the lowest level, and areas at the foot of sloping ground will be far more susceptible to frosts than land higher up the slope. Do not position tender plants, especially fruit trees with susceptible blossom, in frost pockets, and avoid creating pockets by erecting solid fences or hedges across a slope. Cold air flowing down the slope will pond up behind such obstacles, leading to frost and damage to plants. Permeable barriers such as open fences allow cold air to seep through, and are therefore to be preferred.

Wind Frost may be the main problem in low-lying gardens, but strong winds are a constant hazard in exposed or hilltop places where they will physically damage trees and shrubs and cause water to be lost from soil and foliage more rapidly. The answer is not to erect a solid wind break, for wind cannot simply be halted – its energy has to be dissipated. A solid wall or fence presented to the wind will cause the air currents to rise up and then fall directly behind the wall, creating damaging down-draughts and turbulence. The way to cut down damage from strong winds is to erect a relatively permeable barrier such as a hedge or open screen. This will reduce the force of the wind to a level which plants can tolerate, and it will not create eddies or turbulence. A permeable barrier will effectively reduce the wind speed for a distance equal to ten times its height. Thus a 50ft (15m) barrier of poplar or leyland cypress trees will protect up to 500ft (150m) of ground on its leeward side. The prevailing wind in Britain usually comes from the west or south-west, so wind breaks are best erected to run from north-west round through west to south-east. Rows of plants running in the same direction as the wind can create a funnelling effect, and should, if possible, be planted across its path to diffuse the force. Wind tunnels created by buildings and walls should have their entrances sheltered by shrubs, trees or open screens.

Rainfall The wind plays an important part in the distribution of rainfall, and frequently ground at the base of walls or trees to the lee-ward side of the wind will remain dry – most of the rain being blown over the top. Soil below north- and east-facing walls will dry out due to a shortage of rain; and that below south- and west-facing walls will also become dry due to the increased amount of sunlight it receives. Irrigation is essential if plant growth is not to be checked.

Altitude The higher the ground, the colder it will be. For every rise of 250ft (75m) above sea level, the temperature drops by about one degree. This factor may be of little conse-quence in summer, but it can make for a later start to the growing season in spring and an earlier cessation in winter.

Urban heat
The heat generated by a large town or city will greatly influence the minimum winter tem-perature. Large conurbations give off quanti-ties of heat day and night which can artifi-cially lift temperatures and allow a wider range of plants to be grown. The atmosphere in such areas is often charged with pollutants, however, and in some places smoke or haze can cut the amount of sunshine received.

Weather records
The use of simple instruments such as ther-mometers and barometers allows a picture of the local microclimate to be built up. Keep records of rainfall, wind and temperature. After a few years the records will allow opti-mum planting dates to be chosen.

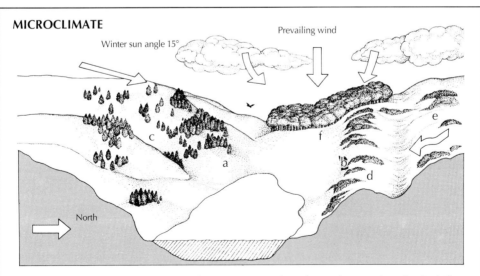

MICROCLIMATE

Winter sun angle 15°

Prevailing wind

North

The lake shore (a) has a moderate climate due to the water's influence. The south-facing slope (b) gets more sun than slope (c) which faces north. Cold air flows downhill at night to form a frost pocket (d). The hilltop (e) is on average one degree colder than (b) due to the effect of altitude. The woodland shelters the field (f) reducing wind.

Plant growth 1

Plant care begins with an understanding of the basics of biology, since it involves the stages of growth from seed to maturity, takes in the elements of propagation and covers the techniques of plant cultivation.

Stages of growth

In order to grow plants successfully the gardener should be aware of how they develop and how their requirements change as they become mature. The vast majority of plants can be raised from seed, which provides a cheap and reliable means of propagating large numbers in a relatively small space. Seed formation is the plant's method of sexual reproduction. Other propagation methods are vegetative, that is they involve removing part of a mature plant and growing a new plant from it.

The seed

Each seed contains one embryo plant (occasionally several) which is usually the product of the fertilization of the female part of the flower by the male. The appearance of the seed varies tremendously from species to species; it may be fine and dust-like or large and hard. It may be carried in a pod, on a fluffy head, in a fleshy fruit or even fitted with wings to enable it to drift on the wind. Whatever its size or appearance every seed has certain basic features.

Seedcoat Known botanically as the testa, the seedcoat is a strong covering that protects the rest of the seed from damage while it is dormant. The seedcoat is usually absorbent and if the environment is suitable the sown seed will take up water to start the process of germination. Occasionally the seedcoat is so hard and impenetrable that it has to be chipped with a knife to allow water to penetrate and germination to take place (sweet peas need this treatment). Other hard-coated seeds can be encouraged to germinate by soaking them in water for 24 hours.

Cotyledons The bulk of the embryo itself consists of one or two (occasionally more) cotyledons, or seed leaves, which in some seeds contain the food supply needed by the young plant during its early stages of growth. These fat seed leaves may remain below ground (hypogeal germination) or they may be carried on the young stem above the soil surface (epigeal germination). As the plant develops and its true leaves appear the cotyledons, no longer needed for nourishment, shrivel and

GROWTH FROM SEED

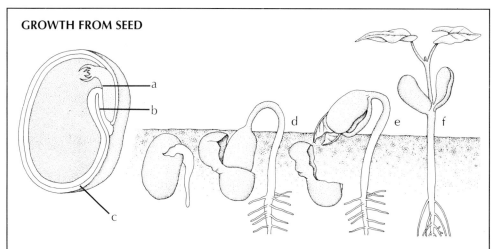

The dormant seed contains the cotyledons, or seed leaves (a), an embryo root system, or radicle (b), and a food store, all within a hard coating, the seedcoat (c).

When germination occurs, the seed leaves swell forcing the seedcoat open. The radicle develops (d), and the seed leaves push upwards (e). True leaves develop (f).

die. In some seeds the bulk of the food supply is carried in the endosperm (a separate food store) rather than in the cotyledons.

Radicle The first root produced by the seed is called the radicle. It generally emerges before the first shoot or the cotyledons and pushes straight down into the soil.

Hypocotyl The stem-like junction between the root and shoot is called the hypocotyl.

Plumule The first shoot, or plumule, is carried above the cotyledons. In some seeds it may be well developed and in others small.

Germination

Water, oxygen and a suitable temperature are all needed to start the seed into growth. As soon as the seed has been provided with these requirements it will start to wake up from its dormancy and put out a root and shoot system. A good compost or good garden soil will provide the first two requirements – moisture and air – and the gardener should ensure that a suitable temperature is provided for the plant being grown. Some seeds need very high temperatures to coax them into growth; others require cold conditions for several weeks before they will germinate; but the majority of seeds will germinate in a temperature of 18°-21°C (65°-70°F).

As the seedlings develop, the first true leaves will appear. These will not be as thick as the cotyledons and are usually an entirely different shape. Both the shoot and root systems will extend and branch out.

Woody plants

Some plants remain fleshy all their lives, but the stems of others become hard and woody as they mature. This process is known as lignification and it occurs in trees and shrubs. Plants which develop woody tissue will usually survive for many years, and they are capable of growing much taller than plants with soft and sappy stems.

Life span

Plants have one object in life and that is to ensure their survival. Most species do this by flowering and producing seeds, and the time it takes to do this varies considerably. Those which grow from seeds and flower, set seed and die within the space of twelve months are

known as annuals; those which take two years to complete this life-cycle are known as biennials, and those which live for many years, usually flowering each year, are known as perennials.

PLANT PROPAGATION

Seeds are the most obvious means by which plants can be increased. However, some plants do not produce seed at all; others produce seeds that are slow or difficult to germinate, or which take many years to reach flowering size, or which give rise to variable and inferior offspring. For these reasons, one of the vegetative methods of propagation may be used.

Spores Ferns do not flower, but they produce spores on the undersides of some of their fronds. These asexually-produced embryos can be sown in a humid environment on moist compost and will eventually develop into mature plants.

Stem cuttings Pieces of plant stem may be severed and encouraged to produce roots. Plants raised in this way will be identical to the parent. There are several different types of stem cutting which are taken at different times during the growing season.

Soft woods These cuttings are taken in spring from fast-growing shoot tips.

Green woods Taken slightly later than soft woods, green wood cuttings are made when the growth of the shoot tips has slowed down but while they are still green.

Semi-ripe woods Semi-ripe cuttings are taken during late summer when growth has slowed down and the stems are thicker and firming at the base.

Hard woods These are taken from deciduous trees and shrubs in the dormant season when the stem is fully woody.

Stem modifications

A modified stem is an organ that stores food, which the plant uses to survive its dormancy period. Often it is a means of reproduction.

Bulbs Bulbs are modified stems equipped with scale leaves. Tunicate bulbs have large scales which overlap one another almost completely; scaly bulbs have smaller scales which do not overlap and are not surrounded by a thin papery covering. Bulbs increase

Plant growth 2

naturally by division. Some produce bulbils in the leaf axils all the way up the stem; others develop bulblets which can be detached and planted. The scales of scaly bulbs can be removed and grown on.

Corms Corms are modified stems which do not possess fleshy leaves, only dry and papery ones which act as a protective covering. A new corm is produced each year under or by the side of the old one, but small cormels may also develop and these can be grown on.

Stem tubers Stem tubers, which are swollen underground stems, can be distinguished from root tubers by the presence of buds. They can be cut into pieces and induced to form roots, or left to multiply themselves before being lifted and replanted individually.

Rhizomes Horizontally growing stems that lie on or just below the surface of the soil, rhizomes can be divided and replanted.

Offsets and runners Lateral shoots sent out from the crown of the plant as a natural means of vegetative propagation are called offsets or runners. An offset will usually have one bud which is capable of rooting and growing away as an individual. A runner will produce several plantlets along its length.

Plantlets Some plants produce miniatures of themselves along their leaves. These tiny plants can be detached and grown on.

Leaf cuttings Leaves may be removed from a variety of plants and encouraged to form roots and shoots. Leaf petiole cuttings consist of a leaf and its stalk, while leaf squares can be cut from some large-leaved plants and inserted so that the roots and shoots are produced from vein ends. Other leaves may be laid on compost and their veins slit. Small plantlets will be produced at the slits.

Division Plants which form a crown consisting of many shoots and roots can be cut up or teased apart and the portions replanted.

Layering Stems are encouraged to form roots while still attached to the parent plant. Later they are severed and grown on individually. In tip layering just the apex of the shoot is buried in soil; in simple layering a central portion of the stem is buried. Air layering is practised on stems that cannot be bent down to the ground. A slit is made in the stem, padded with damp moss and surrounded with polythene to encourage root production.

Root cuttings Certain plants have roots which are capable of developing leaves and shoots. The roots are cut up into convenient lengths,

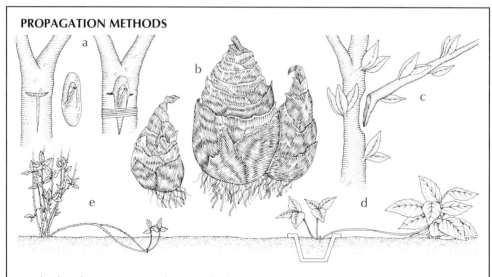

PROPAGATION METHODS

Methods of propagating plants include budding (a), bulbs with developing offsets (b), stem cuttings (c), runners (d) and tip layering (e).

boxed up and transplanted when shoots and fibrous roots have been produced.

Root tubers Unlike stem tubers, root tubers do not possess buds. They can be divided, but a bud from the central stem or crown of the plant must be present if the tuber is to grow.

Budding Dormant buds from a selected plant of good flowering or fruiting ability are attached to the stem of a close relation which has a good root system or a known vigour. The two are encouraged to grow together to produce a healthy plant of the required size and characteristics.

Grafting This technique is similar to budding but in this case an entire shoot is used.

Full details of all these methods of increase will be found in the companion volume in this series: *Plant Propagation*.

Buying plants

To have the best chance of succeeding in their new environment, bought-in plants must be at the peak of health when they are purchased. The gardener usually has several sources of supply to choose from, and the plants may be bought in several states.

Bare-root Available between November and March, bare-root trees, shrubs and herbaceous plants have been lifted directly from the nursery rows in which they grew and will have little soil adhering to the roots. They should be replanted as soon as possible after lifting. If immediate planting is not possible, the plants should be heeled in (see page 61).

Container-grown Available all the year round, container-grown plants should be transplanted with as little disturbance to the rootball as possible, but the container should be carefully cut away and removed.

Bedding plants may be obtained in boxes, pots or plastic strips and should be knocked out and separated before being planted. Avoid choosing those which are covered in blooms and are probably past their best.

Balled Several shrubs, notably rhododendrons and conifers, form a dense, fibrous root system and are often sold with the rootball wrapped in hessian. All the material should be cut away from the sides and base of the rootball once the plant is in its hole, but the roots themselves must be disturbed as little as possible.

Sources of supply

Always buy from a firm with a good reputation to make sure of obtaining plants that are healthy and true to name. Other gardeners may be able to suggest firms with whom they have dealt successfully. Nurserymen who grow their own plants can offer them in a first-class condition and are usually to be preferred to those garden centres that buy in all their stock. However, many garden centres do grow their own plants and may have a large selection raised in containers for year-round sale.

Many specialist and old-established nurseries have a mail-order service and can be trusted to send out good-quality plants which are packed to ensure that they reach their destination in good condition. Always order well in advance of the planting season to be sure of obtaining the required plants, and study the business terms and despatch dates in the catalogue before filling in the order form. Avoid ordering by post from unknown nurseries offering large quantities of cheap plants – they will invariably be inferior.

Supermarkets and chain stores may sell prepacked trees and shrubs in spring. If purchased shortly after they arrive in the shops, there is no reason why such plants should not do well, but avoid buying those which have long, thin, pale green shoots – indicating that they have been packed for some time and will be difficult to establish.

Unwrap all prepacked or mail-order plants as soon as they arrive. Soak the roots of bare-root trees and shrubs in a bucket of water before planting or heeling in.

There is no doubt that the best way to obtain exactly what is required is to go to the nursery concerned and make the selection in person. Plants of good overall shape are to be preferred to those of large size. Small but healthy specimens will often establish themselves more quickly and eventually outgrow those that are larger at planting time.

When an instant effect is required, semi-mature trees and shrubs whose roots have been properly balled up in the nursery may be transplanted with success, but such plants are expensive and should only be used when absolutely necessary.

Growing from seed 1

Growing plants from seed is the easiest and cheapest method of propagation, but cleanliness and attention to detail are needed for quality results.

Sowing in containers
By sowing seeds in containers placed in a heated greenhouse or frame, a close watch can be kept on their development and complete control can be exercised over their environment. Use clean pots or plastic trays. John Innes seed compost (see page 30), or a soilless equivalent, provides the young plants with all they need in the early stages of growth. Use fresh, moist compost. Over-fill a seed tray with compost and firm into place with the fingers – taking care to get the compost into the corners of the tray. Scrape off any excess with a board. Firm the compost with a presser board to leave the surface ½in (1.25cm) below the rim.

Plastic trays have plenty of drainage holes in their bases so they will not need a drainage layer. Plastic pots are equally efficient, but in clay pots a few pieces of broken pot should be placed concave side downwards over the hole. If no such crocks are available use coarse gravel.

Mix very small seeds with a little fine silver sand to make distribution easier. Scatter from the packet so that the mixture is spread evenly over the surface of the compost. Space larger and pelleted seeds individually. Sow very large seeds such as broad beans, marrows and melons individually in small pots of seed compost or in soil blocks.

Cover the seeds with a thin layer of compost put through a ⅛ or ¼-in (0.25 or 0.5cm) sieve. Very fine, dust-like seeds should not be covered at all. Label the container to show the variety of seed and date of sowing, and water with a watering can fitted with a fine rose, or by standing the container in a shallow tray of water and allowing the compost to take up what it wants. Place a sheet of glass covered with newspaper over the top of the tray and keep the tray, ideally, in a temperature of 18-21°C (65-70°F). Do not allow the compost to dry out.

Remove the glass and paper as soon as the first seedlings show, and stand the container in good light. An occasional watering with a proprietary fungicide will reduce the likelihood of damping off (collapse of the seedlings due to fungal attack).

Sowing seeds outdoors
There are two ways of sowing seeds outdoors: in drills, or broadcast. For both types of sowing the soil must be moist but not wet, levelled and broken down to a reasonably fine tilth.

PRE-GERMINATION OR CHITTING
There is always a certain amount of wastage when sowing seeds because not all of them will germinate. In particular, certain crops such as cucumbers and sweetcorn may have erratic rates of successful germination. One solution is to sow a large number of seeds and thin out the seedlings if necessary. However, a more economical and reliable method is to pre-germinate or "chit" the seeds.

To chit seeds sprinkle them on to moistened kitchen paper in a plastic container. Cover the container with newspaper and keep it in a warm place at 21°C (70°F). Germination should begin within 2–3 days and the seeds can then be transferred to individual pots.

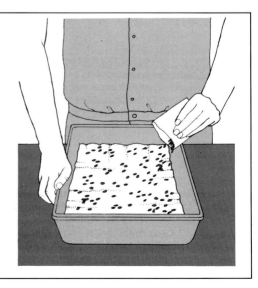

To take out a drill, or shallow furrow, peg a taut garden line against the ground and pull the blade of a draw hoe against it in short jerks so that the corner of the blade removes a 'V'-shaped furrow of the required depth. The drill may also be taken out with the end of a garden cane or the corner of a rake or Dutch hoe. Sow the seeds thinly in the bottom of the drill, mark and label the row, and return the soil carefully with a rake. If the ground is at all dry, water the soil before sowing with a watering can fitted with a fine rose.

Broadcast sowing may be used for lawns, annual flower seeds, or with vegetables being sown in a seedbed for subsequent transplanting. Draw the rake over the ground in one direction to produce ³⁄₄ to ¹⁄₂-in (1.75 to 1.25cm) deep furrows, sow the seeds thinly by scattering them over the area, then very lightly rake the soil at right angles to the first raking direction to cover them.

Pricking out

Seeds sown in trays and pots will produce a dense stand of seedlings which must quickly be transplanted if they are not to become spindly and thus prone to disease. As soon as the first pair of leaves (known as seed leaves or cotyledons) has expanded, the seedlings can be "pricked out" or "pricked off" into another container.

Fill plastic seed trays with compost exactly as for seed sowing, but use John Innes No. 1 potting compost or its equivalent. Prise a clump of seedlings from the seed tray with a label or small knife. About 35 seedlings (5 rows of 7) will fit in a standard plastic tray. Separate the seedlings, and make a hole in the compost for each one as it is planted, using a pencil or dibber. Pick up a seedling by one leaf, spread out the roots in the hole and firm the compost back into place with the dibber. The seedlings should rest at the same depth as they did in the original container, but should now be about 2in (5cm) apart. Label the trays and water the seedlings in with a can fitted with a fine rose.

Very small seedlings such as lobelia can bring problems. Sow the seeds thinly and prick out when slightly larger than normal. Prise out with a pointed stick and gently bed into the surface of the new compost.

Hardening off

Plants that are raised in a greenhouse but which will later be planted outdoors must be gradually accustomed to the cooler temperatures they will later encounter – a process known as hardening off. Gradually reduce the heat as planting time approaches, and move the plants from the greenhouse to an unheated garden frame which is given more ventilation as the days progress. Then remove the light or cover altogether. The plants will then be ready to be transferred to open ground with the least possible check to their growth.

Planting out

Once they are properly hardened off, young plants can be moved to the position in which they are to grow. This should have been cultivated and allowed to settle for several days before planting. All plants should be watered a few hours before they are set out.

To remove plants from their container, knock the sides of the seed tray against the ground to free the soil, and then lift out the plants, separating them but keeping as much soil as possible around the roots. Use a trowel to take out a hole large enough to accommodate all the roots, lower the plant into position and refirm the soil with the fingers. Space the plants sufficiently wide apart to allow them to develop. Water well, using a sprinkler or a watering can fitted with a coarse rose.

Young brassica plants raised in trays or an outdoor seedbed can be planted out with a large dibber made from an old spade or fork handle. Separate the plants, dib a large hole for each one against a line, lower in the roots and firm back the soil with the dibber. "Puddle in" each plant with a rose-less watering can.

Aftercare

To ensure successful establishment after planting, make sure that the plants are watered well when necessary and given shelter from strong, drying winds. Twiggy branches may be pushed into the soil on the windward side of the seedlings to afford some shelter, or a post and hessian screen may be erected as a temporary measure.

Growing from seed 2

Sowing in containers

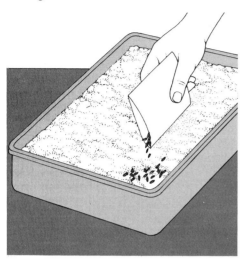

1 Fill a seed tray with moist compost and firm with a presser board to ½in (1.25cm) below the rim. Scatter the seeds evenly over the surface. Space sow larger seeds.

2 Cover the seeds with sieved compost, water in, and label. Place a sheet of glass and paper over the container and keep at a temperature of 18°C-21°C (65°-70°F).

Hardening off

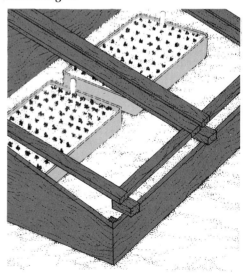

5 Make holes with a dibber 2in (5cm) apart in moist compost in a new container. Transplant the seedlings, firm them in with a dibber and water with a fine rose.

6 Transfer the plants from the greenhouse to an unheated garden frame. Gradually increase the ventilation, eventually removing the cover altogether.

Pricking out

3 When the seedlings appear, remove the glass and paper. Keep the compost moist and spray occasionally with a fungicide to prevent damping off.

4 When the seed leaves have expanded, prise a clump of seedlings from the compost and separate them carefully, holding them gently by the leaves.

Sowing in drills

Broadcast sowing

Take out a V-shaped drill with the blade of a draw hoe. Sow the seeds thinly and regularly in the bottom of the drill. Rake soil over them, water in, and label the row.

Rake the seedbed in one direction to make ½-¾in (1.25-1.75cm) deep furrows. Scatter the seeds thinly over the whole area. Cover with soil, raking at 90° to the furrows.

Cultivation techniques 1

Once the ground has been prepared, the fundamental techniques of cultivation help to keep the soil in the correct state and maximize plant growth.

Hoeing

No gardener can afford to be without at least one kind of hoe to cultivate the soil around his ornamental plants and fruit and vegetable crops. Hoeing serves two useful purposes: it keeps down weeds and so reduces competition for light and nutrients; and it relieves compaction and allows vital air into the soil. It is also claimed that a layer of fine soil on the surface of the ground acts like a mulch and prevents excessive water loss.

There are many designs of hoe to choose from (see pages 115-16). The most popular is the Dutch hoe. It has a flat blade held at the end of two metal arms which allow soil to pass between them. The tool is pushed and pulled back and forth just below the surface of the soil so that it severs the stems of weeds from their roots. If used too deeply the Dutch hoe is less effective at controlling weeds. Pronged cultivators may be used in a similar manner. They are more valuable for breaking down the soil than for weeding.

The Canterbury hoe looks like a three-pronged fork fixed at right angles to the end of a stout shaft. It is used with a chopping and pulling motion and the operator works forwards (instead of backwards as with the Dutch hoe).

Hoes of a similar design but with a solid blade are also available. The draw hoe or swan-necked hoe is a long-handled version. It is the best tool for drawing seed drills and is also very useful for earthing up. The onion hoe is a much smaller version of the draw hoe and can be used effectively with one hand to thin out many crops in the seedling stage –

Earthing up

To protect new shoots of herbaceous perennials from frost in spring, pull a little fine soil over them with a draw hoe or rake.

Support tall brassica plants such as Brussels sprouts by forming mounds of soil around their stalks with a draw hoe, helping to prevent wind damage.

the chosen seedlings are held firm and the rest chopped out with its blade.

Earthing up

The gardener may draw up soil around the stem of plants, or "earth them up", for one of several reasons. Young and tender shoots may emerge too early in spring and a covering of soil will be needed to protect them from frost. This is often the case with potatoes and some herbaceous plants. Pull a little fine soil over the shoots with a draw hoe or a rake.

Brassicas such as cauliflowers, kale and Brussels sprouts will often become top-heavy when nearing maturity. A mound of soil pulled around the base of the stems will give them extra stability. A draw hoe is the best tool to use.

Vegetables grown especially for their crisp, white stems or leaf stalks are surrounded by soil both to keep out the light (a process known as blanching) and to encourage them to extend. With leeks this process can be carried out gradually through the growing season. Celery is earthed up at the end of summer when the plants are almost mature. Hold the leaf stalks together by a tube of paper or card and bank soil up against them with a spade. The paper helps to keep the celery hearts clean.

With potatoes earthing up prevents the tubers from being exposed to the light, which will cause them to become green and unpalatable. A draw hoe or Canterbury hoe will be found useful for this task, which should be carried out at ten day intervals in the early stages of growth.

Blanching

Blanching aims to prevent light reaching certain vegetable crops so that their leaves, leaf stalks or stems become white instead of

Earth up celery every three weeks as the plants grow. Draw soil gently up around the stems with a spade or hoe. Do not let soil fall into the hearts.

Earth up potatoes, using a draw hoe at ten day intervals during the early stages of growth.

Cultivation techniques 2

green. In such a state certain vegetables have a better flavour and are crisper. The blocking of light prevents the production of chlorophyll – the green colouring in plants. Earthing up, a method of blanching celery and leeks, is described above.

The hearts of endives are blanched to improve their flavour. Place a plastic pot over the plant. Cover the pot's holes to exclude light. The pot will prevent light from reaching the leaves and in a few weeks the endive can be harvested with a crisp, white heart.

Forcing
A number of plants can be coaxed into early growth if they are provided with the necessary conditions. In this way the gardener can produce flowers and food when they are out of season and consequently expensive to buy in the shops.

Most plants that are to be forced require some heat, but a low temperature of 10°-15°C (50°-60°F) will suffice. Greenhouses, frames or propagating cases may be used.

Potatoes and French beans can be potted up in 12in (30cm) pots or tubs in December and January and grown on to maturity in their containers. Rhubarb, chicory and seakale require different conditions. To produce the best crops of these three vegetables light must be excluded. When the roots or crowns have been potted or boxed up in compost, put them under the greenhouse staging or in a frost-free place and cover them with a sheet of black polythene supported by wire hoops, or, in the case of pots, place a second inverted pot on top of the first. Should light enter, the shoots will become yellow and, in the case of chicory and seakale, bitter.

Strawberries potted up in summer may be moved into the greenhouse in January to provide early crops, and container-grown

Blanching

Blanch endive hearts by placing an inverted plastic pot on crocks over the plant. Cover the hole to exclude light.

Forcing

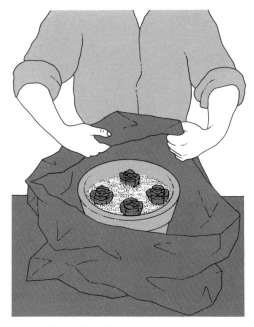

Pot up rhubarb, chicory or seakale in compost. Cover the pots with black polythene and put in a frost-free place.

flowering shrubs may be similarly treated.

Flowering bulbs can be given eight weeks or so in cool conditions to encourage root production and then moved into a greenhouse to bring them into flower early.

Most vegetable plants are best discarded after one forcing, but if necessary they can be planted in the garden and allowed to recover – no crop being taken the following year. Bulbs, too, can be planted outdoors after forcing. Flowering shrubs should only be forced every other year, and forced strawberries should be discarded after use.

Ring culture

Where greenhouse border soil is poor or infected with disease, ring culture offers an alternative means of growing healthy tomato plants. Erect 8in (20cm) high boards down either side of the border, flatten the soil and lay a sheet of polythene over it. Pierce the polythene sheet at intervals with a garden fork to make drainage holes.

On top of the polythene place a 6in (15cm) layer of coarse gravel, pea shingle or weathered ashes. Tomatoes are best grown in 9in (23cm) diameter whalehide or aluminium rings or in 9in (23cm) plastic pots with their bases removed. Before planting, space the rings 18in (45cm) apart on the bed of gravel and fill them with John Innes No. 3 potting compost. Leave them in position a few days before planting.

Water the compost after planting to settle the tomatoes in, but apply all subsequent waterings to the gravel. Apply diluted liquid feeds to the compost. This encourages two distinct root systems to develop: feeding roots in the ring and water-absorbent roots in the gravel. Flood the gravel at the end of each season to remove any impurities and change it every third year.

Ring culture

Alternatively, force rhubarb by covering the plants with a bucket or dustbin in mid-January–February. Insulate with straw. Pick 5-6 weeks later.

Place rings on a bed of gravel, ashes or shingle and fill with compost. Water should be applied to the gravel to encourage root growth.

Cultivation techniques 3

There are many gardening techniques which are specifically designed to improve plant performance and yield. They modify the growth and habit of a plant, changing its natural growth pattern in order to satisfy the gardener's requirements.

Thinning

Thinning is practised on the fruits of such crops as grapes and peaches which the plant produces in large numbers. Some fruits are cut out while they are still small to allow a lighter crop to develop more fully. Such action also saves the plants' energy, so increasing the likelihood of their cropping well the following year. Gooseberries can be thinned from late May, when the fruits are large enough for cooking. Remove every second fruit, leaving the remainder to develop into large dessert fruits. Grapes under glass are thinned in June over a 10-14 day period, removing the interior berries first and then the smallest, leaving a pencil thickness between the developing berries. Thin developing fruit and flowers from melons, leaving one fruit per shoot of frame-grown plants.

Apples and pears should be thinned to one or two fruits per cluster, with the clusters 6 in apart. Thin in mid-June and again a month later. Thin plums similarly, leaving them 2-3in (5-8cm) apart. It is essential to thin peaches if good-sized fruits are to be produced. Thin over a period, aiming for fruits 9in (23cm) apart.

Pinching

Many plants are naturally bushy and form a well-spaced framework of shoots or branches. The stems of others possess what is known as apical dominance – the shoot at the tip of the main stem will grow vigorously and the growth of all other shoots is retarded. Some plants with this habit tend to become tall, spindly and ugly if not encouraged to bush out. Ornamentals such as fuchsias benefit from pinching and develop an attractive bushy habit. The way to reduce apical dominance is to pinch out the terminal shoot. Other shoots will then develop and the plant will become more shapely. Successive pinching of these shoots may be needed.

Vines, cucumbers and melons are pinched

Thinning fruit

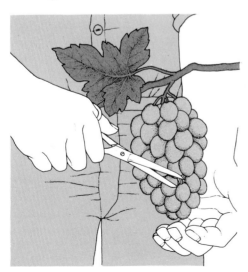

Thin dessert grapes with scissors, carefully removing interior berries in order to leave a pencil thickness between berries.

Thin wine grapes by bunches, removing surplus bunches to leave the required number per spur.

at certain stages to encourage fruit development, and chrysanthemums grown for show are "stopped", or pinched back, to obtain a definite number of shoots per plant if large flowers are required.

Disbudding
On plants such as roses, chrysanthemums, dahlias and carnations, the gardener can choose whether he wants a cluster of small blooms or one large one. Exhibitors usually want plants to produce the largest blooms possible and allow only the terminal flower bud to remain on each stem – all the others being pinched out as soon as they are large enough to handle.

Pollination
The transference of pollen from the male stamen to the female stigma of a flower is the first step in seed production and is known as pollination (see page 73). It is essential that most plants grown for fruit are pollinated, and occasionally the gardener must give nature some help – particularly in the greenhouse where natural pollinators such as bees may not be present at flowering time. Spray the blooms of peaches and grapes with a fine mist of water or dust them with a soft paintbrush or rabbit's tail to transfer the pollen grains. Some flowers may simply be shaken; on those such as melons, which produce separate male and female flowers, detach the male blooms and dust them over the female blooms.

Feeding
Plants both in open ground and in containers must be kept supplied with nutrients to maintain healthy, vigorous growth. Outdoors the rain will leach plant foods from the soil, and the nutrients in container compost are quickly used up by the developing plant.

From March to September all actively growing plants in containers will benefit from being given a fortnightly feed diluted at the recommended rate in water. Only apply such feeds when the soil around the roots is already moist so that the nutrients can be quickly absorbed. There are many proprietary brands, but certain straight fertilizers can be diluted in water and used as liquid feeds (see

Thin gooseberries in May, picking every second fruit and using them for cooking. The remainder will be dessert fruits.

Thin apples and pears to one or two fruits per cluster. Thin in mid-June and again a month later.

Cultivation techniques 4

page 21). Plants such as tomatoes grown for their fruits will benefit from being given high potash fertilizer at an early stage of fruit development. Leafy crops will benefit from fertilizers with a high nitrogen content and root crops from those containing a high proportion of phosphates. Different crops have different nutritional needs and therefore these generalized recommendations should be treated with care. *Fruit* and *Vegetables*, give details.

Liquid feeds may be applied with a watering can or through a special dilutor which can be attached to a hose pipe. This acts as a reservoir for the liquid fertilizer and controls the amount of concentrate mixed with the water.

Certain liquid feeds may be applied to the foliage of plants where they will be quickly absorbed into the sap-stream. Foliar feeds are useful for giving plants a quick boost but they should be used with caution on species with hairy leaves.

Mulching

A 2-3in (5-8cm) thick layer of organic matter spread around plants growing in beds and borders will serve several useful purposes. It will slowly decompose and help to enrich the soil; it will suppress weed growth, and it will conserve soil moisture. Suitable materials for mulching are described on pages 19-20. Mulches are best laid in spring. Remaining material can be forked into the soil in autumn. The soil can then be allowed to weather and absorb the winter rains. It is important to ensure that the soil is moist before applying a mulch. If the soil is dry, the mulch slows down the passage of rainwater.

A mulch of black polythene can be used with crops such as strawberries and potatoes. Stretch yard-wide (metre-wide) strips across the prepared soil, anchor the edges in shallow trenches and make planting holes with a knife or a bulb planter. The strawberries are planted after the polythene has been laid. Potatoes grown under a plastic mulch do not have to be earthed up, as although they develop on the surface of the soil they are protected from light by the plastic. Although such a mulch will not enrich the soil, it does suppress weeds and retain moisture. It is especially useful where organic matter is scarce.

Pollination

Pollinate melons by detaching the male flowers and brushing them against the female flowers.

Transfer pollen from the male stamen to the female stigma using a camel-hair brush.

THINNING SEEDLINGS

Seeds sown where the plants are to grow to maturity will frequently produce dense clusters of seedlings which, if they are not reduced in number, will compete and become weak and spindly. For this reason they are usually thinned out as soon as they are large enough to handle to the distance apart required by the mature crop, or by the growing plants if they are to be further transplanted. Thin seedlings while the soil is damp, pressing firmly on the ground around seedlings to be retained and pulling up and discarding those which are not wanted. Alternatively thin with an onion hoe, which is a tool similar to a draw how only small enough to be used with one hand. Hold the seedlings to be retained with one hand and chop away surplus seedlings using the onion hoe. Carefully remove thinnings and put them on the compost heap. Thinnings left lying on the ground may harbour pests and diseases. Water seedlings after thinning.

Pinching

Pinch out the growing tip of plants such as fuchsias to encourage the growth of sideshoots and a bushy habit.

Feeding

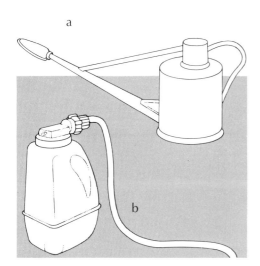

Apply liquid feeds in a watering can (a) or with a reservoir attached to a hose pipe (b).

Mulching

Black polythene can be laid on ground where vegetable crops are to be grown and the plants grown through slits cut in it.

Protecting plants

Staking and supporting

Newly planted trees will be able to support themselves as soon as the roots are established, but require staking initially, particularly in windy places. Other garden plants such as chrysanthemums produce large heavy blooms and need constant support.

Trees Dig the planting hole and check that it is large enough for the tree's roots. Then knock a stake into the soil until one-third of its length is buried. The stake should be either a length of 2in by 2in (5cm by 5cm) timber, treated with a preservative other than creosote, or a larch pole similarly protected. Position the stake to windward of the tree. The top of the stake should be about one-third the height of the branchless stem except in very exposed positions, when it should be just below the lowest branch. With the stake firmly in place, plant the tree. Then fix a tree tie 2in (5cm) from the top of the stake. If it has been necessary to use a tall stake, fix another tie 1ft (30cm) above soil level. Check the ties regularly and loosen as necessary. Another method is to knock a stake into the soil at an angle of 45 degrees so that it crosses the trunk of a planted tree 2-3ft above soil level. The top of the stake should point to windward. Bind the tree to the stake with hessian and strong twine. Guy ropes pegged to the ground and fastened, evenly spaced, around the trunk and lower branches can also be used to hold a tree firm. Cushion them with hessian or by running the ropes through short lengths of rubber hose.

Flowers Support dahlias, delphiniums and other plants which have top-heavy stems either with stout bamboo canes or 1in (2.5cm) wooden stakes pushed into the ground alongside them. Fasten the stems to the supports with soft twine or raffia. Make sure that the support does not touch the flower or damage may result.

Support bushy herbaceous plants by pushing twiggy branches among them while they are small. As the plants grow they mask the branches but are held steady by them. More permanent herbaceous plant supports include wire hoops on legs. These are available in various sizes and can be adjusted as the plants grow.

Staking

Knock a stake into the planting hole on the windward side of the tree. Ensure one-third of its length is below the ground.

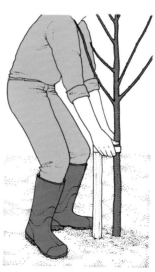

Secure the tree to the stake with a tree tie positioned just below the top of the stake.

Supporting flowers

Support top-heavy flowering plants with bamboo canes. Tie the stems to the canes with soft twine or raffia.

Vegetables Among vegetables only beans and peas normally need support. Runner beans can be grown up wigwams of 8ft (4.2m) canes pushed into the ground in 4ft (1.2m) circles held together at the top with wire or stout twine. Alternatively, grow the plants up canes or poles spaced 18in (45cm) apart. Tie opposite poles together near the top to leave a V-shaped gap. Lay further poles or canes along these gaps and then bind the whole structure together. Support peas with twiggy branches in the same way as herbaceous plants, or with plastic netting on canes.

Wind protection
Wind can cause great damage in the garden, particularly to newly planted evergreen trees and shrubs. The plants may be blown over and they may become desiccated, which causes their foliage to wilt and turn brown.
Anti-desiccant sprays These chemicals seal the pores through which the plant loses moisture, and so help it to remain turgid. Spray with diluted mixture at planting time.
Screens may be used to shelter trees or shrubs. For example, a plastic fertilizer sack, slit at the base to make a sleeve, can be held around a shrub with three or four canes. Alternatively nail a sheet of hessian to two posts knocked into the ground on the windward side of the plant.

Frost protection
The crowns of tender perennial garden plants such as globe artichokes, agapanthus, eremurus and gunnera are susceptible to frost. Protect them by laying a piece of wire netting over each crown. Cover this with dry straw or bracken and fasten another layer or netting over the top to make a warm blanket. Protect larger plants and shrubs by surrounding them with a cylinder of wire netting filled with straw or bracken.

Protection from wet
Some alpines are particularly sensitive to excess moisture in winter. In their natural habitat, they are covered with a layer of dry snow which protects them. To prevent them from rotting off, cover each with a pane of glass supported on wooden or wire pegs. Tie the glass down with wire.

Wind protection

Support herbaceous plants by inserting bushy twigs among them. The plants will grow through the branches.

Wire plant supports can also be used to support herbaceous plants.

Use a plastic sack fixed to four canes to keep down the force of the wind.

Moving and storing plants

It is sometimes necessary to move plants, from alpines to large shrubs and young trees, from one part of the garden to another, or to another garden. The technique outlined here is for large plants. The same basic process, with modifications, should be used for all plants. Always insert sacking or plastic sheet under the rootball and never lift a plant by its neck or branches.

Moving trees and shrubs

Move deciduous trees and shrubs between November and early March, evergreens in October or March-April. First, tie in any spreading branches or wrap the plant in hessian or old sacks to prevent the stem from being damaged and to allow room for lifting. Next, using a spade, cut a vertical slit around the plant. Aim to cut at a distance equivalent to the spread of the top-growth. This cut will sever any side-spreading roots. Using this slit as the inner edge, take out a trench 1ft (30cm) wide and one spit deep all around the plant, severing any roots that protrude.

Ease away any loose soil around the shoulder of the rootball and then thrust the spade underneath the rootball at an angle of 45 degrees to cut off more roots. The aim should be to retain as large a ball of soil around the roots as can be conveniently handled.

When the plant is movable, ease a sheet of hessian or polythene underneath it and then wrap up the entire rootball to retain the soil and prevent moisture loss. Tie the material firmly in place around the stem or trunk. Transport the plant with care to its new site and dig a hole wide and deep enough to accommodate the rootball with 1ft (30cm) to spare all round.

Dig a generous helping of rotted manure or leaf-mould into the base of the new planting hole, together with a slow-release fertilizer to promote fresh root growth. Carefully position the plant at its original depth. Replace and re-firm the soil all round and water it in thoroughly. Spread a 3-4in (8-10cm) mulch of organic matter such as leaf-mould or pulverized bark around the plant.

Considerable amounts of water may be lost by evergreen shrubs and conifers during the move, and an anti-desiccant spray may be

Moving trees and shrubs

1 Tie in any spreading branches to protect the plant during the move. Wrap smaller shrubs in hessian.

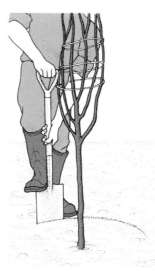

2 Cut a vertical slit in the soil around the plant with a spade. Make the slit 1-2ft (30-60cm) away from the stem, depending on size.

3 Take out a trench 1ft (30cm) wide and 1 spit deep starting from the slit. Sever any roots that protrude into the trench.

applied to the foliage immediately before transplanting to reduce transpiration.

On exposed sites some protection from wind after transplanting will cut down water loss and reduce the likelihood of "wind rock" which will dislodge the roots from the soil and cause them to dry out. Three or four wooden posts can be knocked into the ground around the plant and a screen of hessian or close-weave plastic netting nailed to them. Remove the screen when the plant is established.

Storing plants

Smaller plants can be easily stored in a temporary trench dug in a spare corner of the garden. This technique, called heeling in, should also be used for bare-root shrubs and container-grown plants which are not to be planted immediately. Using a spade, cut a V-shaped furrow at the chosen site. Do this by thrusting the spade vertically into the ground to a spit depth and pulling it back, while still in the earth, to form a trench or slot. Lay the plants against the upright side of the trench and replace the soil loosely.

HEELING IN

Lay bare root plants in a shallow trench at an angle of 45 degrees. Cover the roots with loose, friable soil.

4 Thrust the spade under the rootball at a 45 degree angle, cutting the roots. When it will move, ease the rootball on to a sheet.

5 Dig a hole at the new site 1ft (30cm) wider all round than the rootball. Add leaf-mould or compost and a slow-release fertilizer.

6 Carefully place the plant in the hole. Firm the soil and mulch well. Support with guy-lines if necessary.

Mowing and lawn care 1

Many gardeners pay very little attention to their lawn, apart from mowing it sporadically and giving it an occasional feed. A lawn is, however, a carpet of living plants and, as with any crop, will respond strongly to regular attention. The most important lawn operations are those required by any perennial crop: feeding, watering and pruning (in the form of mowing). Top-dressing, aerating and scarifying also benefit a lawn.

Mowing

Apart from keeping grass neat and attractive, mowing encourages the formation of a dense turf, and helps to deter weeds and moss.

The most suitable height of cut is determined by quality of lawn and time of year. Between late spring and early autumn finest-quality lawns should be cut to ¼-½in (0.5-1.25cm), average turf to ½in (1.25cm), and utility lawns to 1in (2.5cm). Increase these figures slightly during dry spells unless adequate irrigation is available. Between autumn and spring, increase the height of cut by ¼in (0.5cm), since this leaves the turf less open to weed and moss infestation.

A lawn should be mown sufficiently often to keep it as close to the required height as is practicable. For fine lawns, this is every two to three days; for others, once a week.

Generally, it is preferable to remove the mowings from a lawn sice they may harbour cut sections of weeds and weed seeds. The mowings can also impede aeration by forming a compact layer on the surface which can become unsightly as they decompose. Some advantages are claimed for leaving the mowings on the lawn: they return some nutrients to the soil, and they are considered to act as a mulch. Under normal conditions, always remove the mowings except in hot dry weather when irrigation is not available, as the mulching effect is then beneficial.

Irrigating

There is usually sufficient rainfall in the United Kingdom to keep lawns well watered. Occasionally, however, there are dry periods during the spring and summer when irrigation is necessary to prevent dying back.

The frequency of watering varies according to the type of soil, but in general, in dry sunny weather a healthy lawn on an average loam soil needs watering every seven to ten days. Apply at least 2 gallons (18-20 litres) per square yard (metre) (about 10-12 minutes using a garden sprinkler at normal water pressure). Avoid frequent light watering since it encourages shallow rooting.

Keep the lawn well maintained, since this will help the grass to develop a deeply penetrating drought-resistant root system.

Feeding

Feeding serves two important purposes. First, it strengthens and thickens grass, giving it more resistance to drought, disease and weeds. Second, it maintains a good colour and texture.

A single annual dressing of lawn fertilizer usually supplies sufficient food. Do this in early spring during mild showery weather when the grass is starting to grow freely. Apply the fertilizer either by hand or with a distributor at 2oz (55g) per square yard (metre), and irrigate it if it does not rain during

Composting mowings

Small quantities of mowings can be added to the compost heap in thin layers, which should be alternated with thicker layers of other refuse.

the following two days. Even and accurate distribution is important since too much fertilizer can scorch or even kill the grass.

Scarifying

All lawns have a layer of debris, known as thatch, lying between the roots and foliage of the grass. In moderation, that is up to ½in (1.25cm) thick, thatch is beneficial since it acts as a mulch. However, if it becomes too thick, water and fertilizer will not be able to reach the roots, and the thatch has to be removed. This is done by vigorously pulling a rake or special tool along the lawn surface – a process known as scarifying. Powered scarifiers can be hired. Scarify a lawn during the autumn, preferably in September, or in early spring before mowing begins. At other times of the year the process will leave the grass looking sparse and the turf will need special feeding to thicken satisfactorily.

Aerating

Aerating is the process of spiking a lawn to allow air into the soil, which helps the roots of grass to absorb water and nutrients. Few lawns require overall aeration, but most have patches that need regular attention. Aerate wherever the turf appears to be lacking in vigour, particularly on children's play areas, moss-infested patches, and where the turf turns brown quickly in dry weather.

To aerate small areas, drive a garden fork into the lawn and ease it back and forth slightly. Use the fork reversed to obtain vertical penetration. Do this at 4-6in (10-15cm) intervals, working backwards to avoid treading on aerated turf. For larger areas, it is best to hire powered or hand-propelled machines as and when required.

Top-dressing

Top-dressing is the application of a mixture of loam, sand and well-rotted organic matter to a lawn in order to feed the grass, and, to some extent, to even out irregularities in its surface. The term is also applied to the mixture itself. Top-dressing improves the surface soil, thickens the turf and helps to break down thatch. Suitable mixtures can be purchased

How to scarify

Dry large quantities before composting by spreading them out thinly, or by making a loose heap and forking it over.

Pull the scarifying tool vigorously along the surface of the lawn to pull up as much thatch as possible. Keep the tool well pressed down when doing this.

Mowing and lawn care 2

from sundriesmen or made up by mixing (for an average loam soil) one part sieved leaf-mould, three parts sandy loam and six parts sand (not builders' sand). Apply the top dressing in early autumn at 4lb (1.8kg) per square yard (metre), increasing this to 6-7lb (2.7-3.2kg) on very irregular turf. Minor irregularities can also be treated in spring or summer. Broadcast the top dressing then work it well into the grass with the back of a rake.

Controlling weeds

The most troublesome weeds are the low-growing perennials that have a creeping habit or grow from rosettes, since these are unaffected by, or can adapt to, regular close mowing. Many of the most common lawn weeds come into this category, for example, clover, daisy, plaintain and speedwell.

If the lawn is not badly infested, then the most practicable approach is to remove the weeds individually with a hand fork or grubbing tool. Firm the surrounding turf carefully after removing a weed to avoid disturbing neighbouring grasses. Hand-weed only during good growing

conditions in spring when the grass will grow quickly to fill in the bare patches. Later in the year there is a much greater risk of bare patches being recolonized by weeds – or moss if a wet period follows a long spell of warm dry weather. If large numbers of weeds are present in the lawn then hand-weeding is no longer practicable and weedkillers must be used.

Weedkillers

The most efficient way to control weeds in a badly infested lawn is to apply a selective lawn weedkiller. These kill or check broad-leaved weeds but do not harm narrow-bladed erect gasses.

Most lawn weedkillers are sold in concentrated liquid form, to be applied after dilution with water. Apply the weedkiller with a sprayer if the lawn is large. For smaller lawns where there is a danger of the spray drifting on to neighbouring plants, use a watering can with a fine rose or dribble bar attachment. Alternatively, there are some lawn fertilizers on the market that incorporate a weedkiller in dry form. This allows the

Aerating small areas

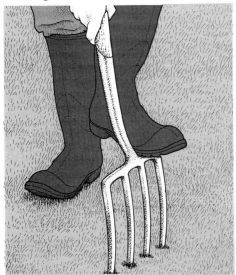

Drive a garden fork backwards into the lawn, since this gives a vertical penetration. Then ease it back and forth slightly before removing carefully.

Using weedkillers

Large areas of weed-infested turf are best controlled by spraying with a proprietary lawn weedkiller.

operations of feeding and weedkilling to be combined into one. However, weeds are better controlled if they are fed beforehand, since they will then be growing vigorously and will absorb the chemical quickly.

Lawn weedkillers are also available in aerosol or solid stock form for spot-treating isolated weeds. There may, however, be some localized temporary scorching of the grass since it is difficult to gauge the amount being applied.

Controlling moss

Moss colonizes lawns for various reasons. Poor fertility or weakness of the turf due to attacks by pests or diseases, lack of aeration, bad drainage, excessive shade or mowing too closely will all result in weak, sparse turf that allows moss to establish.

Moss can be temporarily controlled by using mosskillers but, unless the reason for infestation is established and then corrected, moss will return. Examine the lawn and identify factors causing weak growth. Feed, top-dress, water and aerate it as necessary. If it is prone to waterlogging during the winter, clear existing pipe drainage systems, or install a new system. Do not mow the lawn too closely as this will weaken the grass and allow mosses to establish.

Mosskillers

Moss grows most strongly during cool moist conditions in the autumn and spring, and these are the best periods for applying chemical mosskillers. Lawn sands consisting of sulphate of ammonia, sulphate of iron and lime-free sand have been used to kill moss for many years and are still a useful means of control. Apply at 4oz (110g) per square yard (metre) during fine weather, ideally on a moist, dewy morning with a fine day ahead. Water the lawn two days later if there has been no rain. One to two weeks later carefully rake out the blackened dead moss.

Dichlorophen is an effective chemical mosskiller and the active ingredient in some proprietary lawn moss eradicants. It is marketed as a concentrated liquid formulation. Apply it with a sprayer or watering can.

Hand-weeding

Remove isolated weeds with a hand fork or grubbing tool. Carefully firm the surrounding turf after extracting each weed to avoid disturbing neighbouring grasses.

HOW TO USE LAWN WEEDKILLERS

Do not apply at a rate stronger than that recommended by the manufacturer.

Do not apply when windy, otherwise the spray may be carried to nearby plants.

Do not apply immediately before mowing or much of the leaf surface may be severed before the weedkiller can reach the roots. Allow three or four days before mowing.

Do not apply immediately before rain, otherwise much of the weedkiller may be washed into the soil.

Do not apply early in the year or during drought when there is little growth.

Do not mow immediately before weedkiller application or there will be a much reduced leaf-surface area to receive and absorb the weedkiller.

Do not use fresh mowings as mulches following treatment of lawns. Freshly treated mowings can be composted but the compost should not be used for at least six months.

Basic pruning

Pruning is the removal of any part of a plant to encourage it to grow, flower or fruit in a particular way. The method used and the severity of the pruning depend on the effect required and the natural habit of the plant. Many plants are pruned very lightly just to accelerate the normal process of regeneration and, in general, it is better not to prune at all than to hack a plant indiscriminately.

Basic principles

Before pruning any plant it is important to understand its growth and flowering habit. In most plants, the terminal or apical bud of a shoot grows faster than, and inhibits the growth of, the lateral buds below. This effect is known as apical dominance. If the terminal bud is cut off, the dominance is usually broken, some of the lateral buds below are stimulated into growth and the plant develops a compact bushy habit.

In some plants, such as lilac, the dominance is shared by the uppermost pair of buds, and the natural growth pattern is forked.

It is essential to position pruning cuts correctly: always cut back to a bud facing in the required direction of growth. This bud will then produce a shoot whose terminal bud exerts apical dominance over the lateral growth below. Make a clean cut just above and sloping gently away from the selected healthy bud. If the cut is too low the bud may be damaged, if it is too high the stem may die back. A jagged cut, or one sloping towards the bud so that moisture gathers there, increases the risk of attack by diseases. To avoid jagged cuts, use the correct tools (see pages 114-25) and keep them sharp.

The more of the shoot that is removed, the stronger the regrowth will be, so if strong growth is desired, cut back weak shoots harder than more vigorous ones.

Reasons for pruning

There are four main reasons for pruning, but they all have the ultimate aim of either producing the most attractive plant or the largest crop possible.

Apical dominance

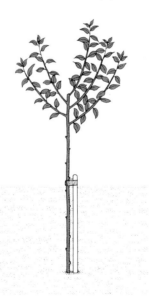

How to cut

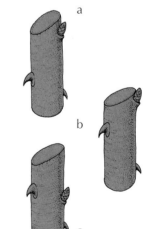

1 Cut back the terminal shoot to a lateral bud to remove the terminal bud and break the apical dominance.

2 Three to five of the lateral buds should then break to give the plant a compact, bushy habit.

Make a clean cut ¼in (0.5cm) above, and sloping gently away from, the selected bud (a). Do not cut too low (b) or too high (c).

Early training Many trees and shrubs need severe pruning in the early stages to establish a good shape, or to train them in a particular restricted form such as an espalier or a cordon. The aim is to produce a balanced framework of strong well-spaced branches. The smaller branches, flowers and fruit will then be evenly distributed over the entire plant.

Maintaining shape Lighter pruning may be needed in subsequent years to maintain this basic shape, and may also be necessary on trees and shrubs that are gowing naturally but have become untidy. It involves cutting out completely any vigorous, awkwardly placed shoots. If there is one more vigorous section of the plant that spoils the symmetry, prune the weak growth harder than the more vigorous shoots to correct the imbalance.

Maximizing flowers or fruit To produce the best display of flowers or foliage, or the largest crop of fruit, it is important to understand the growth and flowering or fruiting habit of the plant. For example, *Buddleja davidii* flowers on the current year's growth and so is pruned hard each spring to encourage new flowering shoots to develop. Shrubs such as *Deutzia*, however, bloom on shoots that are one or more years old and so, if these shoots are cut back as for *B. davidii*, the plant will not flower. Therefore, they are cut back after flowering to new young shoots that will flower the following year.

Maintaining health In order to keep plants healthy and vigorous cut out completely any dead, damaged or diseased growth as soon as it is noticed. Also, thin out any weak, crossing or overcrowding shoots in the centre of trees and shrubs to ensure that there is sufficient air and light. Always cut back into clean healthy wood and burn the prunings, which are a potential source of infection.

Finally, ensure that the plant is well fed and watered, especially if it has been severely pruned, since otherwise its growth may be checked. Plants subjected to severe rejuvenation pruning should be given a generous mulch of organic material.

Maximizing flowers

Maintaining health

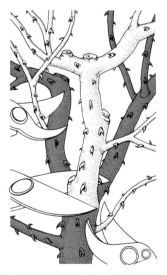

In spring new growth of *Buddleja davidii* should be cut back to promote many new flowering shoots.

In July, cut back the stems that have flowered on *Deutzia*. Strong basal or lateral shoots replace them and flower next season.

Cut out completely any dead or diseased stems (a), weak spindly growth (b), and crossing or over-crowding branches (c).

Crop rotation

It has long been the practice of gardeners to vary the site occupied by each crop from year to year. If the same vegetable is grown on a patch of ground for many seasons without feeding, the soil can become exhausted of certain important nutrients. It is also likely that pests and diseases peculiar to that crop will build up, reducing yields. If the crop occupies a different site each year maximum use can be made of plant food available in the soil, and disease problems reduced.

Crop requirements
For the purposes of rotation, vegetables are divided by their nutritional requirements into three main groups: legumes, salads and onions; root crops; and brassicas.

The first group includes legumes (peas and beans), lettuces, celery, celeriac, cucumbers, tomatoes, sweet peppers, endive, leaf beet, sweetcorn, marrows and courgettes, onions, leeks, shallots, seakale, radishes and spinach. All enjoy a soil rich in organic matter. Peas and beans add plant food to the soil in the form of nitrogen. They are, therefore, followed by brassicas in crop rotation since these plants require abundant supplies of nitrogen to promote leaf and shoot growth.

Root crops include beetroot, carrots, potatoes, salsify, scorzonera, parsnips, swedes and turnips. These crops require ground that is rich in phosphates and potassium, and has been manured for a previous crop. Fresh manure or too much well-rotted organic matter may have adverse effects on root crops, causing them to fork and distort.

Brassicas include cabbages, savoys, cauliflowers, Brussels sprouts, broccoli, calabrese, kale and kohlrabi. Chicory needs similar conditions and may be included in this group. These crops demand abundant supplies of nitrogen and a dressing of lime if the soil is at all acid (see page 20). Apart from decreasing soil acidity (brassicas need a soil pH of 6.5-7.5), lime helps to discourage club root.

Three and four year rotations
A three year rotation system is easy to work, even in a small garden. Divide the plot into three sections: one for legumes and salads, one for roots and one for brassicas. The sections should be of equal size if the same

amount of crops is to be grown each year. In the first year follow this programme:
Section A: Legumes and salads. Dig the ground in autumn, incorporating well-rotted manure or compost (see pages 18-20). If the soil is acid apply lime during the winter (see page 20). Do not add lime at the same time as manure, otherwise the benefits of each will be nullified. In future years the lime applied to the brassica patch should be sufficient to reduce acidity. Three weeks before sowing apply a dressing of general fertilizer at a rate of 2oz (55g) per square yard (metre).
Section B: Root crops. Dig the ground in autumn to allow winter weathering. Apply 4oz (110g) general fertilizer per square yard (metre) in early spring at least two weeks before sowing.
Section C: Brassicas. Dig the ground in autumn and, if the soil pH is less than 6.5, apply 6-8oz (170-225g) lime per square yard (metre). In spring apply a general fertilizer at 4oz (110g) per square yard (metre) two weeks before sowing or planting.

In the second year the brassicas are moved to the site occupied by the legumes and salads; these move to the section where the root crops were, and the roots move to the old brassica site. Each of the new sites is treated as recommended above for the crops being grown. Further moves are shown right.

If a four year rotation is preferred, the plot is divided into four and potatoes grown in the fourth section instead of among the root crops. The ground in plot four should be dug in autumn and, if lacking in organic matter, a light dressing of well-rotted compost or manure is dug in (one bucketful per running yard (metre) of trench). In early spring apply 4oz (110g) of general fertilizer per square yard (metre). Potatoes apart, the four year rotation is carried out as shown in the diagram.

Exceptions to rotation
Certain vegetables will not grow well if they are moved every year. Rhubarb and globe artichokes, for example, should be grown in prepared beds which are cropped for several years. Only when yields begin to show a decline are they dug up, divided and replanted on a fresh site.

Keen onion exhibitors use a site which has

been enriched and improved over many years. The soil is dressed with fertilizer and manure each seson to bring it up to a high level of fertility. Such a system will produce excellent bulbs so long as no specific onion disease such as white rot infests the area, in which case the bed would have to be moved.

Where rotation is impracticable

On very small plots a full-scale rotation may not be a practicable proposition and, if a limited range of vegetables is required, it is difficult to construct a full rotation cycle. In such cases the rows of crops should be alternated if possible so that the ground has a rest from one particular type of vegetable for as long as possible. Careful attention should be paid to manure and fertilizer requirements, with small annual dressings being added as and when necessary.

CROP ROTATION

First year	Second year	Third year
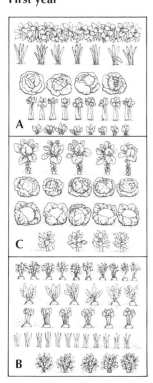	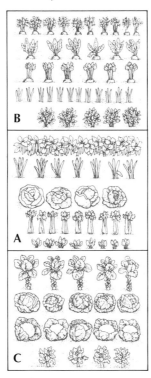	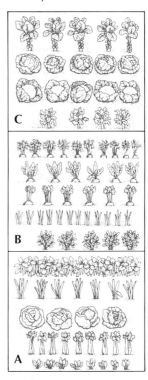

Section A Legumes and salads. Peas, beans, lettuces; celery, celeriac, cucumber, tomatoes, sweet peppers, endive, leaf beet, sweet corn, marrows, courgettes, onion, leeks, shallots, radishes, spinach.

Section B Root crops. Beetroot, carrots, potatoes, salsify, scorzonera, parsnips, swedes, turnips.

Section C Brassicas. Cabbages, savoys, cauliflowers, Brussels sprouts, broccoli, calabrese, kale, kohlrabi, chicory.

Plant names and breeding 1

The Latin names of plants, essential to botanists, may often be confusing to gardeners since some are long and difficult to pronounce, and from time to time names are changed for botanical reasons. However, such a system of nomenclature is essential, for it provides each plant with a universally recognized name which shows its connection with other related plants. Common names, although easier to remember, are inconsistent from country to country and even village to village. Some plants have no common name.

The modern system of naming plants was first put into practice by Swedish botanist Carl von Linné (usually known as Linnaeus) during the 18th century, though the system had been suggested before his time. He gave each plant two names: the generic name, followed by the specific epithet. The generic name indicates the genus to which the plant belongs, and the specific epithet the particular species within the genus. This two-word name fits the plant into the general classification of the entire plant world, which is in essence a reduction from global categories to individual species. Thus, just as species are classified into genera, so similar genera are grouped to form families, similar families are further grouped together, and so on.

Which genus a plant is placed into depends upon its vegetative and reproductive characteristics, and other factors such as genetic and ecological considerations. The most important of these factors is usually the way in which the plant reproduces itself and, since flowers are the sexual organs of many plants, it is the similarities and differences between flowers that govern much plant classification.

The most important groups into which all plants are classified are listed below in descending order of size. Before this stage in the descent from general to specific is reached, the categories of "plant" (as opposed to "animal") and several other groupings have been passed through.

Family In a given family are to be found plants which have several basic features in common but within which can be recognized several distinctly related groups. The heather family, for instance, includes rhododendrons, ericas, callunas, pieris, gaultherias and kalmias. All these make up a natural grouping of plants that appear to "belong" together. The grass family and the rose family have similarly obvious characteristics.

Genus (plural: genera) Plants which bear a strong resemblance and relationship to one another are grouped in the same genus; for example *Primula*. The generic name is always given a capital letter.

Species (plural: species) The species is the basic unit of classification; and is approximately defined as a grouping of very similar plants that in the wild, usually, but not always, breed together to produce consistent offspring. For example, within the genus *Primula* there are many different species, each with a different descriptive name or specific epithet. The primrose is *Primula vulgaris*, the cowslip *Primula veris* and the oxlip is *Primula elatior*.

The specific epithet usually gives some information about the plant. From the names given above the following can be learned: *vulgaris* means common; *veris* means spring-flowering, and *elatior* means taller. Certain specific epithets indicate that a plant was named in honour of a person: *brownii* commemorates a man named Brown and *willmottiae* a woman named Willmott. The ending *"ensis"* commemorates the place where the plant was raised or discovered; for example *kewensis* indicates that a plant was raised at the Royal Botanic Gardens, Kew.

Variety Variation may occur naturally within a particular species, perhaps giving rise to a plant which is identical in every respect except that the colour of its flowers or leaves is different. Such a plant is known as a variety or correctly as *varietas*. For example: *geranium pratense* var. *album* is the white-flowered variety of our native blue-flowered meadow cranesbill; *album* signifies white. Varietal names are written with a small initial letter in the same way as the specific epithet.

Cultivar Should a distinct plant of a certain species arise in cultivation in a garden or nursery, then it is classified as a cultivar (cultivated variety). Variety is often used as a synonym for cultivar and throughout this series of books "variety" is used for both variety and cultivar. Cultivars must not be given Latin names nowadays which might result in them being confused with naturally occurring varieties. Instead they are given names in a modern language; the name has initial capital letters and is enclosed in single quotes. For example: *Geranium endressii* 'Wargrave Pink'.

The botanist uses several other terms to describe variations within a particular species (for example sub-species and forma) but these are relatively unimportant to the gardener. However, the following classifications are frequently used and should be understood.

Sport Occasionally a plant will produce a mutant shoot which is different in appearance to those it normally carries. The shoot may have variegated leaves, unusually coloured flowers or a climbing habit. Such a shoot is said to be a sport, and if propagated vegetatively it may be possible to maintain it as an individual plant. Sporting frequently occurs in chrysanthemums, roses and dahlias, and many of our present-day varieties of these plants arose as sports.

Clone A clone is simply a group of plants propagated vegetatively from one parent. All such plants possess exactly the same genetic make-up as the parent and will therefore be identical to it.

Hybrid A hybrid is a plant which has arisen as the result of crossing any two compatible parents of distinct species, varieties or cultivars. In horticultural terms it usually means a plant raised by crossing two distinct species or variations of a species. Usually the parents are in the same genus, but occasionally successful crosses may be made from two different genera in the same family. Plants in different families are not known to hybridize with one another.

Interspecific hybrids have parents from the same genus but different species, and are designated by the placement of a small "x" between the generic name and the new hybrid

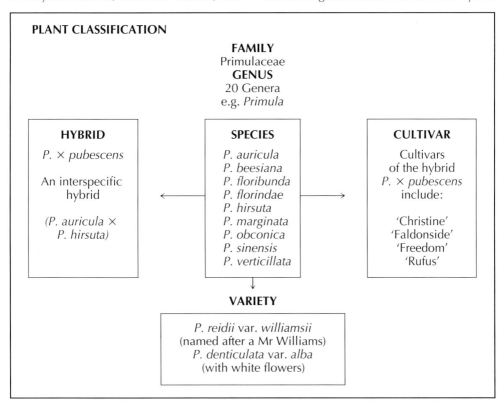

PLANT CLASSIFICATION

FAMILY
Primulaceae
GENUS
20 Genera
e.g. *Primula*

HYBRID	**SPECIES**	**CULTIVAR**
P. × *pubescens*	*P. auricula*	Cultivars
	P. beesiana	of the hybrid
An interspecific	*P. floribunda*	*P.* × *pubescens*
hybrid	*P. florindae*	include:
	P. hirsuta	
(P. auricula ×	*P. marginata*	'Christine'
P. hirsuta)	*P. obconica*	'Faldonside'
	P. sinensis	'Freedom'
	P. verticillata	'Rufus'

VARIETY

P. reidii var. *williamsii*
(named after a Mr Williams)
P. denticulata var. *alba*
(with white flowers)

Plant names and breeding 2

epithet. Intergeneric or bigeneric hybrids have parents from different genera. They have a generic name usually consisting of a combination of the generic names of their parents. The small "x" is placed before this name. Interspecific hybrid: e.g. *Primula* × *pubescens*. Intergeneric hybrid: e.g. × *Cupressocyparis leylandii* (*Cupressus macrocarpa* × *Chamaecyparis nootkatensis*).

If each of the parent plants of a hybrid produces uniform offspring when self-pollinated, it is likely that the offspring produced when the two parents are crossed will be uniform in itself. However, the hybrid race will possess characteristics inherited from both parents.

First filial or F$_1$ hybrids are produced as a result of crossing two specially selected parents which are known to produce offspring of a consistently high and even standard. The plants of this first generation will not, however, produce an even batch of seedlings if they in turn are cross-pollinated, for the characteristics possessed by their parents will not be similarly distributed in the second filial or F$_2$ generation. The fact that F$_1$ hybrid seeds have to be produced afresh by the seedsman each year accounts for their relatively high price.

Stock or selection (strain) Seed-raised plants will almost always show variations in vigour and form, although in plants which are repeatedly self-pollinated to produce a "pure line" these variations may be very minor. However, if such variations are allowed to remain and are used as seed parents, the race might become inferior. For this reason where valued flower and vegetable varieties are concerned, low-quality plants are weeded out and not used as parents. Each variant within the variety is known as a stock or selection (or as a strain) and the importance of buying seed from a merchant who is known to have a good reputation for quality control will be obvious. Certain seed houses will offer their own selection of a particular vegetable variety which may differ markedly from another selection of the same variety offered elsewhere. Any stock or selection recognizably different from the parent should be regarded as a distinct variety.

Plant catalogues and encyclopaedias may use the word synonym, for example: *Crataegus laevigata*, syn. *C. oxyacantha* and *C. oxyacanthoides*. All three names refer to the same plant, a species of the genus *Crataegus*, or hawthorn, which is a member of the family Rosaceae.

Abbreviations commonly used are var. for variety, syn. for synonym, ssp. for subspecies, spp. for several or all species in a certain genus, and sp. for a particular, but unnamed, species, usually so written because only the genus is of interest.

Plant breeding
The subject of plant breeding is a complex one requiring years of observation, selection and rejection, but in its simplest form it can be carried out by the gardener.

Plants known to produce seed which is viable (capable of growing) and true to type can either be left to seed themselves, or hand-pollinated by dusting the flowers with

Structure of a flower

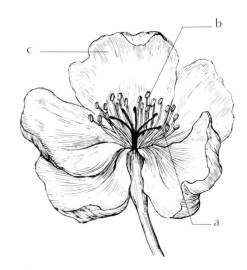

For fertilization to take place, pollen has to be deposited on the stigma (a). Pollen comes from the anther (b), the male part of the flower. Petals (c) attract pollinating insects.

a camel-hair paint brush or by brushing the flowers over one another. Both these methods will ensure that the pollen from the male parts of the flower (the anthers) comes into contact with the female stigma. The transference of the pollen is known as pollination and will, if all goes well, lead to fertilization and the production of seeds. The seeds must be collected as soon as they are ripe.

Where two distinct parents with particular virtues are to be cross-pollinated in the hope of producing offspring with a novelty value, then certain precautions must be taken. The anthers must be removed from the flower which is to act as the seed-producing female. This "emasculation" is necessary to prevent self-pollination which would not produce the required results. To ensure that emasculation is effective, remove the anthers before the flower opens by gently prising the petals apart with a pair of tweezers to allow access. Then cover the blooms with muslin or a translucent paper bag to keep out pollen.

When the anthers on the flower which is to be the male parent are ripe, the pollen from them is dusted over the stigma of the open female flower, which is then re-covered.

Once the female flower withers remove the bag and label the seedhead with details of the cross. Sow seeds that form when ripe.

Professional plant breeders take many years to produce a hybrid which possesses the required characteristics. Parent plants are carefully selected, cross-pollinated and the resulting seeds sown. In the years that follow the offspring are closely observed, and any that do not come up to standard rejected. Apart from the obvious characteristics such as flower and fruit quality, the breeder also looks for resistance to pest and disease attack, weather resistance, vigour and habit of growth. Out of a thousand seedlings maybe one or two will be worth growing on to perhaps form new varieties.

Hand pollination

Hand pollination is done with a soft brush or by brushing the flowers together. Gently dusting the flowers with the brush transfers the pollen from the anthers to the stigmas.

Cross pollination

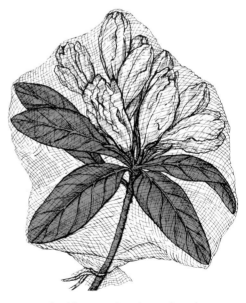

Protect the blooms after the anthers have been removed with a muslin or translucent paper bag to keep out insects and unwanted pollen. The bloom being protected is a rhododendron.

Basic design 1

It is easier to create an effective and workable garden if the design is carefully thought out at the start. The right plants and features can then be incorporated in the best possible positions to make a garden that is not only good to look at but easy to maintain.

Planning

First make a list of the features to be included in the garden and then move them around on a sketch plan until a satisfactory arrangement is achieved. Planning is easier if the basic measurements of the garden are taken and the plans are drawn on graph or squared paper using a suitable scale, such as 1in to 10ft (1cm to 1m). Only when this basic layout has been formulated can other aspects of design be considered.

When deciding what to plant and where to site leisure areas, pools, patios, beds for certain plants, greenhouses, sheds and the like, the following basic features of the garden must be borne in mind.

Aspect The amount of sun received by a patch of earth, or the density of the shade that is present for all or part of the year, govern what will grow there. Greenhouses, flower borders, vegetable and fruit plots, patios and pools should receive good light. Put compost heaps, sheds and beds for ferns and other shade-lovers where the light intensity is low. Take account of different sun angles in summer and winter. Trees and buildings cast long shadows during the shorter months.

Topography The slope of the land and the degree of exposure will impose further limitations (see microclimate pages 38-41). Avoid placing fruit trees and other frost-sensitive plants in dips or hollows where cold air may collect at night and destroy precocious leaves and blossoms. Such frost pockets can only be tolerated by the hardiest of plants. Plots exposed to high winds must be very carefully designed. Windbreaks should be erected or planted to filter strong winds, and plants which can tolerate a degree of exposure grown as shelter against the prevailing wind. Careful choice of plants is particularly important in coastal areas where winds may be laden with salt. On pronounced slopes the design of the garden

should take into account the lie of the land rather than fighting it. Should the angle of slope make cultivation difficult, then terraces may have to be built.

Soil Garden with the soil, not against it. Do not attempt to grow lime-hating plants on alkaline soil, lime-lovers in an acid peat, or moisture-lovers in a sharp-draining sand.

Localized problems The microclimate of a garden is a major influence on its design (see pages 38-41).

Elements of design

While individual taste will govern the final layout, there are certain basic rules of design that are best not broken. Firstly, the house must be made part of the overall scheme. Patios abutted to one or more of its walls will help it to blend with the plot; climbers and wall plants, flower-filled tubs, pots and hanging baskets can be positioned on and around the walls to bring flowers right up to the windows. Mould the garden design around any large trees that are present in the plot and also in neighbouring gardens. These plants are relatively permanent features and should be treated as such.

So-called "hard landscape" (paths, patios, walls and screens) should be constructed from materials which blend in with the house and are freely and relatively cheaply available in the locality. Paths dovetailed with the overall design will make for clean and speedy access to vegetables, herbs and the greenhouse in bad weather.

The garden will be viewed from the house so make all major design decisions from the appropriate windows. Create sweeping curves (not fussy, snakelike ones), and avoid odd-shaped beds and lawns that are difficult to mow. Above all, make each feature as large as possible.

Try to build in an element of surprise – leading the eye from one part of the garden to another by using focal points or by carefully concealing these from view so that the visitor is persuaded to explore.

The plans on this and the following page show "before" and "after" plans of a simple small garden. A landscape consultant has redesigned the garden to show the application of basic design principles.

Before re-design

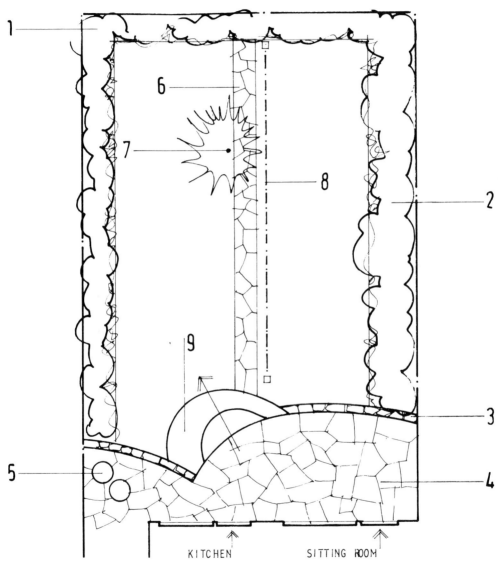

Several features spoil the garden and the whole layout adds up to a poor use of the site. The badly laid crazy paving terrace (4) clashes with the shape of the house. Retaining walls made from broken concrete (3) are unsafe as are the steps (9). The central path (6) divides the rectangular garden into unrelated sections, as do the shrub beds (1, 2) around the lawn and the washing line (8). Other existing features are a sumach tree (7), and an open corner for dustbins (5). The aim of the landscape designer is to provide a family garden, with safe, attractive steps and paving. The design should distract from the straight boundaries.

Basic design 2

After re-design

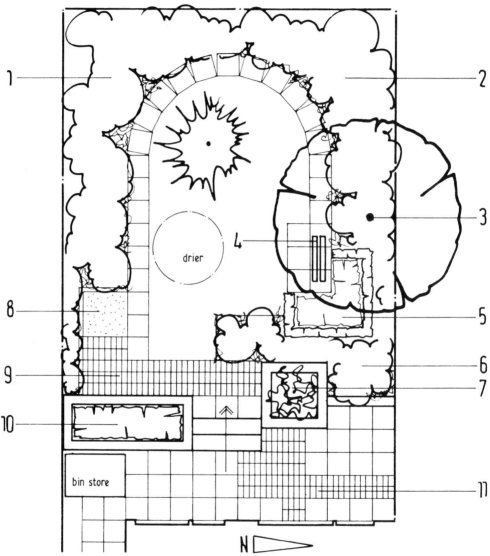

1
2
3
4
drier
8
5
9
6
7
10
bin store
11
N

The terrace has been reshaped to provide room for sitting and eating outdoors. It has been resurfaced with neat precast slabs and bricks to provide contrast. The path (9,11) now sweeps round the garden, ending at a seat (4) under a *Robina pseudoacacia* 'Frisia' tree (3) which provides, with the seat, a focal point. The shape of the lawns and the borders has been changed to give strong, flowing curves rather than straight lines. Raised beds are provided for annuals (7) and shrubs and trailers (10). There is a bed for salad or herbs (5), a mixed shrub and herbaceous border (1, 2) and one for roses (6). A play area with sandpit is provided for the children (8).

Form

The shape and texture of each plant will contribute to the overall appearance of the garden. For this reason it is important to bear in mind more than just the colour of the flowers. Speed of growth and the form of each tree, shrub or herbaceous perennial must be considered before it is incorporated into the planting plan. The blooms will certainly provide vital colour, but they may last only a few weeks and the plant must be able to make a contribution (particularly in a small garden), or else be hidden by other subjects for the rest of the year.

Shrubs and trees form the basic framework of the garden and should be planted first. Some of them must be evergreen if the plot is not to be devoid of interest in winter. Delicate foliaged plants provide a contrast alongside those with large, bold leaves; fastigiate (upright) growers will add height to low plantings, and creepers will cover unsightly bare patches. Consider the habit of each plant when it is chosen and find the right spot for it. Smaller plants are best grouped in threes and fives to display them properly.

Colour

Green in all its many shades is the most important (and most enduring) colour in the garden. It acts as a backdrop for all the brighter hues and is restful to the eye. There are those who despise gardens where flowers of vibrant mixed colours jostle one another; such plots are often described as being in poor taste. However, a glance at photographs of some of the best cottage gardens will prove that such arrangements are very attractive.

Whatever the taste of the gardener, colour planning is important if the plot is to be of floral interest all the year round. One group of plants can be timed to come into flower as another group fades, and particular plant combinations must be equally carefully planned if simultaneous flowering is desired. In small gardens, the longer the flowering season of a plant the more valuable it is.

Only experience will show which colours go best together in the eye of the gardener. Reds, oranges and yellows are fiery and can be planted in small numbers to achieve the same intensity as larger groups of blues and greens. Pink, mauve, cream and pale-blue flowers are especially restful to the eye, and white can bring lightness to dark and heavy plantings. Blues will lengthen the perspective in a garden. Contrasting bright red plants are best kept apart from blue flowers by planting white- or cream-flowered varieties between them.

Plant foliage offers shades other than green. There are greys, maroons, blues, yellows and all manner of variegations to choose from. Position all such plants carefully so that they complement their neighbours and provide a harmonious overall effect.

Scent

Having satisfied the eye by planting subjects of good form and colour, the gardener must not forget to include scented plants to satisfy the nose. Aromatic gardens are a delight both to the blind and to the sighted, for they provide an extra source of enjoyment. Scented carpet plants such as thyme and chamomile can be positioned in paving stones where they will tolerate a modicum of wear, releasing their fragrance every time they are trodden on. Lavender and cotton lavender hedges planted alongside paths will scent the air whenever they are brushed against, and perfumed roses and border plants such as *Sedum spectabile* and *Monarda* will attract bees and butterflies right through the summer.

The right plant for the job

No gardener can complain today at having a poor choice of plant material. Careful scrutiny of nurserymen's catalogues will reveal a wealth of shrubs, trees, herbaceous plants, bulbs, and annuals which will grow in a multitude of situations. One of the secrets of successful gardening is to choose the right plant for a particular place. This involves careful consideration of habit, colour, form, rate of growth and environmental preferences. Occasionally trial and error is the only way of being certain. The following pages include lists of plants suitable for given situations, but be guided, also, by the knowledge of neighbouring gardeners who may be able to offer advice on the likelihood of a particular plant thriving in the locality.

Placing plants 1

Having decided on the layout of the garden, it is time to consider exactly which plants will be grown where. It makes sense to start with trees. These will be the largest and most permanent specimens, acting as focal points to which other plantings can lead.

Trees
Site garden trees where their form can be appreciated and where they will have room to develop unhindered. Avoid planting specimens that will outgrow available space. Consider the habit of the tree as well as its flower, foliage and berry colour. In confined spaces fastigiate (columnar) trees are best; where space needs to be filled, those with spreading branches can be chosen. For small gardens choose trees which have several attractive features and which can be enjoyed for much of the year, rather than those which only have a spectacular but brief blossoming period. Evergreen trees provide form and interest all the year round, though many deciduous trees are attractive even when bare. Trees can affect nearby buildings, causing shade and extracting water from the sub-soil, creating the risk of subsidence. Plant large trees away from buildings if possible.

The ground under deciduous trees will have to be cleared of leaves in autumn. For this reason do not position pools or sandpits under their canopy. Evergreens will also lose a proportion of their leaves during the year and these too can be a nuisance.

Shrubs
Once garden trees have been chosen and plotted on a plan, shrubs can be useful to build up the framework of the planting scheme. Distribute those which have evergreen leaves over the whole of the garden. This is advisable for two reasons: first, it will give a certain amount of form to the entire plot, and second, it will prevent one particular corner from becoming heavy and unchanging, which might be the case if the evergreens were all planted together. In very small gardens where trees cannot be fitted in, shrubs must take their place, acting as focal points as well as a framework.

When designing shrub and mixed borders, plot in the plants on a plan and number them

from one to twelve according to the month in which they are at their best. In this way it is possible to see exactly what will be of interest in the garden at any time of year. Obvious gaps can be filled, or plants repositioned to distribute colour and form more evenly over the garden and over the months of the year. A little careful planning at this stage will help to create a garden for all seasons.

Herbaceous perennials
Strictly speaking, herbaceous perennials are those plants which survive for many years but whose stems and leaves die down each winter and re-emerge afresh in spring. However, some of these plants possess foliage which is more persistent and may be present to a lesser degree through the winter months.

No garden would be complete without herbaceous plants. If shrubs are invaluable as framework then these plants have just as important a role to play as fillers. This is not to say that the plants lack form; some of them are majestic and bold, but their stature is enjoyed only for part of the year.

Plan the herbaceous border in the same

Planning

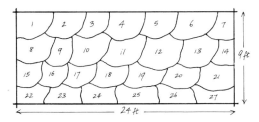

(1) 3 Aster 'Fellowship'. Soft pink, September. 4 ft.
(2) 5 Helenium 'Moerheim Beauty'. Rich crimson, July-Aug. 3 ft.
(3) 3 Echinops 'Taplow Blue'. Metallic blue, July-Aug. 5 ft.
(4) 5 Heliopsis 'Incomparabilis'. Golden orange, July-Aug. 4 ft.
(5) 4 Delphinium 'Blue Jay'. Mid-blue, June-July. 5 ft.
(6) 3 Aster 'Crimson Brocade'. Deep red, September. 3 ft.
(7) 5 Polygonum amplexicaule 'Astrosanguin

Plan a border by numbering plants on a plan according to the month they will be at their best.

way as one devoted to shrubs. In most gardens the two types of plant are intermingled in "mixed borders" which are the best solution where year-round form is required.

Plants for walls

House and garden walls, fences, pergolas, arches and ugly buildings can all be improved by training climbers and wall shrubs over their surfaces. All these plants will benefit from good soil preparation and manure enrichment to encourage moisture retention, for the earth at the foot of walls and fences can become very dry. Many of them will need some form of support. Ivy and Virginia creeper will cling on their own to a vertical surface, but for the rest some horizontal wires stretched between vine eyes, or sections of wooden trelliswork fastened to the wall will help them to remain upright and secure (see pages 98-99). Most shrubs will need tying in and may need regular pruning to keep them trim and close to the wall.

Make sure that the right plant is chosen for a wall of a particular aspect – the planting lists (page 80) offer advice on suitability.

Single colour schemes

In most gardens colour schemes will involve the use of a wide range of shades, although these should be carefully toned so that they do not clash. However, it is possible to plan beds, borders and even entire gardens with plants having one particular flower or foliage colour. White gardens – where grey foliaged and white- and cream-flowered plants are grouped together – have been successfully created in the grounds of several English country houses.

In small gardens such schemes are best confined to individual borders if they are not to become overpowering and monotonous. However, if annual flowers are used there is no reason why such a scheme should not be changed from year to year: blues, violets and purples one year; reds, pinks and creams the next; greens and yellows to follow.

Some form of permanent skeletal planting in shades of green and grey can be used to good effect in single-colour gardens. Not only will such plants set off the flowers well, they will also provide interest during the darker months of the year.

Tree forms

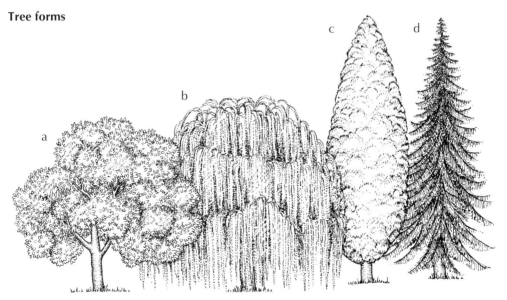

It is **important** to know the habit of a tree before planting it. Trees can be spreading (a), weeping (b), fastigiate (c) or conical (d).

Check the eventual height and spread of the tree and allow it adequate space when planning the garden.

Placing plants 2

CLIMBERS AND WALL SHRUBS FOR WALLS OF VARIOUS ASPECTS

North-facing walls
Camellia species and cultivars
Chaenomeles species and cultivars
Cotoneaster horizontalis
Escallonia rubra ssp. macrantha
Forsythia suspensa and cultivars
Garrya elliptica
Hedera species and cultivars
Jasminum nudiflorum
Parthenocissus species
Tropaeolum speciosum

East-facing walls
Celastrus orbiculatus
Chaenomeles species and cultivars
Clematis species and cultivars
Garrya elliptica
Hedera species and cultivars
Hydrangea petiolaris
Kerria japonica 'Pleniflora'
Parthenocissus species
Pyracantha species and cultivars
Tropaeolum speciosum

South-facing wall
Actinidia kolomikta
Callistemon species
Campsis species
Ceanothus species and cultivars
Clianthus puniceus
Fremontodendron species and cultivars
Lonicera species and cultivars
Magnolia grandiflora
Rosa species and cultivars
Wisteria species and cultivars

West-facing walls
Abutilon vitifolium
Camellia species and cultivars
Carpenteria californica
Chimonanthus praecox
Cytisus battandieri
Fremontodendron species and cultivars
Magnolia grandiflora
Passiflora caerulea
Solanum crispum
Wisteria species and cultivars

TREES AND SHRUBS WITH COLOURED FOLIAGE

	Height		Colour
Abies species and cultivars	20-150ft	(6-45m)	Grey/silver
Acer negundo 'Variegatum'	20-50ft	(6-15m)	Green and white
Acer palmatum f. atropurpureum	10ft	(3m)	Maroon
Calluna vulgaris cultivars	1ft	(30cm)	Yellow/orange/grey
Catalpa bignonioides 'Aurea'	35ft	(10.5m)	Yellow
Cedrus atlantica 'Aurea'	30ft	(9m)	Yellow/gold
Chamaecyparis lawsoniana cultivars	45ft	(14m)	Silver/blue/yellow
Convolvulus cneorum	2ft	(60cm)	Silver-grey
Corylus maxima 'Purpurea'	10ft	(3m)	Deep maroon
Cotinus coggygria 'Royal Purple'	10ft	(3m)	Maroon
Elaeagnus pungens 'Maculata'	15ft	(4.5m)	Yellow and green
Gleditsia triacanthos 'Sunburst'	35ft	(10.5m)	Yellow
Ilex × altaclerensis 'Golden King'	15ft	(1.2-2.4m)	Yellow and green
Juniperus chinensis cultivars	3-25ft	(4.5m)	Grey/green/blue
Juniperis horizontalis 'Plumosa'	1ft	(1-7.5m)	Grey-purple
Juniperus sabina cultivars	2-5ft	(30cm)	Grey/blue
Juniperis virginiana	40ft	(0.6-1.5m)	Blue
Picea glauca var. albertiana 'Conica'	6ft	(12m)	Light green
Pieris formosa var. forrestii 'Wakehurst'	4-8ft	(1.8m)	Red
Robinia pseudoacacia 'Frisia'	30ft	(9m)	Yellow
Thuja occidentalis	50-65ft	(15-19.5m)	Yellow/gold

KEY
E Evergreen
T Texture and colour of bark
B Berries
F Flowers
L Leaves
S Stems
H Habit or form

TREES AND SHRUBS FOR SPECIFIC LOCATIONS

Small garden	Height	
Acer palmatum cultivars	10ft	(3m) LH
Betula pendula 'Youngii'	15ft	(4.5m) TH
Corylus avellana 'Contorta'	10ft	(3m) FSH
Gleditsia triacanthos		
'Sunburst'	35ft	(10.5m) L
Malus 'John Downie'	20ft	(6m) BFH
Pyrus salicifolia 'Pendula'	25ft	(7.5m) LH
Robinia pseudoacacia 'Prisia'	30ft	(9m) TL
Sorbus aucuparia 'Beissneri'	25ft	(7.5m) TBFL

Fastigiate trees		
Chamaecyparis lawsoniana		
cultivars	20ft +	(6m+) EH
Crataegus monogyna 'Stricta'	20ft	(6m) BFH
Juniperus virginiana		
'Skyrocket'	20ft	(6m) EH
Prunus 'Amanogawa'	20ft	(6m) FH
Prunus 'Spire'	25ft	(7.5m) FH
Sorbus commixta	20ft	(6m) BFLH
Sorbus 'Joseph Rock'	25ft	(7.5m) BFLH
Taxus baccata Fastigiata		
'Aureomarginata'	15ft	(4.5m) EH

Weeping trees		
Betula pendula 'Dalecarlica'	40ft	(12m) TLH
Crataegus monogyna		
'Pendula Rosea'	15ft	(4.5m) BFH
Fagus sylvatica 'Pendula'	50ft +	(15m+) LH
Laburnum × watereri		
'Alford's Weeping'	15ft	(4.5m) FH
Prunus subhirtella 'Pendula'	15ft	(4.5m) FH
Pyrus salicifolia 'Pendula'	15ft	(4.5m) LH
Salix × sepulcralis		
'Chrysocoma'	50ft	(15m) LSH
Ulmus glabra		
'Camperdownii'	15ft	(4.5m) LH

Acid soils		
Betula pendula 'Dalecarlica'	40ft	(12m) TLH
Calluna vulgaris & cultivars	1ft	(30cm) EF
Erica species & cultivars	1ft	(30cm) EF
Gaultheria mucronata	2-3ft	(60-90cm) EB
Pieris formosa & cultivars	10ft	(3m) EF
Rhododendron species &		
cultivars	3-15ft +	(1-4.5m+) EF

Coastal gardens		
Arbutus unedo	15ft	(4.5m) TBF
Brachyglottis 'Sunshine'	5ft	(1.5m) EF
Choisya ternata	8ft	(2.4m) EF
Elaeagnus pungens		
'Maculata'	15ft	(4.5m) E

Coastal gardens cont.	Height	
Fuchsia magellanica cultivars	6ft	(1.8m) F
Griselinia littoralis	12ft	(3.6m) E
Hebe species & cultivars	1-6ft	(0.3-1.8m) EF
Lavatera olbia 'Rosea'	6ft	(1m) FL
Phlomis fruticosa	3ft	(1m) FL
Phormium tenax cultivars	3-6ft	(1-1.8m) EL
Pyracantha species &		
cultivars	10ft	(3m) BF
Sorbus aucuparia cultivars	20ft +	(6m+) TBFLS
Tamarix pentandra	10ft	(3m) FL

Chalky soils		
Aucuba japonica & cultivars	10ft	(3m) EB
Buddleja davidii & cultivars	10ft	(3m) FL
Cistus species & cultivars	3ft	(1m) EF
Crataegus laevigata	15ft	(4.5m) BF
Deutzia cultivars	6ft	(1.8m) F
Forsythia species & cultivars	6-10ft	(1.8-3m) F
Genista species & cultivars	1-10ft	(0.3-3m) F
Hebe species & cultivars	1-4ft	(0.3-1.2m) EF
Helianthemum cultivars	1-2ft	(30-60cm) EF
Ilex aquifolium cultivars	15ft	(4.5m) EB
Mahonia aquifolium	4ft	(1.2m) EF
Philadelphus cultivars	8ft	(2.4m) F
Rhus typhina	15ft	(4.5m) LH
Sorbus aria & cultivars	20ft	(6m) FLB

Shrubs for shade		
Aucuba japonica	10ft	(3m) EB
Buxus sempervirens	1-10ft	(0.3-3m) E
Gaultheria shallon	5ft	(1.5m) BF
Hypericum calycinum	1ft	(30cm) EF
Juniperus × media		
'Pfitzerana'	3ft	(1m) E
Mahonia aquifolium	4ft	(1.2m) EF
Mahonia japonica	3ft	(1m) EF
Pachysandra terminalis	1ft	(30cm) EF
Sarcococca confusa	3ft	(1m) EF
Vinca species & cultivars	Trailing	EF

Scented flowers or leaves		
Aloysia triphylla	4ft	(1.2m) E
Buddleja davidii & cultivars	10ft	(3m) F
Chimonanthus praecox	8ft	(2.4m) F
Choisya ternata	8ft	(2.4m) F
Daphne species & cultivars	2-5ft	(0.6-1.5m) F
Eucalyptus species	20ft +	(6m+) E
Hamamelis mollis &		
cultivars	12ft	(3.6m) F
Lavandula species &		
cultivars	1-2ft	(30-60cm) FL
Lonicera periclymenum	8ft	(2.4m) F
Mahonia japonica	6ft	(1.8m) F

Walls and fences 1

Barriers are used to indicate the garden boundary, to provide privacy and shelter and to keep out unwanted animals and people. The range of possible materials is wide, but stone, brick, wood and wire are the most common. For hedges see pages 94-97.

Walls

Brick or stone walls are the most durable barriers and if well made will far outlive their builder. Concrete foundations are essential if stability is to be ensured, and the walling material should fit in with its surroundings. Sadly, walls are very expensive to construct, but it is possible to make certain economies. Brick walls may be constructed from cheap bricks and faced with a more expensive variety to obtain the required effect at a lower price. Reconstituted stone may be used in place of the real thing. In rural districts dry stone walling may be used and local stone can often be bought at a reasonable price.

Open concrete screen blocks can be mortared together and topped with coping stones to provide a permeable but durable barrier. The same effect can be achieved if bricks are used to build a pierced or honeycomb wall.

For privacy, boundary walls should be built to at least 5-6ft (1.5-1.8m). With constructions of this size it is advisable to call in a builder to advise. Foundations will have to be built at the correct depth and of a size large enough to support the wall on a particular soil. Reinforcing piers may be necessary. Mortar for brick walls should consist of 1 part cement, 1 part lime and 5 parts sand. This mix allows a degree of expansion and contraction to take place in hot and cold weather.

Fences

Fences are cheaper to erect than walls, though not so tough or long-lasting. Except where total privacy is required, permeable fences are to be preferred to those that are solid. Solid fences block the wind and in some situations create plant-damaging turbulence on their leeward side. An interwoven fence

Maintaining walls

1 When mortar begins to crumble, repoint with a 1 cement, 1 lime, 5 sand mix. Scrape away old mortar to a depth of 1in (2.5cm).

2 Moisten the joints and pack mortar in firmly. Finish with a trowel to give a chamfered edge.

should be supported by concrete posts which are, in turn, sunk into concrete. The fence can then be expected to last well and only the panels will eventually need replacement – the posts can remain. As an alternative to concrete posts, concrete spurs can be sunk into the ground and the wooden fencing posts bolted to them; or the posts may be dropped into hollow steel supports bedded in concrete. Larch, cedar and pine are the most suitable woods for close-boarded or interwoven fencing.

Hazel or wattle hurdles make good barriers in cottage or country gardens, and like other open fences they provide shelter by filtering the wind. They should be firmly attached with wire to posts knocked into the ground to a depth of 2 or 3 ft (60 or 90cm). All such posts must be treated with a proprietary wood treatment containing creosote or copper naphthenate to prevent rotting. The taller the fence the deeper the posts should be sunk – 6ft (1.8m) fences should be supported by posts driven into the ground for a depth of 2 to 3 ft (60 to 90cm).

There are many variations of the fence theme, from the simple post and rail type seen on farmland, to the picket fence of the old cottage garden, and the more modern ranch-style and board-on-board fencing. All should be made of durable, treated timber held together with galvanized nails or screws.

Wire netting is frequently erected on new housing estates by the builder to mark new garden boundaries. Chain link is the strongest type and will last well if covered in plastic. Such a coating will also prevent the build-up of zinc toxicity on the soil below – this can occur when rain drips from an uncoated fence over a long period. Although chain link fences are not especially pleasant to look at they do last well and can be covered with plants. They should be supported by steel posts and strainers sunk into concrete. Post and wire fencing may be all that is necessary when the garden adjoins open country. Fruit trees can be trained against such a structure provided that farm animals do not have access, when a thorn hedge is more suitable.

Painting walls

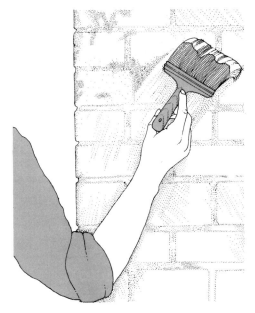

1 Remove loose paint with a wire brush. Seal the wall with chemical sealant if the brickwork is in poor condition.

2 Apply a fresh coat of paint designed for use on exterior masonry.

Walls and fences 2

Wall and fence maintenance

Walls need little attention once they have been built. Only after years of frosting and weathering will some of the mortar fall away, and then repointing will be necessary. Scrape out any loose mortar with a chisel or large nail and repoint using the original mortar mix. If the wall is painted it will need a new coat when the original one starts to bubble or peel. Remove all loose paint with a wire brush before applying the fresh coat of paint which is specifically designed for use on masonry. Brickwork in poor condition can be sealed chemically before repainting.

Treat wooden fences with a proprietary treatment containing a preservative such as copper naphthenate at the outset. Buy only posts which have been tanalized to prolong their life. Creosote should not be used near plants for it will burn their foliage (the fumes are poisonous too). Treat the fence with preservative every two or three years to keep it in good condition. Fences that are to be painted must first be coated with a primer to seal the wood. Further coats of exterior quality paint can then be applied and renewed every few years.

Gates

Gates should be planned and erected at the same time as fences and walls. Position gates carefully, taking into account the dimensions of barrows and mowers used in the garden. Gates should if possible be in a material which complements the wall or fence. Ready-made wood and metal gates are available, in many different designs, or gates can be purpose-made from wood or wrought iron. Metal gates can be hung so that they open beyond 90° around the post, thus creating easier access. Metal gates are also easier to hang as the hinges and other fittings need little work. When hanging a wooden gate, make sure the necessary hinges, hinge brackets, bolts and catches are to hand. When hanging allow for any slope in the ground. When the gate is fully open, it must clear the path, even if the path slopes. Make the outer end of the gate, away from the hinge, slightly high.

Supporting fences

1 Concrete posts should be sunk into concrete. Dig a hole at least a third as deep as the fence is high.

2 Place the post in the hole, pack it with rubble and pour in concrete. Allow it to set for several days.

TYPES OF FENCE

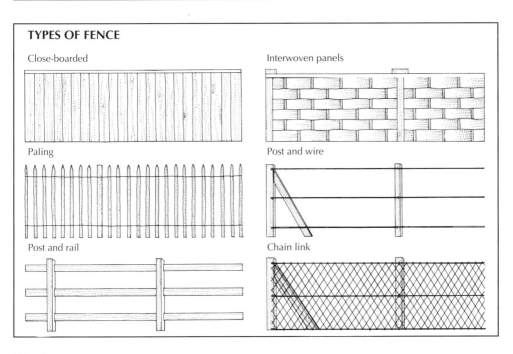

Close-boarded

Interwoven panels

Paling

Post and wire

Post and rail

Chain link

Wooden posts

Treat wooden posts with creosote or a proprietary treatment containing a preservative to prevent rotting.

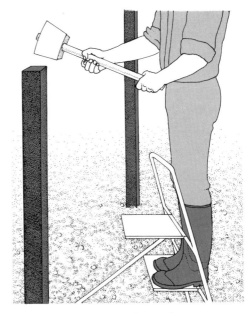

Drive wooden posts at least 2ft (60cm) into the ground. At least a third of the total length should be below ground.

Paths and steps 1

The garden may be full of fascinating features and beautiful plants, but if wet ground has to be crossed to reach them the earth will quickly turn into a muddy mire. Greenhouses, vegetable and fruit gardens have to be regularly visited in all weathers and at all seasons, so some kind of pathway is essential in the garden to provide clean and easy access.

A useful path should conform to some basic rules. It should cover the shortest distance between the two points to be linked. Only in woodland gardens or where the path is deliberately designed to meander should it weave round the plot. A utilitarian path will be ignored if it does not speedily reach its goal. A path should be made from materials which are locally available at a reasonable price, and which blend in with the rest of the garden. It must possess good foundations which will ensure stability. It should allow surface water to drain through or else be given a slope or camber so that the water runs off. It should be wide enough to take whatever "traffic" is likely to pass over it.

Paving materials

There is a wide choice of paving materials, varying in cost and appearance, but all should provide a firm surface which is easy to walk on and to maintain.

Concrete Comparatively cheap and simple to lay, concrete need not look hard and dull if it is textured with a stiff brush while still damp, and edged with bricks or stone setts. It can be mixed at home or delivered ready to lay. Concrete expands and contracts once it has set, so do not make areas more than 10ft (3m) square without allowing expansion joints.

Gravel Retained by boards and laid over hardcore, gravel will make a good-looking path which is relatively cheap to construct. Avoid laying gravel paths near lawns, where stray chippings can foul the mower. Hoggin is similar to gravel but is capable of being rolled firm due to the diversity of its particle sizes. A relatively cheap material, it must be rolled after storms and frost if it is to stay firm.

Stone slabs Real stone slabs are attractive and durable but costly. Many artificial types in

Laying a concrete path

a

b

c

d

Dig a trench 4-6in (10-15cm) deep where the path is to be laid (a). Fill with hardcore and ram into place (b). Peg retaining boards (3in (8cm) deep along the sides (c).

Check for height and level with a straight edge and spirit level. Spread the concrete between the retaining boards, rake and tamp it, and level with the edge of a neutral colours make excellent paths. Avoid harsh pinks and reds in favour of creams, greys and browns, and make sure the slabs are at least 2in (5cm) thick. Local authorities sometimes offer broken paving stones at a reasonable price and these can be used to make crazy paving paths and patios.

Bricks There is such a range of coloured bricks available that it will be possible to find a shade to suit any garden. Bricks are most attractive when laid on edge, but more will be needed in this case, and they are never a cheap paving material. The great advantage of a brick path is that it shows off plants to perfection, and if unmortared it drains well. Interlocking concrete blocks can be laid on a sand base and need no mortar. They are made in several colours.

Cobbles and setts Rounded cobbles bedded in concrete are attractive but not very easy to walk over. Use them to provide a contrasting texture on parts of the path that will receive little wear. Granite setts provide the rustic finish of cobbles but are flatter and therefore easier to walk on. Both materials are expensive.

Logs Sawn-up logs sunk vertically into the soil side by side will make a handsome informal walkway which seems especially natural in woodland and "wild" gardens. The logs can become slippery when wet and should be scored in a cross pattern to provide grip. Where a natural effect is wanted, lay pulverized bark loosely over the path or between retaining boards over firmed ground. It provides a spongy but reasonably well-drained surface which is not slippery.

Stepping-stone paths
The gardener should only construct paths where they are absolutely necessary. Too many will make the garden disjointed. Where a simple path is required across a lawn then stepping stones provide a practical and relatively unobtrusive walkway. Circular, square or crazy paving slabs may be used. Lay the slabs in their position on the lawn (6-9in [15-23cm] apart) and then cut around each one

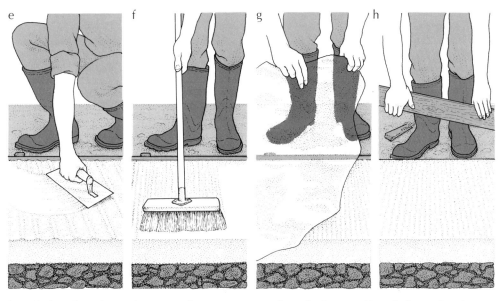

board (d). When the surface water has disappeared, smooth the concrete with a float (e). While the surface is still damp, brush with a stiff broom to roughen the surface (f). Cover with polythene sheeting and allow to dry for 5-10 days (g). A fortnight after laying, remove the formwork (h). The path is now ready for use.

Paths and steps 2

with a spade or half-moon iron. Remove the turf and drop the slab into place so that it rests just below the surface of the lawn. Adjust the height by packing fine soil or sand under the slabs to make them level and secure, and fill any gaps around the sides with the same material. Sunk in this way the slabs will not impede the lawn mower which can pass straight over them.

Laying concrete paths

Paths will need to be constructed over a foundation layer to keep them stable. A 4-6in (10-15cm) deep trench should be excavated and the soil replaced with rammed hardcore. Put vertical boards 3in (8cm) deep into position to retain the sides of the path and check this formwork with a straight edge and spirit level. Allow a fall of ¼in (0.5cm) in 1ft (30cm) from side to side to allow for drainage.

Mix concrete on a solid surface. Combine 1 part cement with 5 parts all-in ballast (sand and gravel), then gradually add water to create a firm but easily spreadable mix. Use the concrete within one hour of mixing. Spread it out between the boards, rake it and tamp it level with a flat board. When the surface water has disappeared but the concrete is still wet go over it with a plasterer's float to smooth out the surface. When the concrete is firmer, but still damp, brush it with a stiff broom to create a rougher, non-slip texture. Alternatively, when the mixture is drier still, use a hose and scrubbing brush to expose the pebbles in the aggregate.

Immediately after laying, cover the concrete with a sheet of polythene to keep out rain and to allow it to dry out slowly. In summer the path will be ready to walk on in about five days, but leave it for at least ten days in winter. The path should not be subjected to heavy loads for at least a fortnight, after which the formwork can be removed.

Foundation construction

The depth and content of path foundations vary according to the nature of the paving material, the traffic that will pass over it and the soil beneath. On firm soils which have been well consolidated, paving slabs, setts and bricks can be laid on a 3in (8cm) deep firmed and levelled bed of sand. Tap the slabs into

place with the handle of a heavy hammer and make sure they do not wobble. Pack any low points with extra sand. Not only does the sand layer make hardcore unnecessary, but as the slabs or bricks are not bedded in concrete it means that the path can be easily taken up in the future without too much trouble. Creeping and carpeting plants can also be grown between the slabs, bricks or setts.

Mortar foundations Sand foundations will be adequate where a path is likely to receive moderate pedestrian use. Where cycle and wheelbarrow use is frequent then the path must be more solidly based. Mark out the strip with pegs and string, excavate 6in (15cm) of top-soil, ram 3in (8cm) of hardcore into place and top this with a 1in (2.5cm) "binding" layer of ashes or sand and lime mixed at the rate of 3 parts sand to 1 part lime. Mix mortar of 1 part cement, 1½ parts lime and 5 parts sand, work it to a spreadable consistency with water and then trowel it on top of the blinding layer to a depth of 1¼in (2cm) before each slab is lowered into position. Lay the slabs to the level of a taut line which should be pegged across the path to allow a fall of ¼in (0.5cm) in 1ft (30cm) so that surface water is shed.

If the slabs are laid close together grouting will be unnecessary. Alternatively lay them ½in (1.25cm) apart and when the foundations are firm brush a dry mixture of the mortar into the cracks. Rain and soil moisture will set the grouting firm – brushed in when dry it produces a cleaner finish.

Edging

Many paths, including those which abut flower beds or lawns, may not need any form of edging; others are distinctly improved by a narrow border of contrasting material. Bricks or setts can be let into the soil alongside concrete or slab paths. Where concrete is used the edging is best put into position inside the formwork before the mixture is laid.

Steps

Where a change of level is needed a flight of steps is usually a better-looking and more practical solution than a simple slope. Only when barrows are in constant use are steps unworkable.

To make them easy to climb outdoor steps must not be as steep as those indoors. Risers (the vertical part) should be no more than 6in (15cm) high and treads (the part that is walked on) should be at least 12in (30cm) and preferably 15-18in (38-45cm) deep. Test steps in other gardens to decide which are the most comfortable to climb. Never make the steps less than 3ft (90cm) wide, and make the rise as gradual as possible.

Steps should be constructed on 3in (8cm) hardcore foundations unless the land is firm and the steps will receive only light use.

Building concrete steps Excavate the bank to a depth 6in (15cm) below the level of the base of the bank. Lay hardcore in the excavation, then build formwork to support each riser. Attach beading to the upper inside edge of the riser formwork to support each rise. Attach beading to the upper inside edge of the riser formwork to give each step a bevelled edge and prevent crumbling. Steel reinforcing rods can be set into the concrete just below the surface of each tread to improve strength. At its thinnest point the concrete should not be less than 4in (10cm) thick. Tamp, level, float and texture the steps in the same way as a concrete path. Build the next step on the first, and proceed up the slope. If a concrete surface is undesirable then the steps can be faced and topped with ordinary or crazy paving slabs cut to fit.

Brick and slab steps are comparatively easy to lay. Calculate the number and height of the steps needed and ram a layer of hardcore into the slope in the required place. To give maximum stability lay a 4in (10cm) deep concrete foundation under the lowest step and bed the first riser on to it. Lay a single or double course of bricks on a bed or mortar over the hardened concrete strip and fill in with rammed hardcore behind them to the level of this first riser. Paving slabs can then be laid as treads. Spread a bed of mortar over the brick riser and ease the slab into place, allowing it to overhang the tread by 1 or 2 in (2.5 or 5cm). An overhanging tread is more attractive. The next rise can be built on the back edge of the first tread and the routine proceeds until the top is reached.

Steps may be constructed from many materials including wooden sleepers, logs, and even large, flat rocks, which are particularly useful in large rock gardens.

Building concrete steps

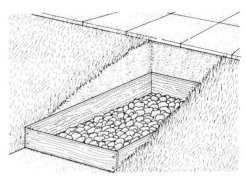

1 **Excavate the bank** to a depth of 6in (15cm) below base level. Ram in a layer of hardcore. Build formwork for the first riser.

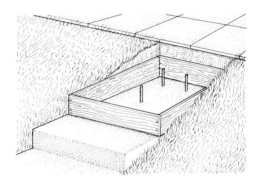

2 **Build formwork** for the second riser on the completed first riser. Place reinforcing rods in the concrete when wet.

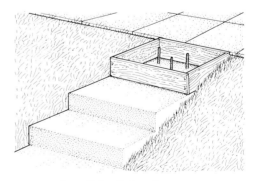

3 **Proceed until the flight of steps** is complete. Make risers no more than 6in (15cm) high, treads at least 12in (30cm) deep.

Rock gardens 1

Plants from mountain and rocky regions are usually called alpines. They are plants which have adapted to very different soil and climate conditions to those found in the normal garden. If they are to thrive they must be provided with the right site and soil. For this reason the plants are usually grown in specially mixed soil among rocks, which provide shaded root-runs and also form the right background to show off these small plants to best effect. Rock gardens should be planned as garden design features as well as plant habitats and carefully integrated into the overall garden plan. Alpine plants have well-defined soil and site requirements. Many rock garden plants are not true alpines and are easily grown, but the special needs of true alpines must be catered for.

Site Nearly all alpines require an open and sunny spot. Shelter from distant fences or trees is beneficial in cutting down drying winds, but avoid heavy shade from trees, which will shed leaves on to the plants. Roots from trees can penetrate rock gardens and inhibit growth.

Drainage and soil In their natural environment many alpines are covered in a dry blanket of snow through the winter. This protects them from severe frost, then melts away in late spring, watering the plants as it does so. Their growing medium is often less soil than rock waste or gravel. Ideally, therefore, plants should be sheltered from winter rain and grown in a freely-draining medium which can nevertheless retain some moisture. In practice, ideal conditions are not obtainable except in an alpine house (see the companion volume in this series, *Growing under Glass*). Efforts must be made to avoid the major problems of damp and summer desiccation.

Construction
The traditional rock garden aims at recreating a natural rock outcrop, with the plants growing between carefully bedded stones.

TYPES OF ROCK GARDEN

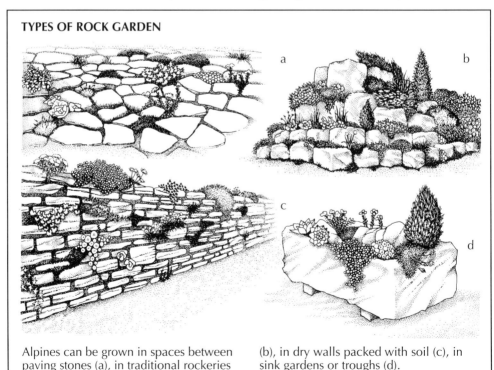

Alpines can be grown in spaces between paving stones (a), in traditional rockeries (b), in dry walls packed with soil (c), in sink gardens or troughs (d).

The true rock garden is on a slope, but rock beds can also be built on level ground with rocks and dwarf conifers or shrubs adding height.

The site can be graded to provide a slope, or a depression can be dug and the sides terraced. Top-soil should be removed first and replaced evenly when the reshaping is complete.

Improving drainage If the site is level, check the soil drainage. If it is at all poor, remove the top-soil to a depth of 12in (30cm), then put down a 6in (15cm) layer of rubble. Top this with a 9-12in (23-30cm) layer of loam, sand, grit and leaf-mould mixed together to form a suitable rooting medium. Ensure that the drainage of the surrounding area is adequate. Lighter, better-drained soils should be improved by the addition of grit, coarse sand and leaf-mould, so that free dainage and adequate moisture retention are ensured. Carefully remove all weeds, and cultivate to a depth of 1ft (30cm).

Rocks Most rock gardens are made from sandstone or limestone, and occasionally from granite. Choose local stone, which will blend with its surroundings and which may also be available more cheaply. The rock should be of a kind that will weather easily to give a natural appearance. Several large pieces of rock are to be preferred to a multitude of smaller boulders which will tend to give a "plum-pudding" effect. Rock is never cheap so use small quantities wisely. It is usually sold by the ton, which is about 14cu ft (0.4cu m) of rock pieces. Specify the largest and smallest sizes required when ordering. Half a hundredweight (25kg) is the heaviest one person can comfortably handle.

Mould the ground into the required contours using a fork and a rake and tread the entire site firm before positioning the rocks. Choose the best faces of the rock and bury any newly broken surfaces which will take a long time to weather. Move the rocks to their sites and position them with their best faces

Construction

 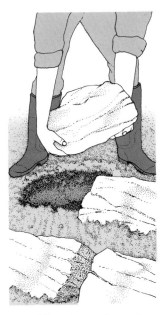 

1 After clearing and draining, if necessary, fork over and rake the bed, moulding the soil into the required shape.

2 Position the rocks on the site, making sure that the strata run the same way. Adjust until the desired result is achieved.

3 When all the rocks are in place, firm soil around them, taking care to avoid air pockets.

Rock gardens 2

forward and with their strata running in the right direction. Group small rocks around one large piece of stone to give the impression that they are part of it, taking care that the strata correspond. Aim to build up natural-looking terraces, with the layers running horizontally with a slight backwards slope. Rocks do not have to be buried deeply. No more than a quarter of the rock need be below the surface.

Once the rocks are in position they can be let into the soil. Have on hand sufficient mixed soil or compost to create planting pockets between the rocks. Excavate sufficient soil with a spade, manoeuvre the rock into position and then ram the soil firmly behind it. Leave no air pockets. When the rock is positioned it should look and feel firm.

Planting
Once the rocks are laid, lightly rake the soil around them to relieve surface compaction. Plant when the soil is moist but not too wet.

In milder areas planting is best undertaken in early autumn. In colder places and where wet winters are common early spring is a better time, but make sure that spells of early summer drought do not check the plants' root development.

Water the rock garden well before planting. Remove each plant from its pot, having first given it a good watering. Excavate a hole in the required place using a trowel or hand fork. Lower the plant in, refirming the soil so that no air pockets are left and the surface of the potting compost around the plant is level with the surface of the soil on the rootball of the plant. Consider the habit of each plant before positioning it, and allow it sufficient room for growth.

When planting is completed, a 1in (2.5cm) layer of coarse grit can be spread over the surface of the soil. This will ensure good drainage around the necks of the plants. It also shows plants off well, keeps down weeds and helps to retain moisture. Label each plant.

Planting

1 Excavate a hole large enough for the plant's roots. Fill it with water and allow it to drain away.

2 Lower the plant into the hole and firm the soil around the roots to avoid air pockets.

GARDEN DESIGN AND CONSTRUCTION

Maintenance

A grit layer will help to keep down weeds, but any which do emerge should be removed at once. In prolonged dry spells between April and July water the rock garden. To check if watering is necessary, scrape any gravel away and probe the soil with a trowel. When the soil is dry 2in (5cm) down it is time to water. Use a sprinkler which will apply a steady and penetrating spray.

Remove all leaves that blow on to the rock garden in autumn and cover any plants that cannot tolerate winter wet with a sheet of glass supported on wire legs. Leave this protection in place from November to February. Top-dress rock garden plants with a mixture of equal parts loam, grit and leaf-mould in early spring. Work a few handfuls around and among each plant. Lightly clip over those alpines which produce untidy seedheads or straggly growth as soon as they have finished flowering. Prune plants which spread too far, using secateurs.

Maintenance

Cover plants that cannot tolerate winter wet with a sheet of glass supported on wire legs. Spread a layer of grit 1in (2.5cm) deep around the plants to keep down weeds.

SCREE BEDS

Rock garden plants which require extremely sharp drainage are best cultivated in scree beds, designed to simulate the naturally occurring conditions at the foot of mountain slopes where there is a deep layer of finely broken rock and a certain amount of humus.

A scree bed is essentially a raised bed with much of the soil replaced by stone chippings. Retaining walls of sandstone, brick or broken paving slabs may be used to support the sides of the bed, and these should be given an inward batter to make them stable. Lay the lowest stones on a concrete foundation; the upper courses may be dry or filled with soil to accommodate plants that enjoy growing in vertical crevices (these should be inserted as building progresses). Leave drainage holes in the base of the wall at frequent intervals. The bed should be at least 2ft (60cm) high over clay soils to provide good drainage; at least 1ft (30cm) high over sandy soil. Place a 4-6in (10-15cm) layer of broken bricks and rubble in the bottom and use the following compost to fill the rest of the space: 10 parts stone chippings, 1 part loam, 1 part leaf-mould and 1 part sand, plus a slow-release fertilizer. Plant in autumn or spring.

Hedges 1

Initial pruning of hedges

Group One
Blackthorn (*Prunus spinosa*), box (*Buxus sempervirens*), hawthorn (*Crataegus monogyna*), *Lonicera nitida*, Myrobalan plum (*Prunis cerasifera*), privet (*Ligustrum ovalifolium*), snowberry (*Symphoricarpos* spp.), tamarisk (*Tamarix gallica*): cut each

Hedges make excellent garden barriers where walls and fences are undesirable. They provide a natural backdrop to other garden plants and thorny hedges are effective obstacles against animals. The traditional garden hedge is formal, close-clipped to give it a regular outline. But there are many shrubs that make excellent informal hedges.

Hedges do have two main disadvantages. First, they must be clipped or pruned annually, and in some cases two or three times in one year; second, they use soil nutrients which may be needed by plants growing close to them. The first problem is eased if a powered hedge trimmer is used for clipping, and the second by applying liquid feed or fertilizer each spring to the plants growing alongside the hedge and to the hedge itself. Mulching with rotted manure is beneficial as it makes the hedge's roots less likely to spread in search of food.

Planting

The time of planting will depend on the shrub being used. Deciduous shrubs lifted from the open ground and supplied "bare root" should be planted between November and March. Evergreens and conifers may be planted in late September and October or late April to early May. If the plants arrive at an inconvenient time or when the ground is unfit for planting, heel them in (see page 61). Container-grown shrubs can be planted at any time of year providing attention is paid to watering in dry spells.

Ground preparation Hedges usually remain in place for a long time, so make sure that ground preparation is thorough. Use bamboo canes and stout twine to mark out the strip of ground to be occupied by the hedge. Excavate a trench 2-3ft (60-90cm) wide and one spit deep along the line that the hedge will take. Fork over the base of the trench, incorporating well-rotted compost, manure or leaf-mould. Set aside more of the organic matter to mix with the soil when it is firmed back around the plants. Two or three handfuls of compound fertilizer can be forked into each running yard (metre) of the trench.

Choosing plants It is tempting to choose very large plants so that an instant effect is achieved. Avoid doing this. Smaller plants, around 12-18in (30-45cm) high, are not only cheaper but will usually establish themselves much more quickly than older specimens. If immediate protection is needed, erect a post and wire fence alongside the young hedge.

How to plant Plant when the soil is moist and easily workable, not when it is very dry, frozen or muddy. Trim any broken or damaged roots from the plants with sharp secateurs and space them out in the trench at the required distance (see table pages 96-97). Remove the containers from container-grown shrubs but do not disturb the rootball unless the roots are pot-bound, when they should be gently teased out.

Where hedges of 3ft (90cm) or greater thickness are required, use a staggered double row of plants. Set the rows 12-15in (30-50cm) apart, against garden lines stretched along the trench.

Spread out the roots of bare-root plants and replace the soil, firming it around the roots with the foot. The old soil mark on the stem of each plant should rest at or just below soil level. Container-grown plants should have their rootballs just buried, so that the new soil level is about 1in (2.5cm) above the old. Firm the soil around the stem.

Immediately after planting neatly cut off any ungainly or damaged stems or branches with a pair of secateurs. Prune most deciduous hedges to a third of their height, and hawthorn and privet to 6in (15cm) from ground level. Evergreens and conifers may be sprayed with an anti-desiccant solution to reduce transpiration and encourage the rapid establishment of the young plants.

Aftercare

Spread a 2-3in (5-8cm) mulch of pulverized bark over the soil at the foot of the hedge in the first spring after planting. Do so immediately in the case of spring-planted conifers and evergreens. Make sure the soil is moist before the mulch is applied.

The hedge must not be neglected after planting if it is to grow unchecked and establish itself rapidly. In dry weather frequent waterings will be necessary. In frosty weather the ground should be refirmed around the plants every day, if necessary, so that the roots do not dry out in the lifted earth.

plant back to 6in (15cm) from ground level.

Group Two
Beech (*Fagus sylvatica*), flowering currant (*Ribes sanguineum*), hazel (*Corylus avellana, C. maxima* 'Purpurea') hornbeam (*Carpinus betulus*): cut back leading shoots and longer side-shoots by one-third.

Group Three
Conifers and evergreens such as cherry laurel (*Prunus laurocerasus*), gorse (*Ulex europaeus*), *Griselinia littoralis*, holly (*Ilex aquifolium* and vars), laurel (*Aucuba japonica*), Lawson cypress (*Chamaecyparis lawsoniana* and vars), Leyland cypress (× *Cupressocyparis leylandii*), New Zealand daisy bush (*Olearia* × *haastii*), *Osmanthus* × *burkwoodii, Osmanthus delavayi, Poncirus trifoliata, Viburnum tinus*, Western red cedar (*Thuja plicata* especially 'Atrovirens'), yew (*Taxus baccata*): cut back untidy laterals, do not prune the leader.

Planting

Excavate a trench 2-3ft (60-90cm) wide and 1ft (30cm) deep where the hedge is to grow.

Fork over the base of the trench, adding organics and compound fertilizer at 4oz per yard (110g per metre).

Trim any broken or damaged roots from bare-root plants with secateurs.

Spread out the roots of bare-root plants, place them in the trench and replace soil, firming well.

Initial pruning

Cut plants back on planting to encourage strong basal growth. See chart at top of page.

Cutting

Trim formal hedges at least twice a year. Stretch a garden line taut along the hedge to ensure straight cut.

95

Hedges 2

Clipping and pruning

For most formal hedges twice-yearly clipping is necessary, though privet may need three clips. May and August are the best times to carry out the operation and the shears (or electric trimmer) should be sharp and well lubricated. Aim to create a hedge which is slightly narrower at the top than at the base so that light is allowed to reach the lower portions and snow is shed more easily.

Informal hedges, which are often grown for their flowers, may be pruned to shape with a pair of secateurs immediately after flowering and then left untouched until the same time the following year.

Cut all formal deciduous hedges and small-leaved evergreens with shears or an electric trimmer. For informal hedges and large-leaved evergreens such as laurel and holly use secateurs, which will leave the foliage unmarked and produce a better shape. Shears can be used if the hedge is very long. Remove damaged leaves and stems with secateurs after cutting with shears.

Gather up and burn all the clippings as soon as the job is finished; do not allow them to lie on lawns or among border plants.

Chemical retardants are available to reduce the growth of most widely grown hedges. They are applied in spray form shortly after the spring clipping or pruning. After application, the hedge will retain

HEDGING PLANTS

		Site	Features
Aucuba japonica	Laurel	C D	2
Berberis darwinii	Barberry	C D	1 2 4
Berberis × *stenophylla*	Barberry	C D	1 2 4
Buxus sempervirens	Box	C	2
Carpinus betulus	Hornbeam	C D	2
Chamaecyparis lawsoniana and cultivars	Lawson cypress	D	2
Corylus maxima 'Purpurea'			2
Cotoneaster simonsii		A C D	1 2 3
Crataegus monogyna	Hawthorn/Quick	A B C D	1 2 4
× *Cupressocyparis leylandii*	Leyland cypress	A	2
Escallonia rubra ssp. *macrantha*		A D	1 2
Fagus sylvatica	Common beach	B C	2
Forsythia × *intermedia* 'Spectabilis'	Golden bells	C D	1 2
Fuchsia magellanica		A C	1 2
Ilex aquifolium and cultivars	Holly	A D	2 3 4
Lavandula angustifolia and cultivars	Lavender	A	1 2
Ligustrum ovalifolium	Privet	C	2
Lonicera nitida		C D	2
Metasequoia glyptostroboides	Dawn redwood		2
Olearia × *haastii*	New Zealand daisy bush	A C	1 2
Poncirus trifoliata			4
Prunus laurocerasus	Cherry laurel		1 2 3
Rhododendron ponticum	Common rhododendron	B	1 2
Rosa rubiginosa	Sweet briar	A C D	1 2 4
Rosa rugosa	Ramanas rose	A C D	1 2 4
Tamarix gallica	Tamarisk	A B	1 2
Taxus baccata	Yew	B C D	2
Thuja plicata 'Atrovirens'	Western red cedar	C D	2
Ulex europaeus	Gorse	A B	1 2 4
Virbunum tinus	Laurustinus	A B C	1 2

Key to hedging plants table

Site	Features	Pruning	Growth rate
A: suitable for seaside sites	1: flowers	For pruning groups see	The figures give the number
B: suitable for windy sites	2: foliage	list at top of pages 94-95.	of years taken by the
C: suitable for chalk soils	3: fruits	S: cut with secateurs	plant to grow to 5ft (1.5m).
D: suitable for heavy soils	4: thorns	Sh: cut with shears	

its shape, with reduced growth rate, until the following spring, when a further cut and spray will be necessary. Follow the instructions on the label closely and do not apply the retardant to those species listed as being unsuitable for treatment.

Weeds have a tendency to grow unnoticed at the foot of hedges, and leaves and litter may also collect there. Clear out all this rubbish during the winter when it can easily be seen and removed and apply a weedkiller such as simazine to inhibit germination.

Screens and windbreaks
Where strong winds severely limit the types of plant that can be grown in a garden, it is a good idea to establish a row of trees to act as a windbreak. Such barriers may also be useful in hiding an ugly view. Trees make excellent windbreaks for they filter the wind, so slowing it down, rather than stopping it dead like a wall and creating turbulence and damaging eddies. Plant the screen at right angles to the wind. It will cut down the force of the wind on its leeward side for a distance up to 20 times greater than its height.

Suitable upright windbreak and screening trees include: *Chamaecyparis lawsoniana* (Lawson cypress), × *Cupressocyparis leylandii* (Leyland cypress), *Populus alba* (white poplar), *Populus nigra* 'Italica' (Lombardy poplar), *Thuja plicata* and cultivars.

Planting distance	Pruning	Evergreen/ deciduous	Formal/ Informal	Growth rate
24in (60cm)	Group 3 S	E	F/I	5
18in (45cm)	Sh	E	F/I	6
18in (45cm)	Sh	E	F/I	5
12in (30cm)	Group 1 Sh	E	F	8
12in (30cm)	Group 2 Sh	D	F	6
24in (60cm)	Group 3 Sh	E	F	5
	S	D	F	
18in (45cm)	S	E	F/I	5
12in (30cm)	Group 1 Sh	D	F	7
30in (75cm)	Group 3 Sh	E	F	3
18in (45cm)	S	E	F/I	4
12in (30cm)	Group 2 Sh	D	F	5
18in (45cm)	S/Sh	D	F/I	4
12in (30cm)	S	D	I	5
18in (45cm)	Group 3 S/Sh	E	F	8
12in (30cm)	Sh	E	I	Only 2ft (60cm)
12in (30cm)	Group 1 Sh	E	F	4
12in (30cm)	Group 1 Sh	E	F	5
24in (60cm)	Sh	D	F	5
12in (30cm)	Group 3 S	E	I	7
	Group 3 Sh	D	F/I	
24in (60cm)	Group 3 S/Sh	E	F/I	3
24in (60cm)	S	E	I	5
18in (45cm)	S	D	I	3
18in (45cm)	S	D	I	5
12in (30cm)	Group 1 S	D	I	4
24in (60cm)	Group 3 Sh	E	F	8
24in (60cm)	Group 3 Sh	E	F	5
18in (45cm)	Group 3 S	E	I	6
18in (45cm)	Group 3 S/Sh	E	F/I	5

Plant supports

As a means of giving height to a flat plot, or providing a colourful screen, climbing plants are invaluable. To grow well, all climbers, ramblers and scramblers need some means of support. Plants can be grown up walls and fences, but there are other structures of a more decorative appearance that can be erected purely for the plants' convenience.

Arches The rustic arch looks especially at home in cottage gardens covered in honeysuckle, roses or clematis. Larch poles (treated with a wood preservative to prolong their life) can easily be joined together in a suitable shape. The top of the arch may be straight or rounded, and the wood fixed together with long screws or nails. Brass screws will certainly last longest and provide the best effect, but the wood will perish before they do.

Sink the base of the poles into concrete, into purpose-made post supports or into earthenware pipes bedded into concrete to hold them firm (see illustration below). If removed when the wood has rotted beyond repair, another can be lowered into place.

Pergolas A pergola is simply a series of arches linked together. Use rustic poles or prepare tanalized timber and secure the bases of the posts as with those of an arch. Alternatively construct brick or stone columns and bolt wooden cross-members to them. Knock galvanized staples into the wood and tie plant stems to the frame with twine.

Tripods In small, flat gardens, tripods of larch poles can be used to support climbers in flower beds, so giving height to the planting. Simply knock treated poles into the ground 2-4ft (60-120cm) apart – and fasten them together at the top with strong twine or wire. Tie in the stems of the climber as it grows.

Colonnades Useful more as a visual screen than an impenetrable barrier, the colonnade consists in garden terms of a series of vertical posts linked by one or two stout ropes. The posts are secured in the same way as those of the arch and should be positioned 6-8ft (1.8-2.4m) apart. Plants growing on colonnades will need to be tied in regularly if the feature is to be seen to best effect.

Arches and pergolas

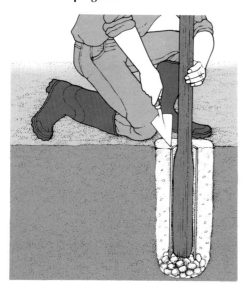

Sink wooden posts into concrete or into 2ft (60cm) pipes bedded into concrete. Replace the posts in the pipes when they rot. Always use treated timber.

Walls and fences

Fix trelliswork to walls with screws, using cotton reels as spacers to hold the trellis away from the wall.

Trees Garden trees that are past their best but still strong enough to stand up can be brightened up considerably if climbers are planted at their bases and allowed to grow up them.

Thin out the branch canopy if necessary and plant a vigorous climber in a prepared patch of soil at least 18in (45cm) away from the tree, leading the stems towards their support with bamboo canes. Old tree stumps can also be covered with scrambling plants if their removal is difficult or impossible. However, honey fungus, which often colonizes old tree stumps, can kill nearby plants.

Plant supports on walls and fences
Plain-faced fences and most walls will need to be provided with some kind of plant support if climbers and wall shrubs are to be grown against them.

Ordinary wooden trelliswork can be fastened to a wall which has been drilled and plugged to accept screws. Use cotton reel spacers to allow the trellis to be held an inch or so away from the surface so that the climb-

ing shoots can pass between trellis and wall. For ease of maintenance, the lower edge of the trellis can be hinged to a horizontal 2in by 1in (5cm by 2.5cm) batten fixed to the wall. The upper edge is held against a similar batten with bolts and wing nuts. The entire structure, with its plants, can then be eased away from the wall to allow painting or pointing to take place.

The traditional way of supporting climbing plants on walls and fences is to fix horizontal wires to the surface at 1-1½ft (30-45cm) intervals. These can be held in place with masonry nails if they are required for one season only, but metal vine eyes inserted into drilled and plugged holes provide a more permanent fixing. The wires will be held 2-3in (5-8cm) away from the wall, allowing the stems to twine around them. Wire netting, which can be plastic-covered, is an alternative to trellising and wires. Annuals can be grown up plastic or cord nets.

For lists of plants suitable for walls of a given aspect see page 80.

Hinge the base of the trellis, fixing it to a 2 × 1in (5cm × 2.5cm) wooden batten with brass hinges. Fix to a batten at the top with wing nuts.

To support plants on walls, attach wires horizontally at 1-1½ft (30-45cm) intervals with masonry nails, or vine eyes fitted to drilled and plugged holes.

Water 1

Water is used in the garden both for irrigation and as a feature, in the form of a pool or stream. Water allows a wide range of aquatic and marginal plants to be grown. Fish can be introduced, and amphibians such as newts and frogs may find their way to the pool.

Siting a pool

Position the pool where it can be seen to best effect and where the reflections on its surface can be enjoyed. Avoid siting a pool under trees. Not only will the shady conditions make for poor plant growth and minimal flower production, but the pool will also become clogged with fallen leaves, which can be harmful to fish and are laborious to remove. An open site which is sheltered from strong winds is best.

If pool lights or a pump are to be installed, make sure that the pool is within reach of the electricity supply.

Size and shape

Larger areas of water look more effective and are easier to manage than small ones, so give the pool as large a surface as possible. Pools as small as 6ft (1.8m) long by 3ft (0.9m) wide may be constructed in small gardens and on patios but they will have to be planted carefully and maintained regularly if they are not to become overgrown bogs.

The water should be at least 15in (38cm) deep, though 18ins (45cm) is more satisfactory. Pools with a surface area of more than 100sq ft (9.3sq m) may be 2ft (60cm) deep, and very large pools up to a maximum of 3ft (90cm) deep. This depth will allow the pool to heat up and cool down relatively slowly, and it will ensure that fish can avoid being frozen in winter. Pools less than 2½ft (75cm) deep may be more troubled by algae than those of greater depth. The pool should contain steps or shelves where the water is about 9in (23cm) deep. This allows marginal aquatic plants to be positioned at the best depth.

The shape of the pool will depend entirely on the effect required, but as a rule it is best to use bold and simple shapes rather than intricate ones which look fussy and are more difficult to maintain. Formal pools (in the shape of rectangles, squares, circles and ovals) can be constructed to fit into formal gardens and terraces. Uneven shapes will create a more natural sheet of water in a natural garden. Experiment by laying a hose pipe or a trail of sand to mark the proposed shape of the pool and adjust the curves until the desired effect is achieved. Mark the final shape with wooden pegs.

Natural water courses

A stream running through the garden will present the owner with the makings of a superb garden feature, but also with some possible problems. Moving water will not support water lilies and other aquatics that need calm conditions; the speed and level of the water may be very variable, and bog plants may even be washed away in heavy downpours. Fish will be difficult to retain, and the water may contain harmful mineral salts. Certainly, part of the stream may be dammed to make a pool, but the constant displacement of water and the infiltration of fresh supplies may cause a build-up of algae and blanket weed. Trial and error alone will reveal what can be done with individual garden streams, but the safest approach would be to establish bog plants on the banks and to experiment with one or two marginal aquatics. If the scheme does work the feature will become a spectacle rivalled by few pools. Any changes to the bed or course of the stream may have to be approved by the local river authority.

Domestic water supply

Where no natural water course is present, the pool maker will have to rely on the domestic supply both for initial filling and any subsequent topping up of the pool. An ordinary hose pipe connected to an internal or external tap is used. Domestic supplies will have higher levels of mineral salts than the water in the pool, which has been modified chemically by plant and animal growth. Thus topping up with mains water can lead to faster build-ups of algae and weed.

Poor balance

A garden pool must be managed with the aim of establishing a balanced ecology. A balanced pool will stay clear, and no single species of plant or animal life will become dominant.

WATER CONSERVATION AND STORAGE

Gardeners cannot always rely on un-limited and cheap supplies of water from the mains. By conserving and storing rain-water, gardeners may save money on metred water and they will have a supply to fall back on when there are hose-pipe bans. For garden use, rainwater has the advantage of being free of calcium, which may be present in damaging quantities in the tapwater of some areas, adversely affecting rhododendrons and other lime-haters.

Butts and tanks If there is space, butts of around 50 gallon (225 litre) capacity can be used to store rainwater, down pipes channelling water to the butts from the gut-tering of a dwelling house or a greenhouse. A butt should be equipped with a tap 3-4in (8-10cm) above its base, and it should be raised off the ground on bricks or a con-crete base so that a watering can or bucket can be placed under the tap.

Flooding can be avoided if an overflow pipe is fitted just below the rim of the butt to divert surplus water to another butt or to a drain or soakaway. Proprietary fittings are also available to cause the water to bypass the butt when it is full.

To prevent leaves and other debris from falling into the water, fit a lid to the butt, and fasten one foot from a pair of nylon tights over the end of the inlet pipe as a filter.

If the stored water is required for green-house use, then a tank sunk into the border soil below the staging will provide an accessible supply at the same temperature as that prevailing in the greenhouse. Fit a removable lid to greenhouse water storage tanks to prevent compost, faded leaves and flowers from fouling the water and algae from growing.

Storage vessels should be emptied and scrubbed clean at least once a year, pre-ferably in the winter months.

Siting a pool

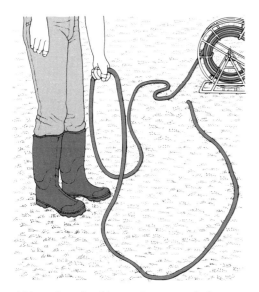

1 Use a length of hose pipe to mark the boundaries of the proposed pool.

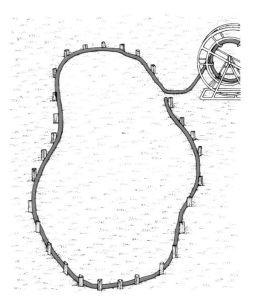

2 Adjust the pipe until the best shape is achieved. Mark the line with pegs.

Water 2

There was a time when all garden pools were made either of puddled clay or of concrete. Concrete is still used today, but it has largely been replaced by lightweight pool liners that are far less laborious to install.

Pool materials and construction

Once the shape of the pool has been marked out, the soil can be excavated with a spade to the required depth. Slope the sides of the pool to an angle of 20 degrees, allow shelves for marginal aquatics, remove all sharp stones and then line the hole either with a 2in (5cm) layer of sand, or with old newspapers, to prevent the liner from being punctured. Choose from the following types of pool liner.

Polythene Black polythene is preferable to the transparent types, but even heavy duty grades (500 gauge) will usually have a life expectancy of no more than a couple of years. Polythene containing an ultra-violet inhibitor will resist breakdown by sunlight more effectively than ordinary types. The material will not stretch and must be pleated to lie flat on corners and curves. Punctures are impossible to repair, but the entire liner is relatively cheap to replace. Polythene is good for temporary pools or for creating bog gardens.

PVC PVC is far more durable than polythene and also stretchable so pleating is unnecessary. Punctures can be repaired. Reinforced PVC contains nylon for added strength and a longer life. Generally sold specifically for pool construction, these types of PVC are usually blue on one side, and fawn on the other.

Butyl A matt black material, butyl rubber will stretch well to fit the pool shape and is available in large sheets. The material will last for many years and punctures are repairable. The black colouring is a distinct advantage in the early life of the pool, for algal growth and sediment will not be quite so noticeable and the reflective properties greater.

Size of liner Butyl and PVC liners are stretchable and the size needed can be calculated on the following basis: maximum length plus twice maximum depth times maximum width plus twice maximum depth. Therefore a pool 12ft (3.6m) long by 6ft (1.8m) wide with a maximum depth of 1ft (30cm) will need a liner 15ft (4.5m) long by 9ft (2.7m) wide.

With all flexible liners a further 12-18in (30-45cm) should be allowed on the width and length of the material so that the edges can be anchored under stones or soil.

Filling and edging the pool

Butyl or PVC liners should be spread out over the prepared excavation and held in place at the edges with bricks or flat paving slabs. It is not necessary to smooth out the material against the sides of the hole – the water will stretch the fabric into place when it is run in through a hose pipe. Polythene liners should be smoothed into place on the bottom of the pool and the edges carefully pleated to lie flat as the water rises.

Construct the edges of the pool as soon as the water has reached the required level, so that unsightly glimpses of the liner can be avoided. Flat paving stones, bricks, large pebbles or smooth logs can all be used to mask the edges of the liner and hold it in place. Bog plants will soften the effect later.

Cut off any surplus material to leave an overlap of 9in (23cm), and let paving stones or brick coping overhang the edge of the pool

Building a lined pool

1 Excavate a hole of the planned shape. Slope the sides at an angle of 20 degrees and leave shelves for marginal plants.

by 2-3in (5-8cm). The slabs should be laid on level ground and made firm; they may be bedded on cement if necessary.

Moulded pools
Glass-fibre and a number of less resilient but rigid plastics are used in the manufacture of pre-formed pools. Most of these pools are too small to be of much practical use, but they can be incorporated into patios to provide small features of interest. Take out a hole to the required size, lower in the pool, make sure that the soil is refirmed around and under it to give support, and then mask the edges with paving or plants.

Concrete pools
It must be stressed that concrete is not the best material from which to construct a pool. It is inflexible and likely to fracture in extremes of temperature and if the earth below it settles or moves. It is difficult to repair and labour intensive in construction.

If, however, concrete is the chosen material, construction should proceed as follows. Mark out the area of the pool and then ex-cavate a hole 9in (23cm) deeper, 18in (45cm) wider and 18in (45cm) longer to allow for the foundations and the concrete mix. Ram a 3in (8cm) layer of rubble hardcore into position on the bottom and sides of the pool. Make a concrete mix consisting of 5 parts all-in ballast to 1 part cement, adding a proprietary waterproofing agent to reduce the likelihood of leaks. Mix the concrete with water to a thick but spreadable consistency, shovel it into the pool and then tamp it evenly over the base to a depth of 4-5in (10-13cm), smoothing with a float.

Sloping sides may be constructed in the same way as the base, but if they are too steep to support the mixture then wooden formwork should be constructed and the concrete shuttered behind it (see page 105). It is important that the sides of the pool are as thick as the base and that they are shuttered into position before the base sets so that a good bond is achieved. Polythene sheeting or damp sacks should be laid over the concrete so that it dries out slowly.

When the concrete has set, the formwork can be removed and the entire surface

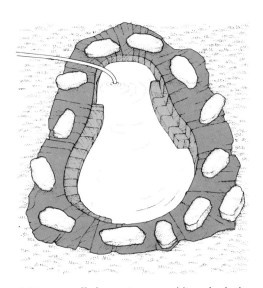

2 Remove all sharp stones and line the hole with a 2in (5cm) layer of sand. Spread the liner over the hole and anchor the edges with stones.

3 Mask the edge of the liner, using, for example, paving stones. Polythene sheet will need to be carefully pleated to lie flat.

Water 3

rendered with a mixture of 3 parts sand to 1 part cement. Replace the polythene until the rendering has set.

Whereas pools constructed from liners can be planted up immediately, those made from concrete must either be filled and emptied three or four times over the course of several weeks, or else coated with a bituminous sealant. If this precaution is not taken, the concrete will give off chemicals which are harmful to fish and aquatic plants.

As with pools constructed from liners, bricks or paving slabs may be mortared into place as copings and allowed to overlap the edge of the pool. It is not esssential that pools are built so that their rims rest at ground level. Although pools in gardens look more natural if this is the case, formal pools and those on patios may be constructed with raised brick or stone sides, which will provide seats.

Fountains and waterfalls

Although fountains and waterfalls are not essential to the well-being of the garden pool and its contents, they do have several advan-tages. The sight and sound of moving water is always appealing and fish will benefit from the additional oxygen that falling water brings to the pool. However, some plants, water lilies in particular, will suffer from the disturbance strong currents cause.

Pumps

If the water in the garden pool is circulated by a purpose-designed pump, there will be no need to install an additional water supply. There are two types of circulating pump which can be used to power waterfalls or fountains: the submersible pump is the better of the two because it can simply be stood on the floor of the pool where it will take in water and expel it through a fountain jet or through a length of hose pipe that can be placed above the waterfall system. Some pumps are equipped with both waterfall and fountain outlets.

The pump should be connected to the mains electricity via a thick, water-proof cable run from the pump to the power point. Suitable cables are usually supplied with the pump. Position the pump as near to

Constructing a concrete pool

1 Excavate a hole 9in (23cm) deeper, 18in (45cm) wider and 18in (45cm) longer than the planned pool.

2 Ram hardcore into the base of the hole to provide a foundation.

3 Shovel concrete on to the base and tamp it evenly to a thickness of 4-5in (10-13cm).

the base of the waterfall as possible so that it does not have to move the water very far and so that turbulence is kept to a minimum. Check with the supplier that the pump is powerful enough to lift the water to the required height, but remember that 6-12in (15-30cm) steps in a waterfall will be quite large enough to give a good effect.

A surface pump should be placed in a dry, brick-built chamber at the side of the pool as near to the waterfall or fountain as possible. It draws water from the pool through a pipe fitted with a strainer. Although a surface pump may cost slightly less than a submersible pump, the saving may well be lost in the cost of the pump chamber. Surface pumps are also noisier.

Fountains

Fountains are best suited to formal rather than informal pools. They are usually placed in a central position and they may distribute their water in a variety of patterns. Place them where the falling droplets will not land on the leaves of aquatic plants but on the water – the fountain will then sound better.

Waterfalls and spillways

Waterfalls look most natural in informal settings and where pools are built into rock gardens. The water may be allowed to cascade over rock steps, down narrow channels and even through hollow tree trunks or bamboo pipes until it finds its way into the pool. Glass-fibre cascades are available at garden centres, but it is difficult to make them appear natural.

Spillways are best constructed from PVC or butyl rather than concrete, which is likely to leak and cause the water level in the pool to drop.

Lighting

Pools can be displayed at night if they are illuminated. Fully insulated garden spotlights can be directed on to them (see pages 110-11), or water-proofed underwater lights may be submerged behind waterfalls and fountains, where they will produce spectacular effects.

Pool lights and pumps should be installed by a qualified electrician, and inspected regularly to ensure that they are in safe working order.

4 Build a wooden formwork and fill it with concrete to form sides 4-5in (10-13cm) thick.

5 Lay polythene sheeting or damp sacking over the concrete so that it dries out slowly.

6 When the concrete has set, remove the formwork and render the entire surface with 3:1 concrete.

Water 4

Once a pool has been filled with water for a week or ten days, aquatic and bog plants can be introduced. These plants are divided into groups according to their habit of growth and their moisture requirements.

Submerged aquatics Some plants grow entirely beneath the surface of the water, producing oxygen beneficial to fish and other pond life. They are not usually decorative but are essential for the health of the pool. Submerged oxygenators are usually supplied as bunches of unrooted cuttings. They should be planted (at the rate of one small bunch for every 2-3sq ft (0.2-0.3sq m) of the pool's surface area) either in the baskets or soil occupied by other plants, or in small mounds of soil on the bottom of the pool.

Fixed floating aquatics Plants whose roots are anchored in baskets or mounds of soil, but whose foliage floats on the surface of the water, are fixed floating aquatics. Water lilies are included in this group. Very vigorous varieties will thrive in water 4ft (1.2m) deep, but some of the smaller types will tolerate as little as 3in (8cm) of water above their crowns. Consult specialist catalogues for details.

Free-floating aquatics Free floaters simply lie on the surface of the water and need no soil at all. They vary from those with tiny green leaves, to plants which consist of floating rosettes. When they become overcrowded the unwanted plants can be discarded. The duckweeds (*Lemna* spp.) may become a severe nuisance if allowed to get out of hand, and should never be introduced on purpose. If necessary, remove them with a fine mesh sieve.

Marginal aquatics Plant which grow in shallow water are called marginals. They should be planted in baskets placed on submerged shelves.

Bog plants A permanent site for bog and moisture-loving plants can be created by extending the pool liner under a marginal band of soil, so that the earth remains moist. The soil depth should be at least 9in (23cm). Pockets can be constructed at the edge of concrete pools to house bog plants.

How to plant
Marginal aquatics, water lilies and other fixed floating aquatics can be planted in purpose-made plastic baskets, in plastic bins provided with holes, or old cane baskets. Mounds of soil on the pool bottom are seldom satisfactory. Ordinary fibrous garden soil can be used and so, too, can old manure. Composts rich in manures and fertilizers should usually be avoided.

Line the basket with clean coarse sacking or some other coarse material to keep the soil in. Cut all old leaves and long, straggly roots from the plants and set them in the containers. Firm soil round the plants, leaving a gap of 1½in (3.75cm) between the surface of the soil and the rim of the basket. Spread a layer of coarse gravel over the soil to prevent it floating off and to keep fish from disturbing it. Containers 10-12in (25-30cm) square are suitable for most vigorous aquatics; smaller versions 8in (20cm) square may be used for pygmy water lilies and less invasive marginal plants. Put freshly planted containers into a bath of water before placing them in the pool. This expels air, which can bring up debris and cloud the water if the container is put straight into the pool. All aquatics are best planted and put in place during late April and May, though the planting season may be extended through the summer.

Do not place the baskets on the bottom of the pool immediately, but instead stand them on bricks so that they are 6in (15cm) below the surface of the water. Gradually lower them into their final positions as the plant grows.

Pool management
The greatest problem facing the pool owner is that of green water, which is the result of colonization by algae. All newly made pools will turn green shortly after they are filled, but if plenty of oxygenating plants are present, and the pool is sufficiently deep, the water will eventually clear and remain clear. Blanket weed should be removed with a garden rake or sieve as soon as it is seen. On no account remove and replace all the water in the pool, for the algae will soon reappear and the clearing process will have been delayed. Each spring may see a recurrence of the problem but if the pool is left alone the murkiness will clear.

Throughout the summer the pool may

need topping up to replace water lost by evaporation. Allow a hose pipe with a piece of sacking tied over the end to trickle water into the pool, so oxygenating the water as it replenishes the loss.

Like all herbaceous garden plants, most aquatics die down at the end of the season and their foliage can be cut down to within a few inches of the rootstock. Remove flowers as soon as they fade to encourage further flushes.

Once planted in their baskets, aquatics can be left undisturbed for several years, after which time it is advisable to remove, divide and replant them, discarding any dead or weak portions. Feeding will generally be unnecessary, but water lilies lacking in vigour can be given a little bonemeal. A handful of this fertilizer should be moulded into a handful of clay soil and the lump of mixture then pushed into the soil around the plant in mid-summer.

Fish

Fish should be added eight weeks or so after the plants have been introduced, otherwise they may eat most of the submerged oxygenators before they have become established. Rocks or other shade-casting features must be present to allow the fish shelter when they choose.

Select brightly coloured fish such as golden orfe, shubunkins and common or comet gold-fish, and avoid dull-coloured varieties and catfish, which will stir up the sediment in the bottom of the pool. Allow at least 1sq ft (0.09sq m) of pool surface to each fish.

Buy the fish from a reputable supplier, and submerge the travelling container in the pool before the fish are set free. This allows the water temperatures to equalize and the fish to become acclimatized to their environment.

From April to September feed the fish once or twice a week. The floating type of food pellet is best for it will not add to the pool sediment. In winter a patch of ice should be kept melted at all times in small pools, to allow the fish to breathe.

Other pond life

Frogs, toads, newts, dragonflies and many other varieties of native wildlife may make their home in and around the pool, and ram-shorn snails are of value in reducing, to a certain extent, the detritus in the pool. Take care not to introduce sticklebacks or water snails such as the freshwater whelk, which can damage the leaves of aquatic plants.

Planting aquatics

1 Line a plastic basket with clean sacking and fill it with ordinary garden soil.

2 Plant the aquatics, firming them in well. Spread a layer of gravel over the soil surface.

3 Carefully submerge the basket in a bath of water to expel the air before placing in the pool.

Electricity in the garden

However self-sufficient the gardener may be he should leave the installation of outdoor electrical wiring and apparatus to a qualified professional. Electricity is potentially lethal, and stringent safety measures are essential if electrical equipment, especially outdoor equipment, is to work correctly and without endangering life.

Having established this principle, it is as well if the gardener understands some of the requirements which must be met when a power supply is being installed. It is sometimes possible for the gardener to do a certain amount of preparatory work to ease the electrician's task and lessen the expense. Consult the electrician before starting any such work.

Cables and power points

When a power supply is to be run from a dwelling house to a garden shed or greenhouse, or to outdoor lighting points, the safest course is to have the supply cable laid underground. Overhead cables not only present safety problems – unless they are carefully positioned, for example, there is the risk of them being chafed by branches – they also look unsightly.

When electricians lay a supply underground they should use a fully armoured cable, for it can stand a certain amount of damage should it be struck inadvertently when the garden is being dug. To minimize the likelihood of such an accident, all armoured cable should be buried to a depth of 20in (50cm) under paths and hard surfaces, and to a depth of 24in (60cm) under lawns, beds, borders, and other cultivated soil. Before the soil is filled in, tiles and warning tape should be laid on top of the cable. The circuit must have its own fuse or miniature circuit breaker (MCB).

Gardeners can save a lot of money and avoid possible damage to plants by excavating the trenches themselves to the specifications of the electrician who is to carry out the wiring. A permanent record should be kept of the position of underground cables and this information should be checked and passed on to new occupants when a property changes hands.

All switches, sockets and plugs used outdoors or in a greenhouse must be weatherproof; those used for domestic supply indoors are not suitable. Control boards especially designed for greenhouse use are available.

Underground cables

1 Dig a trench for the cable at least 24in (60cm) deep, 20in (50cm) under paths and other hard surfaces.

2 Protect the cable by placing a row of roof tiles over it in the trench.

3 Lay warning tape along the top of tiles to indicate the presence of a live cable.

A permanent outdoor electrical supply

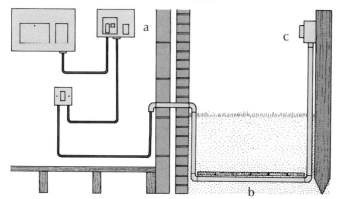

An outdoor electrical circuit installed by a qualified electrician should include a switching unit (a) that incorporates an MCB or fuse and a residual current circuit breaker (RCCB). This diagram shows a circuit in which armoured cable (b) has been laid underground (minimum depth 24in (60cm) in cultivated soil and 20in (50cm) under hard surfaces) to a weather-proof socket (c).

SAFETY PRECAUTIONS

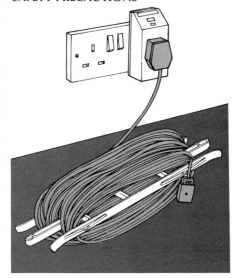

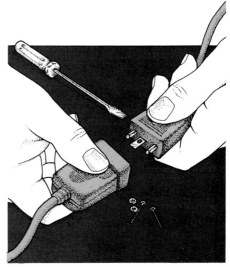

When electrically powered lawnmowers, hedgetrimmers and other tools are used in the garden and the circuit itself is not protected by an RCCB, always use a plug-in RCCB with individual items of equipment.

Use only equipment that complies with the relevant British standard and has been tested for safety (look for the Kite Mark or BEAB label).

Check that metal-cased power tools are properly earthed before use. Plastic-covered power tools will be double insulated but should still be used with a three-core extension cable.

Before switching on the current, check all equipment for worn or loose parts and check flex and extension leads for damage to insulation and loose connections.

Should a cable be damaged, cut out the damaged section and join the two ends with a purpose-made weather-proof connector (above right) – not with tape.

Do not use electrical equipment in damp conditions.

Garden lighting

Lighting can be used to great effect in the garden to illuminate shrub beds and borders, pools, fountains and trees. It can be designed to highlight those parts of the garden that are viewed from the house, thus allowing the garden to be enjoyed after dark. If the observer is indoors the internal lighting and the barrier of the house windows will make it hard for the eye to appreciate the garden lighting. Very powerful bulbs will therefore be necessary to overcome this. It may also be worth while fitting dimmer switches inside the house to enhance the effect of the outside lights.

Securing lamps

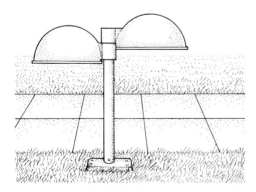

Push lamps fitted with spikes into firm soil or turf. Direct the beams onto features.

Positioning lamps

For functional lighting of paths and steps, use mushroom lamps directed downwards. This avoids dazzle.

Installing a circuit

A garden lighting system must be installed by a qualified electrician: it can be extremely dangerous if the equipment is incorrectly installed or is unsuitable for outdoor use. The mains cable should be laid underground as described on page 108. The sockets must be fully weather-proofed if they are not under cover and an RCCB should be fitted unless the whole circuit is protected by an RCCB. Keep the cable which runs from the socket to the lamp as short and as obviously displayed as possible to minimize the risk of damage. The cable must be weatherproof, resistant to

Fix exterior spotlights to walls or posts with screws and if necessary plugs.

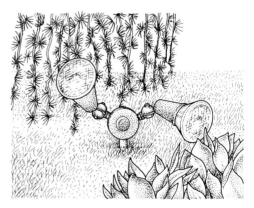

Illuminate trees and shrubs with floodlights placed low down and shining up into the foliage.

ultra-violet light and vermin-proof, and all equipment should be properly earthed.

Low-voltage sets are also available. A transformer, housed inside, usually converts mains voltage to a 12-volt supply. The lights are a weak source of illumination but the cumulative effect can be attractive and the lights can be moved around the garden to create a diversity of moods.

Choice of fittings

Choose only those lamps that are especially constructed for use in the open. They must be waterproof, resistant to corrosion, and able to

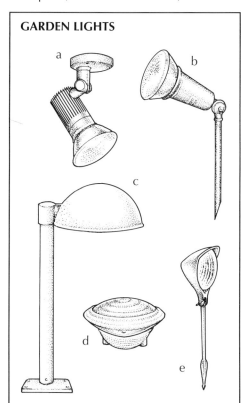

GARDEN LIGHTS

Spotlights (a) can be fixed to any solid surface, or to spikes (b) so that they can be moved. Mushroom lamps (c) light paths and steps. Pool lights (d) can be floating or submerged, and floodlights (e) coloured.

withstand frost, snow and damp. Most garden lamps are made of aluminium alloy or high impact plastic and fitted with rubber or plastic gaskets to keep out water.

Positioning the lamps

Only experiment will reveal the best positions for garden lights, but the following points should be borne in mind. Make sure that all the lights point away from the onlooker so that they do not dazzle and mar the view. Use white rather than coloured bulbs to bring out the natural beauty of the plants. A tree or large shrub can be floodlit to act as a backdrop to a carpet of low-growing plants in the foreground. Alternatively, use floodlights to illuminate large areas in a pool of light; and position smaller spotlights to pick out specimen trees or shrubs. An illusion of greater distance can be created by the strategic positioning of bright illumination in the foreground and dimmer illumination in the background.

Securing the lamps

Dome lamps have spikes that are simply pushed into the ground to hold them firm. Others may possess drilled brackets which will have to be mounted on the house wall or a convenient garden building, or on a wooden post which has been treated with preservative and knocked into the ground in front of the plants to be lit.

If lights are to be positioned in trees among the branches, they should either be firmly screwed to a strong branch, or secured with padded brackets that can be adjusted to prevent constriction.

Pool lighting

Spotlights turned on garden pools and streams can be especially effective, but they can also be positioned under the water to give waterfalls and fountains another dimension. Use only fully waterproofed lights especially designed for pools. The best effect is achieved by lighting waterfalls and fountains from behind. The lamps should be directed towards the onlooker so that they shine through the curtain of water. Experiment with various coloured bulbs if particularly bright effects are required.

Electricity in the greenhouse

A mains electricity supply in the greenhouse is a considerable aid in the propagation and growth of a wide variety of plants. Lighting also allows the greenhouse to be used on winter evenings. While heating by electricity can be expensive compared with other fuels, growing aids such as propagating cases, extractor fans and soil-warming cables can only be run on mains electricity. Fan heaters, which though electric are relatively cheap to run, are useful adjuncts to other heating systems, or they can be used on their own to provide background heat.

Lighting

Fluorescent strip lights are the most suitable kind for lighting greenhouses. Lighting can be used to stimulate plants as well as to supply general illumination. Light is the factor that most frequently limits plant growth in greenhouses during the winter. Additional lighting, using high pressure mercury vapour lamps, is used commercially to stimulate the growth rate of various crops. However, it is seldom economic for amateurs because of the high equipment and running costs. Special lighting installations are useful however as an aid to propagation. Extra light will help to maintain the growth of rooted cuttings of deciduous plants during autumn and early winter when they would normally lose their foliage and cease growth for the season.

Lighting can also be used to increase the day-length, or period during which there is enough light for growth to go on. Some plants will not flower unless they have a certain number of hours light per day. This process is used commercially, but due to cost is seldom viable for the amateur. Only certain plants respond to "long days". Some are "short day" plants, others are "day-length neutral". Manipulating the responses of various plants to produce useful results is a complicated process.

Using fluorescent tube lighting Install lighting tubes about 3 ft (90cm) above the greenhouse bench, with a reflector above the tube so that the light is focused on to the plants. Do not use a reflector so large that it blocks daylight. A timeswitch is essential, allowing the lights to be switched on for the optimum period required to stimulate the plants.

Heating

Electricity may not provide the cheapest form of heating but it is clean, flexible and efficient. Fan heaters will expel their heat quickly, and care must be taken to position them where the heat can be evenly distributed and not blown directly on to plants.

Soil and air-warming cables can be used to heat greenhouse beds and propagating cases. Such a form of heating is cheap and is only applied where it is needed, not diffused as with general heating systems. A thermostat, or pair if soil and air cables are used, is essential.

Use only those electrical heaters designed specifically for greenhouse use – domestic types are likely to be dangerous in the humid greenhouse environment.

Air circulation

Air circulation is vital if the greenhouse atmosphere is not to become excessively humid, hot or stale. An electric extractor fan positioned high up at one end of the greenhouse will draw out the hot, humid air and, provided that some ventilators are open, fresh air will be drawn in.

A simple circulating fan can be similarly positioned to keep the air moving and avoid a stagnant atmosphere. Such provision is particularly valuable in winter when air temperatures must be maintained at a reasonable level and frost avoided.

Lighting

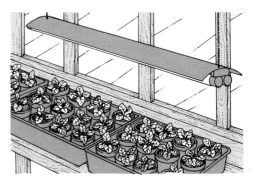

Fluorescent lighting can be used to speed plant growth. Mount a reflector above the tubes to direct light onto plants.

Electric propagating cases

Mains electricity in the greenhouse makes possible the use of heated propagating cases. These can be used for raising seedlings, cuttings or grafted plants. The combination of warm growing medium and relatively cool air provides the best possible growing conditions for many plants. The heat is provided by cables in the base of the soil tray. Propagating cases should have a thermostat to allow the correct temperatures to be maintained. Most cuttings root best at 18-21°C (65-70°F). For full details see the companion volume in this series, *Growing under Glass.*

Mist propagation

Cuttings of many shrubs, herbaceous and pot plants root more quickly if they are sprayed regularly with a fine mist of water. The mist propagation unit is a system for automating this operation. A moisture-sensitive "electronic leaf" governs the frequency of the spray which is emitted through fine jets mounted above the plants, and soil-warming cables provide the necessary bottom heat to prevent the growing medium from becoming too cold. More efficient control switches which operate the mist spray according to light intensity may be installed as an alternative to the normal electronic leaf. Mist units are often used in conjunction with electric soil-warming cables, which are controlled by a separate thermostat.

GREENHOUSE CONTROL PANEL

If the greenhouse is fitted with a mains supply, it is worth adding a special control panel. This is a switch and socket panel which is fitted to the end of the mains cable. It allows all electrical apparatus to be controlled from one safe, fused point, avoiding the installation of several sockets, each of which is a possible source of trouble. Only the mains supply has to be connected. Such panels can be bought with adjustable fixings to allow them to be mounted between two glazing bars in any size of greenhouse.

Ventilation

An electric extractor fan should be mounted high up above the greenhouse door. Provide ventilation at the other end.

Mist propagation

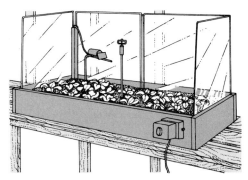

Mist units produce a humid atmosphere ideally suited to cuttings. They are often used with soil-warming cables.

Basic tools 1

Every gardener should aquire a few basic tools of good quality, rather than a large selection of cheap implements that will be uncomfortable to use, short-lived and of little practical value. Although a good spade or fork is not cheap, with care it will probably have as long a life as its owner.

Shafts and handles
The shafts of tools can be made from several different materials, including wood, metal and plastic. Wood is traditional and long lasting. Make sure that the wood of the shaft is close grained and that the grain runs down the length of the shaft. Check that it is smooth and not likely to splinter.

Shafts made from polypropylene are lightweight yet strong, and lighter tools such as hoes and rakes are often equipped with tubular aluminium alloy shafts which are coated with plastic. All these materials will offer good service if they are not ill-treated.

Spades and forks are fitted with handles in three shapes: 'T', 'D', and 'YD'. If possible try all three when choosing a tool so that the most comfortable is selected.

Spade
Spades are available with shafts of different lengths and blades of different sizes. The standard spade blade measures 11½in by 7½in(29cm by 19cm); that of the ladies' spade 10in by 6½in (25cm by 16cm), and that of the border spade 9in by 5½in (23cm by 14cm). Choose whichever is most comfortable to use; heavy digging will probably be easier with the middle size. Choose a shaft length to suit the height of the user.

The shaft of the spade should have a gentle crank to allow maximum leverage, and the strapped or tubular socket should be securely attached to the shaft. Metal treads welded to the upper edge of the blade make digging heavy soil less painful to the foot.

Spades with stainless steel blades are far more expensive than those equipped with blades of forged steel, but they are exceptionally long-lasting and penetrate the soil more easily than ordinary steel spades.
Uses An essential tool for digging and trenching, the spade is also efficient for skimming weed growth off the soil before cultivation

begins. Always hold the spade upright when cutting into the soil prior to lifting it, so that the ground is cultivated to the full depth of the blade. The spade is also useful for planting trees and shrubs, and for mixing compost.

Fork
The fork is just as useful as the spade and is similarly manufactured. The four tines may be square in cross-section, as in the general purpose or digging fork, or flat, as in the potato fork, which is designed to avoid tuber damage. The head of the digging fork measures 12in by 7½ in (30cm by 19cm), and that of the small border fork 9in by 5½ in (23cm by 14cm). Stainless and forged steel types are available.
Uses A fork is easier to use than a spade for digging heavy soil, though it cannot be used to skim off weeds. It is essential for breaking down rough-dug soil and for lightly cultivating well-worked ground before sowing and planting. The smaller border fork can be used to cultivate herbaceous plants and shrubs, and the larger fork for moving compost and manure. Both can be used to aerate lawns.

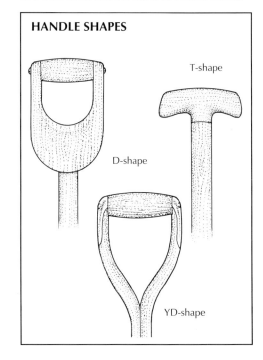

HANDLE SHAPES

T-shape

D-shape

YD-shape

Hand fork

Of the same size as a trowel, the three- or four-pronged hand fork is similarly made.

Uses For transplanting seedlings, for working among tightly packed plants such as alpines in the rock garden, and for intricate planting and weeding, the hand fork is unsurpassed.

Rake

The most popular type of garden rake has a steel head 12 in (30cm) wide which is fitted with teeth 2in (5cm) long and smooth to allow a good backwards and forwards motion. Larger wooden rakes are useful for raking up leaves, grass and debris, which clog in steel rake teeth.

Uses The main use of the rake should be to level soil which has been previously broken down to a reasonable tilth with a fork. Although the rake will make the soil texture even finer, it should not be over-used or the soil will be inclined to pan. Move the rake backwards and forwards over the soil in a sweeping motion, first in one direction and then at right angles to ensure an even distribution and level finish.

Hoe

There are many different types of hoe but the two most important are the Dutch hoe and the draw hoe. Both have 5ft (1.5m) handles and forged or stainless steel blades. The head of the Dutch hoe consists of a horseshoe-shaped piece of metal, across the open end of which is attached a flat 4-5in (10-13cm) blade designed to cut almost horizontally through the soil. The rectangular or semi-circular head of the draw hoe is of a similar width but is attached at right angles to the handle and is used with a chopping or scraping motion.

Uses The Dutch hoe is perhaps the best tool for general weeding, for the operator skims it backwards and forwards just below the surface of the soil while walking backwards. In this way the cultivated ground is not walked over and the weeds (severed from their roots) are left to dry out in the loose soil. The Dutch hoe is also used for breaking up surface pans.

With the draw hoe the operator must move forwards, chopping the soil and pulling it towards him slightly, or scraping the weeds off the surface. The draw hoe (despite

Using a spade

Keep the blade vertical when cutting into the soil. This ensures that the ground is dug to the full depth of the spade.

Using a hand fork

Aerate the soil around rock garden plants by the careful use of a hand fork. Hold plants back with one hand.

Basic tools 2

its disadvantage of forcing the operator to walk over the cultivated soil) is safer to use among closely spaced plants than a Dutch hoe.

Both types of hoe can be used to draw seed drills against a taut garden line, and the draw hoe is used to earth up vegetables such as potatoes, leeks and celery.

Trowel

An invaluable planting tool, the trowel may have a wooden or polypropylene handle 4-6in (10-15cm) long. Longer-handled versions are available but these may be less comfortable to use. If possible buy a trowel with a stainless steel rather than a forged steel blade for it will be somewhat easier to use and less likely to bend.

Uses The trowel may be used like a shovel or flour scoop and also as if it were a digging claw. Either method may be used depending on the preference of the gardener. Scoop the soil out of the hole. Insert the plant in the hole and refirm the soil around the roots with the hands. Use the trowel for planting bedding and vegetable plants, herbaceous plants and bulbs.

Wheelbarrow

In larger gardens and on the vegetable plot a wheelbarrow can save a lot of time and energy. Always check the weight distribution of a barrow before buying it – as much of the load as possible should be placed over the wheel so that the barrow, and not the operator, takes most of the weight. Barrows are available with large, inflated, ball-shaped wheels, and these are especially useful if the land to be traversed is soft. Small, two-wheeled barrows can be easier to load, unload and push than single-wheeled types. Solid tyre models are adequate where sinkage will not be a problem. Make sure that the chosen barrow is large enough without being too heavy. Two-wheeled trailers can be obtained which can be towed by cultivators or garden tractors. Before purchasing a trailer check the widths of garden paths and gates.

Uses Compost, manure, soil, sacks of fertilizer and all manner of tools and equipment can be moved around the garden with the aid of a barrow. Stand the barrow upright against a wall or under cover when it is not in use to prolong its life.

Using a rake

Level previously dug soil by moving the rake backwards and forwards across the soil surface to give an even finish.

Using a Dutch hoe

Skim the blade of the hoe just below the soil surface while walking backwards. Keep the blade horizontal to cut cleanly.

TYPES OF BARROW

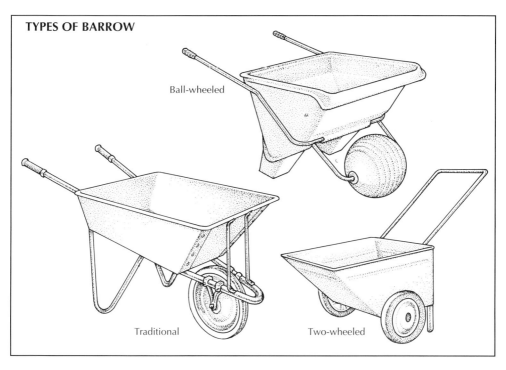

Ball-wheeled

Traditional

Two-wheeled

Using a draw hoe

Use a chopping motion, moving forward and drawing the soil towards the feet.

Use a trowel to make a planting hole

Scoop soil out of the hole, insert the plant and firm the soil with the hands.

Basic tools 3

WATERING CANS, HOSES AND ATTACHMENTS

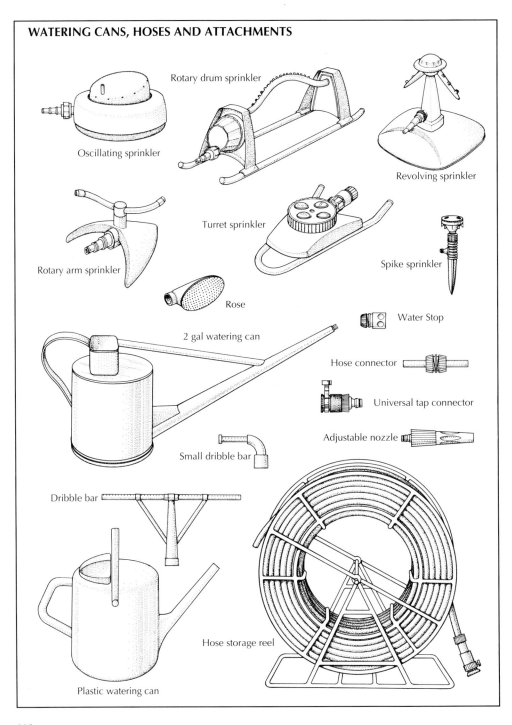

Rotary drum sprinkler

Oscillating sprinkler

Revolving sprinkler

Turret sprinkler

Rotary arm sprinkler

Spike sprinkler

Rose

Water Stop

2 gal watering can

Hose connector

Universal tap connector

Adjustable nozzle

Small dribble bar

Dribble bar

Hose storage reel

Plastic watering can

Secateurs

There are two distinct types of secateurs – those with a scissor action, and those which possess one sharp blade that cuts against or directly on to an anvil. Both types will do a good job if they are kept sharp. Check that the secateurs are strong enough for the task they are bought for, and that the hand grips are comfortable – the type with one swivelling hand grip is especially easy to use.

Uses For dead-heading roses and herbaceous plants, and for all general pruning, a good pair of secateurs is essential. Avoid trying to cut branches which are obviously too thick or the secateurs may be irreparably damaged.

Shears

Garden shears are usually manufactured with wooden, polypropylene or tubular steel handles and carbon steel blades. Check that the shears are comfortable to hold; that the blades close without jarring the wrists and that there is a notch in each blade to allow individual thick stems to be cut.

Uses Use shears for clipping all formal hedges and for cutting long grass around trees and where bulbs are naturalized. Alpines and other mat-forming plants can be quickly cleared of dead flowerheads if lightly clipped over. When cutting hedges, check that the blades of the shears are presented flat against the top and sides – the handles have a slight crank and this should be allowed for.

Garden line

A stout nylon or hemp garden line is essential to the vegetable gardener, and it is best if the twine can be wound on a special steel reel which will keep it tidy. Lines wound around stout stakes are easy to make at home but they have a tendency to become tangled and knotted. Knots should never be allowed to remain in the garden line for they will throw a drill-drawing hoe off course.

Uses For marking out formal shapes of lawns and beds the line is very useful, but it comes into its own on the vegetable plot, where it is used as a guide-line for the hoe when drills are being drawn. The line should always be taut and it should always lie flat against the ground. Stand on it when drawing drills so that it moves as little as possible.

Using shears to cut hedges

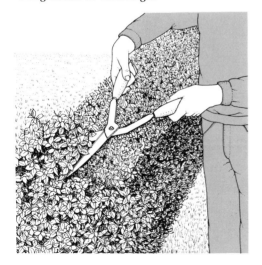

Shear handles have a slight crank to allow the blades to be kept flat against the top or sides of the hedge. Check that a flat cut is being made at all times.

Using a measuring rod

Mark a 6-8ft (1.8-2.4m) length of planed square-section timber with saw cuts at 1in (2.5cm) intervals. Make the 1ft (30cm) cuts deeper. Use to measure spacings.

Basic tools 4

Besom

Although brushes have taken over from the old-fashioned birch broom or "besom", this is still unsurpassed when it comes to certain tasks. Ensure the twigs are securely fastened to the shaft and that they are supple.

Uses The besom should always be held so that it lies almost flat against the ground; in this way it will sweep up leaves and work top-dressing material into the lawn more effectively. Make broad sweeps from side to side or in one direction only, depending on the nature of the task.

Dibber

For general greenhouse work a dibber made from ½ in (1.25cm) dowelling and cut to a length of 3-4 in (8-10cm) will be found to be convenient. It should have a sharp point at one end. In the garden an old spade or fork handle may be cut to a length of 12in (30cm), sharpened at the tip and given a new lease of life as a large-size dibber. Similar tools with a steel cap over the point are also sold in garden centres and hardware shops.

Uses The small version may be used to prick

out all seedlings into boxes and pots; the larger version for planting brassicas and other plants which do not need a lot of root room (in which case a trowel should be used). Insert the dibber; withdraw it, and then push it down alongside the newly inserted plant, firming the soil inwards around the roots.

Measuring rod

A measuring rod is most easily made at home from a piece of straight 1 in (2.5cm) square timber 6-8 ft (15-20cm) long. The timber should be treated with a preservative such as copper naphthenate, or else coated with exterior quality paint. A saw should be used to mark off every 1ft (30cm), and a smaller mark made every 3in (8cm). In the first 1ft (30cm) the 1in (2.5cm) gradations can also be shown.

Uses A measuring rod is invaluable on the vegetable garden for measuring the distance between plants when thinning or planting; and in the fruit garden when setting out.

Watering can

There are many kinds of watering can available, but for general purposes a 2 gallon

Using a line

Fix the line taut along the line of a drill to be taken out in the vegetable garden. Then draw a hoe along it to form a sowing drill.

Using a besom broom

Hold the besom almost level with the ground and make broad sweeps to remove leaves or to work top-dressing material into the lawn.

(9 litre) long-handled type will be found the most convenient to use. It may be constructed of painted or galvanized metal, or of polythene – both types have their advantages and disadvantages. The metal type may leak in time but it is repairable; the plastic type will last a long while if looked after, but once it leaks it must be discarded. Balance is important – test the can when full – and reach must be adequate. A coarse and a fine rose (the name given to sprinkler heads) should be obtained with the can.

Uses Use for watering plants both outdoors and under glass (though here a 1 gallon (4.5 litre) can will be found easier to work with in the confined space). If the can is used to apply weedkiller then it should be kept especially for that purpose to prevent other plants from being damaged by herbicide residues. See also Irrigation (pages 34-36).

Hose pipe
A very wide range of hose pipes is available, but the best type to buy is undoubtedly that with nylon reinforcement running through it. This material will not only give the hose a longer life but it will also prevent it from "kinking" when in use. Various attachments are available and the two most useful of these are the tap connector and the spray nozzle.

Uses For all garden and greenhouse watering a hose pipe will be found to be labour saving. Store it on a reel to make it easily accessible and to prolong its life. Keep it out of the sun.

Sieve
A sieve with a medium mesh is a useful garden tool, especially in the greenhouse and when propagation is carried out. A ½ in (1.25cm) mesh is best for general purposes.

Uses Sieve soil or sand for mixing compost, and ready-mixed compost when sowing.

Sprayer
A trigger-action hand sprayer or mister of 1-2 pints (0.5-1litre) capacity is useful even if larger-scale equipment is also needed.

Uses Use a sprayer to apply liquid pesticides, fungicides and weedkillers (reserving one for weedkillers only). Use also to give foliar feeds and for misting a greenhouse. Wash out thoroughly after use to avoid contamination.

Using a small dibber

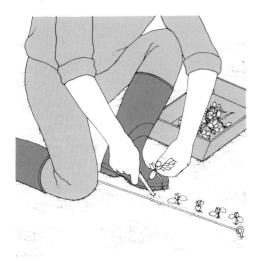

Use a ½ in (1.25cm) dowelling dibber to make planting holes when planting out seedlings.

Using a large dibber

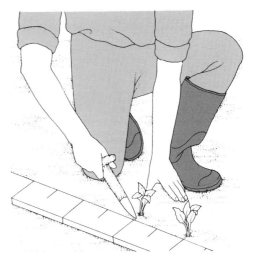

Insert the dibber, withdraw it, insert the plant, then push the dibber into the soil beside the plant to firm the soil around the roots.

Specialist tools 1

Wire-toothed rake (n) Fan-shaped with long, springy teeth of either heavy-gauge wire or split bamboo – the wire type being more durable. The handle should be smooth and the head securely attached.

Half-moon iron (f) With a semi-circular blade of forged or stainless steel, and a wooden or polypropylene shaft, usually with a 'T' handle.

Turfing iron Similar to a spade but with a heart-shaped blade.

Knives At least one sharp knife is essential. It should have a comfortable grip, and a tempered steel blade since stainless steel blades quickly become blunt. The budding knife (b) is strong, yet relatively lightweight, and has a slight protrusion at the end of the handle or on top of the blade for prising open the bark once the cut has been made. The grafting knife (c) is heavier than the budding knife and has a straight, slightly wider blade. The pruning knife (d) has a fat handle that can be gripped securely, and a curved blade.

Edging shears (m) Shears with long handles. They are preferable to ordinary shears for cutting along the edge of a lawn since they can be used standing upright.

Loppers (g) Pruners with long handles and a sharp blade, they are essential for pruning all stems between ½in (1.25cm) and 1in (2.5cm) in diameter.

Pruning saw (l) Used on large branches where loppers or secateurs are inadequate. It usually has a narrow, curved blade that is easily worked between the branches of trees and shrubs. The English pruning saw (k) has a double-sided blade with fine teeth on one side and coarse on the other.

Scythe (e) A tool with a curved blade, and a shaft with two handles. The blade may be long – a mowing scythe, or short – a bramble scythe. It should be kept razor sharp.

Sickle (a) Also called the grass hook, it is smaller than a scythe and has only one handle.

Special hoes Most useful are the onion and the Canterbury. The onion hoe (i) is a smaller version of the draw hoe. It has a draw hoe blade attached by a swan neck to a very short handle which is held in one hand. The Canterbury hoe (h) has a 4 ft (1.2m) shaft with a fork-like head. The hand cultivator (j) has 3-5 tines.

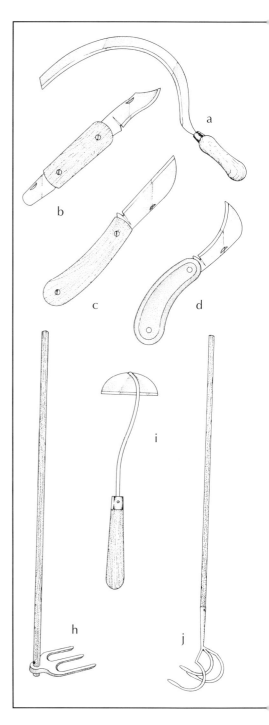

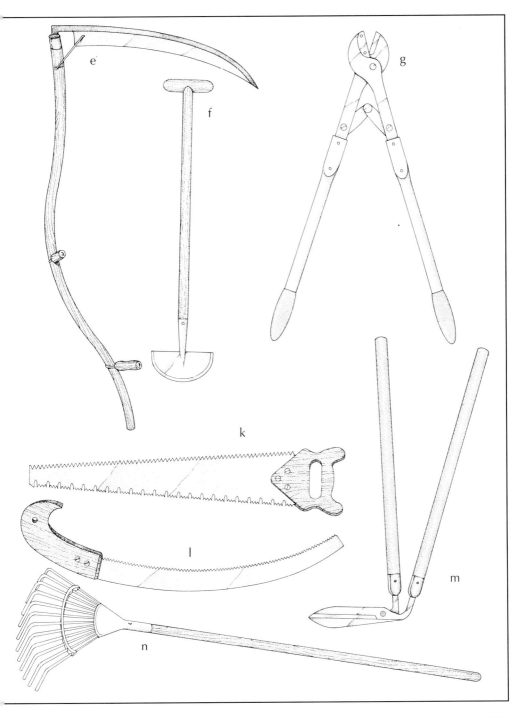

Specialist tools 2

Wire-toothed rake

Pull the rake across the lawn to comb it free of dead grass and leaves. Use some force so that debris is torn away, leaving the living grass with more space to grow. The operation is called scarification.

Half-moon iron

Use a half-moon iron for cutting the edges of newly laid turf lawns and for re-cutting the edges of existing lawns. Hold it vertically against the side of a flat board on which the operator stands, or against a garden line. Mark curves with a hose pipe.

Loppers

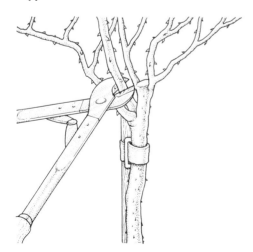

Use loppers on branches up to 1in (2.5cm) in diameter. Cut cleanly and square to the branch, without leaving a snag. They simplify the pruning of thorny plants.

Pruning saw

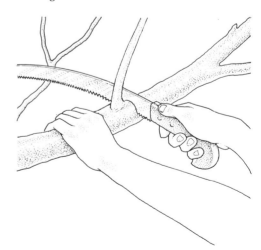

The teeth of a pruning saw are angled to cut on the pulling rather than the pushing motion. Take care not to damage other branches with the saw's teeth.

Budding knife

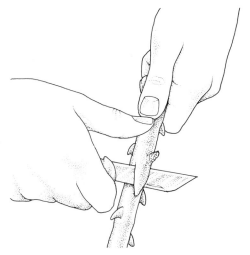

Budding Use a budding knife to remove a bud from the stock to be propagated. This bud is grafted on to a rootstock. Make a shallow cut behind the bud with the knife pointing upward. Lift off the bud.

Edging shears

Hold the handle attached to the bottom blade steady at all times, and move the handle of the top blade in and out to make the cutting motion. This method produces an even cut faster and more easily than if both handles are moved.

Scythe

Adjust the two handles so that the scythe can be used without bending. Make long sweeping motions with the blade parallel to, and as close to, the ground as possible.

Onion hoe

This tool is used one-handed. When thinning, chop out unwanted plants between those to be retained. It can also be used for weeding.

Power tools and machines 1

Lawn mowers

There is a large range of lawn mowers available which falls into two basic categories: the cylinder and the rotary mower.

Cylinder mowers

The cylinder mower cuts by means of a scissor action. Blades attached to a cylinder revolve horizontally against a fixed blade; the grass is cut when trapped between the two. The number of blades in the cylinder varies. The more blades, the more cuts per yard (metre) of travel. The number of cuts per yard (metre) is also governed by the speed at which the cylinder revolves. High cutting rates are for high-quality lawns only. Cylinder mowers provide a fine, even cut on good turf but are of no use on rough ground.

Cylinder mowers can be of the simple hand-propelled variety or powered. Not all power mowers, however, are self-propelled. The simplest cylinder mower is the hand-propelled, side-wheeled version with a small roller at the rear. The cylinder has five or six blades and will make around 25-30 cuts per yard (metre), suitable for coarse lawns. The width of cut will be between 10 and 14 in (25 and 35cm). The disadvantages of the side-wheeled mower are that it will not cut along the edge of the lawn, and the lack of a large rear roller means that no "stripes", which some find decorative, will be produced.

Hand-propelled mowers with large rear rollers are available in widths ranging from 12-16 ins (30-40cm), and are equipped with grass boxes to catch the clippings. These machines are best for average, small lawns.

Power mowers Where larger areas of grass are to be cut, a powered mowing machine is desirable. Models powered by petrol engines, batteries and mains are available. Petrol mowers can be noisy and difficult to start and require regular maintenance. However, they can be used for long periods of time and in isolated corners far from an electricity supply. Mains powered mowers are relatively quiet, and easier to start and run but a convenient power source must be available. It is important to make sure that the cable is not left in the path of the machine. Battery powered mowers combine the advantages of both petrol and electric models, but they must be recharged from the mains electricity supply at regular intervals.

Cylinder mower

Rotary mower

Hover mower

Cylinder mowers cut by means of a multi-bladed cylinder which revolves against a fixed blade.

Rotary mowers power one or two horizontal blades which spin around a drive shaft beneath a cowl.

The hover mower's motor creates an air cushion beneath the cowl, supporting the machine.

Where an exceptionally fine cut is required, a mower with a ten or twelve-bladed cylinder that will make between 100 and 140 cuts per yard (metre) should be used. For the average close-cropped lawn 60 to 80 cuts per yard (metre) will be satisfactory.

The grassbox Considerable controversy surrounds the use of the grassbox. Some gardeners believe that it should be left off in dry spells so that mowings return to the lawn and act as an organic mulch, increase drought resistance, deter moss, and, as they decompose, return nutrients to the soil to give a greener, lusher turf. The disadvantages can, however, outweigh the advantages. In wetter weather mowings often lie on the surface for a considerable period and are increasingly unsightly as they slowly decompose. In drier weather seeds of weeds and annual meadow grass are scattered to extend infested areas. Worm activity is encouraged and in milder, moister autumns the softer lusher turf is more susceptible to disease attack with lack of aeration. The lawn must then be scarified in spring and autumn. It is better to use the grassbox in normal circumstances but to cut the grass less closely so that the living blades

themselves shade the soil from sun and so retain moisture. In very dry or drought conditions the grass may be left uncut or cut less close. Grass clippings can be placed on the compost heap but not used fresh as a mulch if weedkillers have been applied recently.

Rotary mowers
For cutting rough grass in orchards and on verges and banks, the rotary mower is the best choice. They cut by impact, a bar with sharpened edges or a rotary disc with up to four small fixed or swinging blades revolves at high speed under a protective canopy. The blades slash at the grass in a way very different from the scissor action of the cylinder mower. Some models are equipped with grassboxes or bags, others are not. Some rotary mowers have powered wheels, while others have to be pushed.

Rotary mowers are petrol or electric, with mains electric models suitable for small areas. It should be remembered that rotary mowers are not intended for use on fine lawns, and , if there is no grassbox, a build-up of dead grass will occur unless clippings are raked up regularly. Rotary mowers will not

Hedge trimmer

Use a powered trimmer in a series of short sweeps, gauging the height of the cut by means of a fixed line.

Power saw

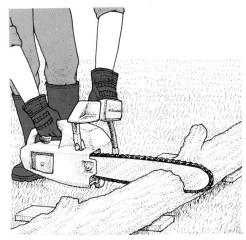

Trees and branches can be cut with a power chain saw. Keep the cable of electric saws away from the blade. Check the chain tension before use.

127

Power tools and machines 2

help to keep lawns level as they do not have rollers. No mower or roller for that matter will keep a lawn level. It may assist in a minor way but to eliminate undulations a very heavy roller would be needed, involving the risk of compaction.

Hover mower The hover mower works on the rotary principle, but instead of being supported by wheels it hovers on a cushion of air produced by the engine. The height of cut is achieved either by raising or lowering the blade or spindle. The hover mower is especially useful for cutting the grass on banks, where it can be swung from side to side in large sweeps on a length of rope if necessary. It cuts by the rotary method.

Hedge trimmer

Shears will produce the best finish on a hedge, but where long, tall hedges are to be cut, an electric trimmer will make light work of an arduous task. The machine must be double insulated to prevent the operator from receiving an electric shock should the cable be inadvertently cut. The machine should have two operating switches, requiring it to be held by both hands, and the 18-24in (45-

60cm) blades (single or, preferably double-sided) should have blade extensions beyond the moving part.

Wear eye-protectors when trimming a hedge and have the flex over one shoulder so that it is kept away from the blade. It is useful to mark the proposed height and width of the hedge with a guideline and to cut to this. Make short sweeps backwards and forwards to obtain an even finish. Oil the blades after each clipping session to keep them moving smoothly.

Chain saw

The chain saw is a very useful tool for heavy pruning and tree felling. It is, however, a very dangerous tool in the hands of someone who is inexperienced and unsupervised. The operations where it is most useful should almost always be carried out by a professional tree surgeon. Another person should always be present when the saw is in use. Electrically powered chain saws are lighter and consequently easier to use than their petrol-driven counterparts. They are also quieter and maintenance is simpler. They must be double insulated to protect the oper-

POWER CULTIVATORS

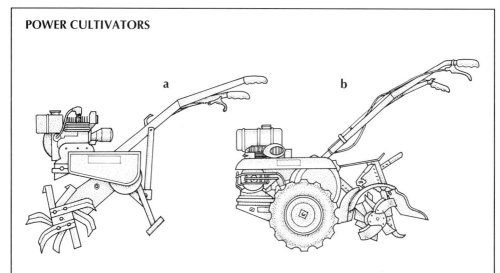

The two main types of power cultivator are the front-bladed non-wheeled type (a), with a rear skid; and the rear-bladed wheeled type (b). The first type is pulled along by the action of the blades, while the second type has powered wheels.

ator and the cable must always be kept away from the blade. All chain saws should have two-handed switches, a short chain-stopping time and a chain brake that operates if the saw jerks upwards (kicks back). A low profile blade reduces the risk of kick-back.

Power cultivators

Although there are many different kinds of powered cultivator on the market, they all operate on the same principle – that of turning the soil over by steel blades rotating on a central spindle. There are two main types: those with blades which are at the front of the machine and which are unprotected by any cowl; and those with blades which are positioned at the rear under a stout metal hood. The blades of the first type rotate quite slowly, pulling the machine along against the restraint imposed by a rear skid which is pulled through the soil. The second type has driving wheels and rear-mounted blades which create a fine tilth.

The two types work in different ways and serve different purposes. The front-tine type digs deeper and produces a rougher tilth. The wheeled, rear-tine type is capable of producing a finer, though shallower, tilth. Wheeled machines are capable of working closer to crops and can undertake tasks such as destroying weed seedlings and digging in green manure. However, where there is heavy perennial weed growth the cultivator should not be used since it will only disperse sections of stem, leading to regrowth.

Cultivators have to do a lot of hard work, so look for one that is sturdily built and of a size that is manageable and suited to the plot being worked. Some models have handles that can be swung to the side so that the operator need not walk on the land that is being turned over, and all are equipped with petrol engines. Regular maintenance is essential plus oiling and cleaning immediately after use. The depth of cultivation should be varied from season to season to prevent the formation of a pan. Most machines are equipped with depth adjusters. Mechanically cultivated soil is very loose and should always be firmed with the feet and raked level before sowing or planting.

Roller

For garden use a 2cwt (100kg) roller made of steel, concrete or tough plastic filled with water will be adequate for most jobs. New lawns may be rolled just before being given their first cut when the soil is moist but not wet, and established lawns may be firmed if lifted by frost by a spring rolling.

Fertilizer spreader

Over large areas the even distribution of fertilizer may present something of a problem. A simple spreader which will apply a measured dose to the soil will not only save time and money, but will also ensure that plants are not over- or under-fed. Most fertilizer spreaders consist of a metal or plastic trough-shaped hopper, in the bottom of which is a grooved or pitted roller driven by wheels at either end. The hopper is filled with granular or powered fertilizer and then the machine is wheeled over the lawn or soil in straight lines. To ensure even application do not overlap areas already covered by fertilizer. Most spreaders are adjustable so that the dose can be altered, and some have a cut-out handle so that the flow of fertilizer can be stopped while corners are being turned. At all times follow the manufacturer's instructions on fertilizer application rates and machine adjustment. Clean the machine immediately after use to prevent corrosion.

Leaf sweeper

A birch broom or besom (see page 120) will prove quite adequate for collecting fallen leaves in small gardens. Where there are large amounts of fallen leaves a large wooden rake is also useful. But where there are many trees and large areas of lawn a leaf sweeper may be useful. The simplest type consists of a cylindrical brush held between two drive wheels in front of a large bag. When the machine is pushed the brush rotates and throws the leaves backwards into the bag (which must be emptied regularly). Wet leaves are particularly difficult to remove with this machine. Powered models which work on the vacuum cleaner principle are more costly. Hiring is probably the best solution as the machine has a relatively short season of usefulness.

Caring for tools

Every gardening tool and machine should be thoroughly cleaned after use so that it remains in good working order and easy to use. Neglect can shorten the life of tools.

Hand tools

Immediately after use, brush or scrape hand tools free of earth. An old screwdriver or spoon (adaption illustrated page 131) can be very useful for removing earth. Next, rub over the blades of tools with an oily rag to prevent rust forming. Carry out this cleaning process each time a tool is used.

Mowers and other machines

Lawn mowers should always be cleared of grass clippings after use. Clean with a stiff handbrush, and remove any long stems from around the cylinder or rotor spindle. Wash the machine down with a hose if necessary to remove dirt. The undersides of rotary machines may become rusty if left dirty. Wash them clean, rub down any rust present with emery paper, and rub the metal surfaces with an oily rag.

It is not essential to oil and grease mowers every time they are used, but regular lubrication is important. Carefully follow maintenance instructions given in the manufacturer's handbook. Cultivators should be oiled and greased after use on every occasion. Change the engine oil in four-stroke engines after every 25 hours of use. Keep the carburettor air filter clean. Cultivator rotor blades must be kept clean and lightly oiled. Hedge trimmers and chain saws should be treated similarly. Check the tension of the chain every time a chain saw is used. Make sure that wheels and bearings on mowers, barrows, spreaders and cultivators are kept lubricated.

Servicing Have lawn mowers, cultivators and other machines serviced annually by a recognized dealer. Correct sharpening and adjustment once a year costs relatively little, but will help to ensure many years of life. Routine oil and spark plug changes can be carried out at home, as can a certain amount of stripping down and cleaning, but it is a mistake to attempt such tasks as regrinding a cylinder mower blade, for this is an operation needing specialized equipment. During the winter in-spect machines for rust on painted surfaces. If rust is present, rub down painted areas thoroughly with emery paper, prime any bare metal, then apply a paint recommended for metal surfaces.

Sharpening

Few gardeners think of sharpening hoes and spades, but both tools cut better if their edges are kept keen. Clamp the tool in a vice and use a file to hone up the leading edge of the blade. Sharpen the upper edge only.

The gardener's knife should always have a really keen edge. An oilstone is necessary to produce the best results. The side of the knife which does not have the thumbnail indentation should be sharpened in a circular motion flat against the stone, which should first have been moistened with a few drops of oil. The side which carries the indentation is then laid on the stone with its sharp edge pointing away from the operator. The top (un-sharpened) edge of the blade is tilted upwards to an angle of 25 degrees and the blade pushed forwards against the stone, lightly drawn back and then pushed again repeatedly until a sharp edge is produced.

Some manufacturers of secateurs recommend that the tool is returned to them for sharpening; others make no provision for such maintenance. The gardener will find that secateurs stay reasonably sharp at all times if they are rubbed over with emery paper to free them of congealed sap.

Storage

Store all tools and machines in a dry shed, garage or outhouse. Provide a rack or a series of hooks for tools to keep them tidy. At the end of their season of use thoroughly clean, oil and grease mowers and other machines. Dust sheets will help to keep machines clean, but polythene sheeting covers may cause condensation which can lead to rust.

Keep the metal parts of all tools in store lightly coated with oil or grease. The tanks of all petrol-driven power tools should be emptied before storage. Keep petrol-driven machines in a cool place to prevent fuel evaporating. Always keep a fire extinguisher in the shed or other store used. Mount it by the door so that it is easily accessible.

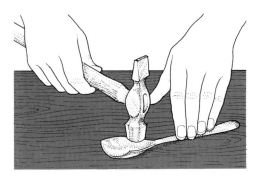

Adapt an old spoon to form a scraper by cutting in half and hammering the stub flat. Use to scrape earth from hand tools.

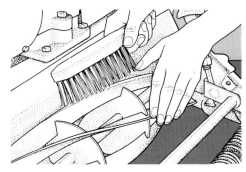

Clear grass cuttings from mower blades after use using a stiff hand brush. Remove long stems from the spindles.

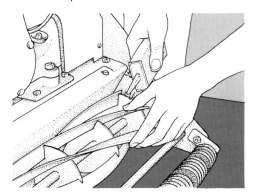

Oil mowers and other machines regularly. Apply light lubricating oil to the wheel bearings and other moving parts.

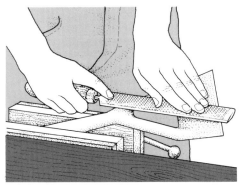

Keep hoes and spades sharp by honing the upper edge of the blade with a file.

Sharpening knives

1 Sharpen knives on moistened oilstone. Sharpen the edge without a thumbnail indentation first, using a circular action.

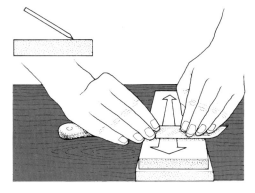

2 Sharpen the other edge with a back and forward motion. Keep the blade at 25° to the stone. Moisten the stone with oil.

Safety

The gardener should always dress sensibly when using power tools or implements with sharp edges. Stout shoes or boots are essential, as are old clothes when dirty jobs are being carried out. Long hair should be tied back or pushed under a hat when hedge trimmers or chain saws are being used. Carry out preparatory work, such as clearing stones from lawns, before using power tools. Never attempt to adjust any machine while the engine is running, and, if possible, have another person standing by when power tools are in use.

Fuel storage

Always store mower and rotavator fuel in sturdy, purpose-built cans which are labelled to show their contents (petrol, 2-stroke or diesel oil). To prevent a build-up of condensation, which can cause stalling, keep the cans as full as possible (though allow for a little expansion of fuel in warm weather) and in a cool, dry place. Children and pets should not have access to places where fuel is stored, and naked lights should be forbidden at all times. Cans showing any signs of corrosion should be discarded. Diesel oil should not be stored in galvanized cans for the fuel will attack this protective coating.

Never re-fuel a machine with the engine switched on, and never smoke while handling fuel. A generous-sized funnel should be used to minimize spillage.

Electrically powered tools

There is an ever-present danger with electrical gardening tools that the cable will come into contact with the blade. All tools which carry this risk should be properly insulated to prevent the operator from receiving a shock. Socket outlets should be protected by an RCCB (see page 109). An essential precaution is to keep cables clear of mowers, hedge trimmers and chain saw blades. When using hedge trimmers and chain saws lead the cable over the shoulder, so that it runs away from the machine. When using a lawn mower it may not be possible to drape the cable over the shoulder but it should always lie behind the machine. Bright orange cable can easily be seen when laid across lawns and against hedges.

When not in use electrical cables should be stored in coils or around drums or reels. If they are piled in a heap there is a danger that they will become tangled and kinked and the internal wires may eventually rupture. Replace any cables showing signs of wear. Never use cables which are longer than recommended by the manufacturer for the equipment being used.

Wiring a plug

It is extremely important that electrical plugs are correctly wired, and every gardener should be able to attach a 3-pin plug to the cable of an electrical appliance.

Use a screwdriver to remove the back of the plug and then slacken off the two screws which hold the cable anchoring plate in position. Slacken off or remove the screws which hold the three wires in position against the pins of the plug. Check that the fuse is of the correct size for the implement being wired (see the manufacturer's instructions).

The cable may possess two or three wires (or cores) – again consult the manufacturer's instructions to see which is necessary if no extension cable is fitted. If the cable possesses two wires, one of them will be coated in brown plastic and the other in blue. If three are present they will be coated in brown, blue, and yellow with a green tracer.

The brown-covered wire is the live; the blue is the neutral wire and the yellow and green the earth. Double-insulated implements such as hedge trimmers will not be fitted with an earth wire.

Looking into the plug the wires are connected in the following manner: brown – on the right, blue – on the left, green and yellow – at the top. Replace the back of the plug and the equipment is ready to use.

Chemicals

It is important to read carefully and follow closely instructions on pesticide and other garden chemical containers. Keep chemicals in a cool, dry, safe place out of the reach of children. Do not transfer chemicals into other containers, especially those formerly used for food or drink. Wear rubber gloves and old clothing when handling chemicals, especially when mixing or spraying.

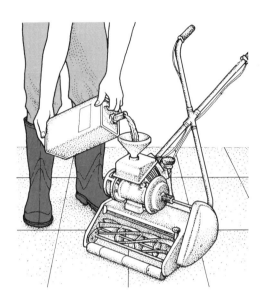

Use a large metal funnel to transfer fuel or to fill a tank. Do not re-fuel machines when the engine is running.

When using electric tools, drape the cable over one shoulder to prevent it being cut by the machine.

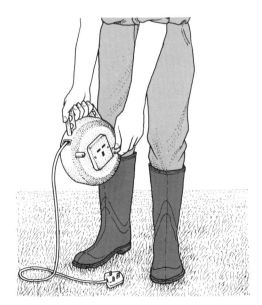

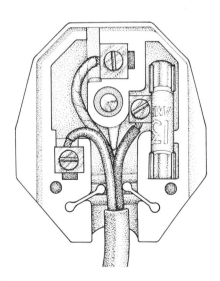

Store cables on drums or reels to prevent kinking and tangling.

Wire a plug with the brown (live) wire on the right, the blue (neutral) on the left, and the green and yellow (earth) in the centre.

Garden buildings 1

Greenhouses, sheds and summerhouses can play an important part in the garden, but for best results they should be thoughtfully sited and carefully maintained.

Site
All buildings should be easily accessible from the dwelling house, particularly in the case of sheds and greenhouses which have to be visited in wet weather. If electricity and water services are to be incorporated then the nearer the buildings are to the mains supply the cheaper and more convenient will be installation.

Do not erect buildings on exposed sites, which may result in the building being damaged by wind, and in the case of greenhouses avoid frost pockets and excessively shady spots. Bear in mind that shade angles alter considerably over the course of the year. All buildings should be sited clear of overhanging trees. Not only will the leaves cut out some light (many greenhouse plants need high light levels), but if the trees are deciduous the leaves will be shed on the building in autumn, fouling the glass and the gutters. Honeydew may be secreted by aphids colonizing the leaves of trees, and if a heavy branch is shed or blown down, then the building may be severely damaged.

Make sure that the ground is well drained, and that there is adequate provision for access when the ground is wet. Check with the local authority to see if planning permission is required for the structure to be erected.

Choice
There are so many different greenhouses, sheds and summerhouses that the gardener can soon become bewildered when it comes to choosing the right one for his particular purpose. Firstly, buy from a reputable manufacturer who has had plenty of experience in making garden buildings. Always inspect the erected model before deciding to buy, and, if possible, consult a friend or neighbour who possesses a similar building to discover how well it works in practice. Some manufacturers will supply addresses of previous customers who will be able to comment on the virtues and drawbacks of the design.

Materials
Sheds and summerhouses may be constructed from ordinary deal (often Baltic pine) or from western red cedar. The latter is more durable and consequently more expensive. It is essential that both types of wood are treated with preservative to prolong their life. Western red cedar looks attractive unpainted and is the more durable wood. Many manufacturers supply buildings which have been pre-treated; others supply the preservative which must be applied by the purchaser.

Greenhouses are available in western red cedar, deal and aluminium alloy. The latter needs no maintenance, though on sites which are exposed to sea winds and spray a timber house might be a wiser choice, for salt is known to corrode some aluminium alloys. In any situation the alloy will tend to develop a white powdery deposit, but this is quite normal and should not lead to problems. Some manufacturers supply alloy houses which are coated with white or green acrylic paint for protection and to improve their appearance. Untreated aluminium may look out of place in some gardens.

Prefabricated foundations

Bed the corners of ready-made foundations in concrete placed directly on the soil. Fix the building to the foundations, following the maker's instructions.

Choose a greenhouse that pleases the eye, is strong and well made, large enough for the needs of the garden and well equipped to allow good ventilation and light transmission. For further details see *Growing under Glass* in this series.

Foundations

Solid foundations are essential for all permanent garden buildings, both to hold them firm and level and to reduce the risk of rot and corrosion, which stem from contact with the soil. Some manufacturers offer ready-made steel or precast concrete bases for their buildings. These are simply laid in place on firm ground, bolted together and checked with a set square and a spirit level before the building is erected on top of them. It is wise to bed the corners of these foundations in concrete to ensure stability in high winds.

Marking out Home-made foundations will have to be constructed for all buildings which are not supplied with custom-built bases. Mark out the area to be occupied by the building by pushing four bamboo canes into the soil. Use a large wooden set square to check that the corners are right angles. Excavate a trench between the canes which is the depth and width of the spade blade. Half-fill the trench with rammed rubble.

Position one brick at each end of all four trenches and check with a spirit level and a straight edge that all eight bricks are at the same height. The bricks mark the level of the finished concrete. Mix together 6 parts all-in ballast and 1 part cement, adding water to make a firm but moist concrete mixture. Pour the concrete into the trench on top of the rubble and tamp it using a wooden straight edge until it is level with the tops of the bricks.

When the concrete is dry, cement a row of bricks into place, using a mixture of 4 parts sand to 1 part cement, in the exact position of the base of the building. Check the bricks as they are laid to make sure they are square and level. Coach bolts or metal brackets may be bedded into the cement at this stage to allow the framework of the building to be attached. Allow the concrete several days to dry, covering it in cold or wet weather with damp sacking or polythene sheets. Lay

Constructing foundations

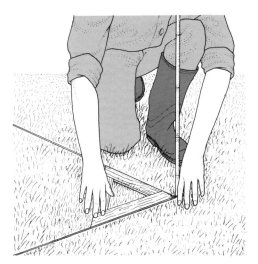

1 Mark out the area of the building and place canes at the corners. Measure the angles between the lines so drawn and ensure they are 90°.

2 Excavate a trench for the foundation one spit deep and a spade's width wide between the canes.

Garden buildings 2

roofing felt over the bricks to act as a damp-proof course before the building is erected.

Maintenance

All timber buildings should be coated with preservative once every two or three years. A proprietary treatment containing copper naphthenate is suitable for both cedar and deal, though the latter can also be coated with exterior quality paint if first treated with a primer undercoat. Apart from retaining the smart appearance of the building, painting or preserving will also lengthen its life.

Greenhouses should be thoroughly cleaned once a year in winter or early spring. The contents – plants, pots and movable fixtures and equipment – should be removed. Fixed stagings and the main structure should be washed or scrubbed down with a dilute solution of a proprietary horticultural disinfectant, and all debris and unwanted plant material removed. Thoroughly clean pots and containers and equipment before restocking the greenhouse.

Hinges and catches on windows and doors should be oiled regularly throughout the year to keep them operating smoothly. All glass, particularly in greenhouses, should be kept clean to allow maximum light penetration. Carefully clean overlaps between panes.

Re-glazing Should a pane of glass be broken, then it should immediately be replaced. In aluminium alloy greenhouses (and in some wooden models) this may simply be a matter of removing the broken pieces and slotting in a new one which is held in place either by clips or grooves.

On buildings where the glass is held in place by putty, proceed as follows: Extract the old glazing sprigs with a pair of pliers and then remove all the broken glass. Strip out the old putty using a hammer and an old wood chisel, or a special glazing knife. Lay a bed of new putty along the rebate of the glazing bar, and push the new pane of glass into place, slotting it underneath the pane above if necessary. Press the edges of the glass firmly into contact with the putty and then secure the pane with glazing sprigs. Strip off the excess putty (inside and out) with a damp knife and immediately wipe the glass clean with a damp cloth.

3 Half-fill the trench with rubble or hardcore. Ram it firm. Use hardcore of even size and free of plaster rubble.

4 Position a brick at the ends of each trench and, using a spirit level and a straight edge, check that the eight bricks are at the same level.

RE-GLAZING

Immediately replace any panes of glass that are accidentally broken. Remove the old glazing sprigs with pliers and take out all the broken glass. Remove the old putty. Lay a bed of new putty and push the new pane of glass into place. Secure the pane with new glazing sprigs, which are knocked into place using a light hammer. Clean off excess putty with a damp knife and clean the glass with a damp cloth.

5 Mix concrete from 6 parts ballast and 1 part cement. Pour into the trench up to the top of the bricks. Tamp it level.

6 When the concrete is dry, cement a row of bricks into place using 4:1 mortar. Check that they are square and level. Lay a felt damp course over them.

Container gardening 1

City gardeners and flat dwellers are particularly reliant on containers to bring colour and plant interest to windowsills, steps, paths, balconies and patios, but even large gardens benefit from the addition of containers. Containers on terraces and beside paths add variety of scale to the garden design, and allow small plants to be singled out for attention and enjoyed in detail. However, container-grown plants require more care than those grown in open ground.

Windowboxes

Wooden or strong plastic troughs are especially suitable for use as windowboxes. They should be at least 6in (15cm) wide and 8in (20cm) deep, and as long as the window ledge. Choose plain colours which will be unobtrusive – the plants should provide the interest and brightness. Holes in the base are essential to allow free drainage, and the trough should be fitted with two or more feet to hold it 1-2in (2.5-5cm) above the windowsill so that excess water may escape.

Wooden boxes are easy to make. Ordinary planed deal may be cut to the required dimensions and fastened together with brass screws, which should be lightly greased to allow the box to be dismantled if necessary. To make the box last paint it with primer and exterior quality paint or coat it with polyurethane varnish or timber preservative containing copper naphthenate. Do not use creosote which is poisonous to plants as long as it is giving off fumes. Allow all preservatives to dry off before planting up.

Proprietary plastic troughs may not have enough drainage holes. Use a drill to make more before planting. Windowboxes and troughs on balconies can be a hazard because of dripping water, damp, or even falling boxes. Standing the box on a galvanized or plastic tray will prevent drips. The danger of falling boxes, however, is far more serious. The windowbox or trough on a balcony must be absolutely secure, especially if placed where it could fall on anyone.

Plant up as described on the next page, or alternatively place plants in pots in the box and surround the pots with gravel. The plants can be changed when they fade for new ones prepared beforehand.

Making and planting a windowbox

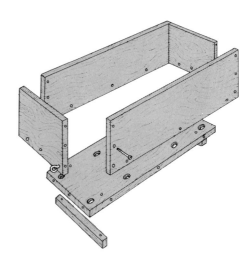

1 Construct the box from wood, using brass screws. Paint or treat with preservative. Fit low feet to hold it clear of the sill.

4 Fill to within 2 in (5cm) of the rim with moist John Innes No. 2 potting compost or a soilless equivalent.

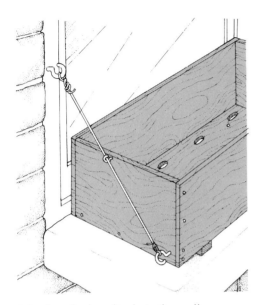

2 Anchor the box firmly to the wall or windowframe, using screw eyes and wire or chain, to prevent accidents.

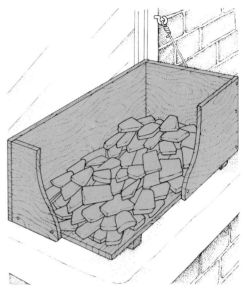

3 Place a layer of drainage material such as crocks or coarse gravel in the bottom of the box, which should have adequate drainage.

5 Water the plants, knock them from their pots and plant in the box, carefully firming the compost around the rootball.

6 Alternatively, place plants in pots in the box and surround with peat or gravel.

Container gardening 2

Pots

As a general rule, clay or plastic flower pots less than 8in (20cm) in diameter should not be used for plants that are to be grown on hot and sunny patios and paths. Such pots will hold relatively little compost, and the plants will thus require frequent feeding. The compost will also dry out exceptionally quickly, not only checking the growth of the plants but also making more work for the gardener. Small pots are subject to excess cold as well as excess heat. The soil in containers may freeze, killing normally hardy plants.

As with troughs, large plant pots should have adequate drainage facilities, and they should be stable when placed on a flat surface. Most plastic pots are held a fraction of an inch above the ground by a protruding rim; clay pots may have to be raised on two bricks if there is a risk of the drainage hole becoming blocked. Both types of pot are durable provided that they are carefully treated. The white or green deposits on clay pots can usually be removed with a scrubbing brush and water.

Wall-mounted pots are useful for bringing flowers and foliage close to the house and alongside windows. They can be supported by masonry nails or wired to vine eyes. Planting and maintenance are the same as for free-standing pots.

Tubs and planters

There are many different kinds of tubs, boxes and planters available. Those selected should be stable, capable of holding plenty of compost, and equipped with good drainage facilities. Oak barrels sawn in half are frequently offered as tubs. They are attractive and functional but need to be strong. The process of cutting can weaken the barrels so that they fall apart. Check that the hoops are firmly attached and that the wooden sections are securely held in place. Drainage holes should have been drilled in the base, and at least the inside of the tub coated with mastic or timber preservative. Tubs, like large plant pots, may have to be supported on bricks so that drainage is not impeded and damp patches are not created below them, especially on rooftops.

Large precast concrete or plastic containers can sometimes be fitted with removable liners which make the changing of bedding schemes a simple operation. The set of liners containing the faded plants is removed and a set planted up with the new bedding is immediately slotted into place. Thus the scheme need never look faded or underdeveloped, especially if the new plants are established in the liners some weeks before the changeover.

Siting and filling containers

Unless the containers are to grow shade-loving plants they should be positioned in good light. Give them a sheltered spot whatever they contain so that growth can proceed without the likelihood of wind damage.

All large troughs and tubs are best filled with compost *after* they have been positioned. It is foolish and dangerous to attempt to lift a 4 ft (1.2m) long windowbox full of moist compost and plants on to a high windowsill.

When the container is in position place a layer of drainage material such as broken clay plant pots (crocks) or coarse gravel in the bottom. Then fill to within 2 in (5cm) of the rim with moist John Innes potting compost No. 2, or a soilless equivalent, and lightly firm the mixture into place. Bear in mind that the soilless type will be exhausted of nutrients more quickly than the John Innes. It does, however have the advantage of being lighter – an important consideration on balcony and rooftop gardens. Always use the John Innes mixture for perennials.

Planting

Make sure that the compost around the plants is moist before they are transferred to their new container. When planting up windowboxes, troughs, tubs and other large containers the compost can be scooped out by hand, the plant tapped from its pot and inserted and the compost refirmed around the rootball.

Containers of all descriptions may be planted up with permanent plantings of shrubs, dwarf conifers or herbaceous plants, or with spring and summer bedding schemes which are lifted and replaced as they fade. When planting bulbs and spring bedding plants, the bulbs should be planted last so that they are not subsequently disturbed.

TYPES OF PLANT CONTAINER

141

Hanging baskets

Suspended containers filled with plants are of great value in linking the garden and the house. They will quickly brighten up dull walls and can be planted with a range of hardy and tender plants to provide flower and foliage colour right through the summer. The only way in which their care differs from that of pots, tubs and troughs is that they are inclined to dry out more quickly. In warm weather, water twice a day.

Types of basket
The commonest type of hanging basket is made from heavy-gauge galvanized wire and equipped with three "arms" by which it is suspended. Baskets made from green or white plastic-covered wire are also available and these are preferable to the plain wire type as they have a longer life.

When a basket is to be positioned over a doorway or path, water drips can be a problem. In this case a plastic bowl-type "basket" with a built-in drip-tray will eliminate the nuisance. Individual pot plants may be suspended in the same way as hanging baskets if a simple wire cradle is made for each.

Preparation
Compost may be placed straight into the plastic hanging basket which is equipped with a

drip-tray, but open mesh baskets must be lined to prevent the compost from falling out. The traditional lining material is sphagnum moss (a spongy type of moss which grows in moorland bogs). Black polythene is a more convenient, though less attractive, substitute lining. It must be perforated at intervals around the base of the basket to allow surplus water to drain away. Put the sphagnum moss in place bit by bit as the basket is filled and the plants inserted. Cut polythene liners to shape before planting starts.

Compost
John Innes No. 2 potting compost is the best mixture to use in hanging baskets, as its loam base retains moisture well. Soilless composts, while being lighter and therefore easier to use, tend to dry out very quickly and are difficult to re-moisten. With both types the inclusion of polymers will increase moisture-holding capacity and reduce watering frequency.

Planting
Hanging baskets are usually planted up in May and hung outdoors towards the end of that month. Place the basket on top of a bucket or large plant pot to hold it steady while planting. If sphagnum moss is being

Filling a basket

1 Line the basket with a 1in (2.5cm) layer of damp sphagnum moss. Weigh it down with a layer of damp compost.

2 Insert one or two trailing plants, pushing the rootball through the basket from the outside, and firm compost around them.

used as a liner, place a 1in (2.5cm) layer over the bottom of the basket and weigh it down with moist compost. Insert one or two trailing plants. Push the small rootball of each plant through the wires from the outside so that it rests on the compost. Add more compost to cover the roots and firm this lightly into place. Gradually build up the layer of moss (keeping it above the level of the compost) and insert more trailing plants, spacing them 4-6 in (10-15cm) apart. Bring the moss right up to the rim of the basket, but make sure that the compost is about ½-1in (1.25-2.5cm) below the rim to allow for watering. A black polythene liner will have to be slit at intervals and the roots of the trailing plants pushed through.

Once the trailing plants are in position, taller and more bushy plants may be inserted in the top. Position a large plant in the centre, scooping out the compost by hand and re-placing and firming it when the rootball is in position, and surround it with plants of smaller stature. Plants already in flower will provide an instant show, but younger ones will soon come into flower.

Greenhouse baskets
Many trailing half-hardy plants can be shown off to best effect in hanging baskets which are slung from the rafters of the greenhouse.

Plants grown in baskets under glass are treated in the same way as those positioned outdoors, but they may be kept growing all the year round and only disturbed when their performance starts to deteriorate or when they are excessively overcrowded.

Aftercare
Soak the compost in the basket immediately after planting by using a watering can fitted with a fine rose. Greenhouse-grown plants may need to be hardened off before being placed outside permanently. Put them in a cool greenhouse for a week, or place them outside during the day for a few days, bring-ing them in at night.

When placing the baskets outdoors make sure that their supports are secure. Large screw eyes may be attached to wooden per-golas to support baskets, or brackets may be fastened to walls with screws held firm by wall plugs. Check the supports each year before the baskets are hung up. Avoid placing hanging baskets in exposed parts of the gar-den where they may be damaged by wind, or in very shady spots.

Should a hanging basket dry out during the summer, it can be plunged in a tank of water for ten minutes, then allowed to drain before being put back in position.

3 Add more moss to the side of the basket and insert further plants in the sides and top, keeping them 4-6in (10-15cm) apart.

4 Fill the basket with compost to within ½-1in (1.25-2.5cm) of the rim. Water thoroughly.

Caring for container plants

The most common cause of failure with outdoor container-grown plants is neglect. Plants grown in containers are more sensitive to extremes of heat, cold, damp and drought than plants grown in open ground. To provide the anticipated display the plants' needs must be studied and feeding and watering must be attended to regularly.

Watering
On sunny patios, windowsills and balconies, soil-filled containers dry out with surprising rapidity during the summer months. From May to September they should be checked for water at least once a day (twice in warm weather) and the container filled to the rim with water if the surface of the soil is dry. There is little danger of overwatering at this time of year if the container has adequate drainage. Neglect watering for just two or three days in the height of summer and the plants may never recover.

It is particularly important to retain a moist rooting medium at all times where larger shrubs, fruit trees or bushes and dwarf conifers are being grown. Extremes of waterlogging or desiccation will lead to fruitlet drop on fruit trees and may kill the plant. In hot weather, place moist sacking around the pots to protect the roots.

During the winter months waterlogging can become a problem in large containers if no adequate provision has been made for drainage. Follow the recommendations on pages 138-40 and the plants should grow well, but if heavy downpours are more than the compost can cope with then the plants should be brought under cover until the compost dries out a little.

Heavy frosts can kill container-grown plants by freezing the entire root system. In winter, protect the plants by burying the container in well-drained ground up to the rim. Alternatively, move the plants to a sheltered position. If neither precaution is feasible, wrap the container with sacking or wire netting packed with straw.

Feeding
With a limited supply of compost in which to sink their roots, plants in containers are completely dependent on the gardener to provide them with an adequate supply of nutrients. Soilless composts should be watered with diluted liquid fertilizer at fortnightly intervals some 4-6 weeks after they have been planted up. Feed fruit trees in leaf at 7-10 day intervals. Loam-based mixtures such as John Innes will last two months or more before additional food is necessary, then apply at

Feeding and watering

In summer check the containers once a day and if the compost is dry fill to the rim with water. Any surplus will drain away.

In summer feed plants fortnightly with diluted liquid general fertilizer. Apply the liquid feed when the compost is moist.

the same rate as for soilless composts. Use a fertilizer formula suitable for the plants being grown.

Feeding is unnecessary during winter months and should only be undertaken during the growing season – from April to September. Apply liquid feed when compost in the container is moist so that it can go straight into action without burning the roots.

Dead-heading

Remove faded flowers and foliage as soon as they are noticed whatever the time of year. Decaying blooms and leaves look untidy and may harbour pests and diseases and fungal infections which might spread to living parts of the plant. Not only will the removal of faded flowers tidy up the display, but it will also encourage the plants to bloom more continuously – those allowed to run to seed will invariably stop flowering before those which are dead-headed.

All weeds should be removed from containers. Apart from competing with the cultivated plants for light and nutrients, they may harbour pests and diseases.

Repotting and top-dressing

If the container is planted up twice in one year, first for a spring show and then with summer bedding plants, the compost should be replaced at the end of this cycle. Take the opportunity to clean the container thoroughly at this point. Timber tubs and troughs should be repainted or treated with preservative every two years. Scrub terracotta and plastic pots with water and dilute fungicide.

Permanent shrubs and trees which will resent disturbance may be top-dressed each spring. Scrape away 2 in (5cm) or so of compost from the surface of the rootball and replace it with fresh John Innes No. 3 potting compost, firming this against the rootball. Repeat this operation each year, unless the plant requires potting on when it should be potted into a slightly larger container.

Pot on in late autumn, gently teasing out the edges of the rootball. Fill the gap around the rootball with John Innes No. 3 compost or an equivalent. Care should be taken to use lime-free compost when potting or top-dressing ericaceous plants.

Pests and diseases

It is important to deal rapidly with pest and disease outbreaks. A hand mister containing diluted insecticide can be kept close to hand so that pests such as greenfly can be speedily controlled. Occasionally badly infested plants may have to be removed and replaced.

Dead-heading

In winter bring containers under cover to dry out if heavy rain saturates the compost.

Remove faded flowers and foliage. They may harbour pests and diseases. Dead-heading encourages further blooms.

Renovation: lawns

Gardens require constant care if they are to remain gardens and not degenerate into jungles. Renovation is a task faced frequently by those who move house and have to counter previous neglect.

Lawns

Lawns run wild faster than most areas of the garden. If a lawn is not mowed regularly and if other maintenance measures are skimped, weeds and rough grasses will invade it and the lawn grasses will be displaced.

Before doing anything to a neglected lawn examine it to see if it can be saved. If weeds, moss and coarse grasses predominate it may be simpler to start again with fresh turf or seed. If the lawn grasses appear to be surviving despite neglect, the lawn can be reclaimed. The best time to begin renovation is spring, for the grass then has the summer to grow and recover.

First remove stones, branches and any other rubbish. Then cut to 2-3in (5-8cm) using a rotary mower, or if necessary a sickle or scythe, removing dead grass, weeds and seedheads. Rake thoroughly to remove grass cuttings and dead material. If a scythe or sickle has been used, cut again with a cylinder mower to reduce the height of the grass to 2in (5cm). The lawn will appear yellow because the dead grass at the base has been exposed. New growth should soon begin, however. A week after the rotary cut begin mowing with a cylinder mower set as high as possible. Continue using a cylinder mower at weekly intervals, progressively reducing the height of cut. When normal grass height has been attained, apply a general-purpose turf fertilizer. Ten to fourteen days later apply a lawn weedkiller. Five to six weeks after applying the first dressing of fertilizer, feed again with sulphate of ammonia dressing. Apply this dressing at a rate of $\frac{1}{4}$-$\frac{1}{2}$ oz (7-14g) per square yard (metre) mixing it with a spreader of sand to ensure even distribution. Water the lawn beforehand if conditions are dry to reduce the possibility of scorch. This cutting and feeding programme should enable the turf to grow strongly throughout the summer. In September fork out patches of coarse grass and re-seed with a suitable lawn seed mixture. In early autumn scarify the lawn, using a spring-tined rake to remove patches of moss and dead grass. Then apply an autumn turf fertilizer at a rate of 2 oz (55g) per square yard (metre). The following spring a normal routine can begin (p. 62-65).

Bare patches

If the lawn has bare patches, first attempt to discover why the grass is bare. If excessive wear is the cause, consider resiting paths or gates while the grass is replaced or lay a hard-surfaced path. Other possible causes of bare patches are compaction, the removal of weeds, oil drip or fertilizer spillage. If the turf is thin rather than bare, aeration, scarifying, feeding and irrigation may stimulate growth. If these measures fail, investigate drainage.

Bare or sparse patches can be renovated by seed or turf. Sow seed in September or April, first forking up any rough grass, raising the soil level to that of the surrounding turf if necessary. Sow, at a rate of 1-1$\frac{1}{2}$ oz (28-40g) of seed per square yard (metre), lightly rake the soil, and erect some form of bird deterrent. When using turf, first cut out from the old turf a small square that includes the bare area. Break up the underlying soil with a fork. Cover with new turf, firming it so that it is level. Brush in a sandy top-dressing mixture.

Bumps and hollows

Bumps in the lawn show up as bare or sparse patches. The grass is worn down by excess wear and by the action of the mower. Minor bumps can be eliminated using a hollow tine aerator. This tool removes plugs of turf from the lawn. Do this at intervals allowing the turf time to settle back into the holes created, until the lawn is level. To remove larger bumps, make a cut with a sharp knife or half-moon iron across the bump. Fold back the turf in flaps and level by removing excess top-soil. Replace the turf flaps and seal the cuts with a top dressing.

Hollows can be filled by the use of a light top-dressing, applyed in no more than $\frac{1}{2}$ in layers. Larger hollows can be treated by rolling back the turf as described above for hollows and adding top-soil. If there are many bumps and hollows, raise the height of the mower until they have all been dealt with, or bare patches will result.

1 After clearing rubbish, use a rotary mower to cut the grass to a height of 2-3in (5-8cm).

2 Scarify the lawn with a wire-toothed rake to remove dead grass and thatch.

3 Apply a dressing of a general-purpose lawn fertilizer, using an applicator or by hand.

4 When healthy growth begins, mow closely with a cylinder mower set to a medium setting.

5 Apply a herbicide designed for use on lawns to control broad-leaved weeds.

6 Apply lawn sand in spring and summer to discourage moss. Seed-in bare patches.

Renovation: roses

Although roses are long-lived plants they need regular pruning if they are not to become straggling and choked with dead wood, with a consequent decline in quality and quantity of blooms. Roses that have suffered neglect can often be saved, however. Most roses are tough plants and will stand a renovation regime that consists essentially of cutting them back to the ground level and stimulating new growth.

Before carrying out any renovation treatment examine the plant carefully. There may well be vigorous young growth amid the tangled, dying and dead branches. If such young shoots exist, the aim should be to preserve them.

Suckers
Most roses are budded on to a selected rootstock of a wild rose species. If shoots are allowed to grow from the rootstock they will weaken and eventually replace the rose variety. In summer or autumn identify their shoots, which are known as suckers. They frequently have different leaves from the main plant. Clear away the soil from around the roots and gently pull the sucker from the rootstock. Do not cut the sucker off at ground level for this will stimulate the growth of more suckers.

The first year
In winter cut out all dead, thin, tangled and diseased wood from the rose. Check for and remove any further suckers. Cut up to half the existing main stems back to the base of the plant, leaving any on which there is young vigorous growth. Cut any weak, dead or crossing twigs from those stems that are left. Cut any strong laterals on the remaining shoots back to 2-3 eyes or 6in (15cm).

In spring, apply a heavy top dressing of well-rotted manure or compost around the base of the plant. Foliar feed the plant during the growing season, at 2-3 week intervals if possible, to encourage the growth of strong replacement shoots from the base.

In the summer the plant will flower on laterals of the older wood left when pruning. The new shoots that appear will provide flowering wood for subsequent years, though some varieties flower on the new wood.

The second year
In winter cut back to the base all the old wood left from the first winter pruning. Enough new growth should have been formed in the 12 months since renovation commenced to provide a framework. Cut laterals on these new growths back to 2-3 eyes or 6in (15cm). Manure or compost should be applied as a top dressing to maintain vigorous growth the following summer.

The rose is now ready for any pruning that is necessary for the variety in question. For full details, see the volume *Pruning* in this series. By the summer of the second year sufficient new growth should have been stimulated to bring the rose back to health.

Climbers and ramblers
Climbing and rambling roses should be treated in the manner outlined above. However, it will be necessary to untie the rose from the wall, fence or other support on which it is climbing and to lay the stems on the ground. Cut out dead wood and retie, renewing the supports if necessary.

CLIMBERS AND RAMBLERS

Renovate climbers and ramblers in the same way as bush roses. The stems will have to be untied and laid on the ground.

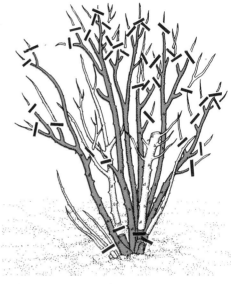

1 Summer and autumn Remove all suckers. Scrape away soil and gently pull the sucker from the rootstock. Do not cut it off.

2 Winter Cut out dead, weak and diseased shoots. Cut half existing older stems to base. Prune laterals to 2-3 eyes or 6in (15cm).

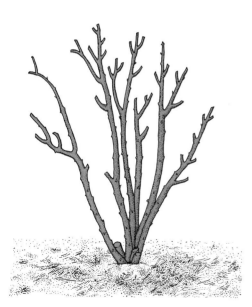

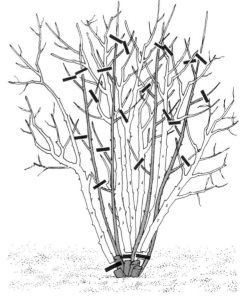

3 Spring Apply a heavy top dressing of well-rotted manure or compost around the base of the plant.

4 Second year: Winter Cut remaining old growths to base. Prune any laterals on new growths to 2-3 eyes or 6in (15cm).

149

Renovation: trees and shrubs

Renovating full-grown trees is often a major task and one best left to an expert tree surgeon. However, neglected fruit trees and smaller ornamentals such as cherries and *Prunus* can often be restored to health by careful pruning and feeding.

The first priority is to remove all dead, damaged and diseased wood. Then examine the tree and decide which framework branches upset the balance, are too large, or are crossing others. Aim to create an open centre and an evenly spaced framework. After the necessary framework branches have been removed, thin the side-shoots allowing for new growth. When planning the cuts it may be necessary to prune over two seasons in order to ensure that the tree grows into the required shape. In spring feed with a slow-release fertilizer and apply a mulch of well-rotted compost.

Removing branches

If it is necessary to remove a branch, and the branch does not need to be dealt with by a tree surgeon, carefully follow the sequence illustrated if the branch is long and is too thick to be cut with secateurs. The work is best done in late autumn or early winter.

Fruit trees

Fruit trees which have suffered neglect may be stunted or overvigorous. The treatment of an overvigorous tree, which may have plenty of vegetative growth but little fruit, is essentially the same as outlined in the first paragraphs. Trees which through old age have stopped bearing a good crop are usually past redemption and should be replaced, unless their ornamental value as mature specimens is greater than that of their crop. The aim with overvigorous trees which seem worth saving

Removing a branch

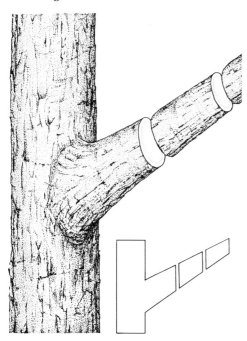

1 Using a sharp saw, cut the branch back to a 12in (30cm) stump. It may be desirable or necessary, if the branch is long or very heavy, to cut it in sections.

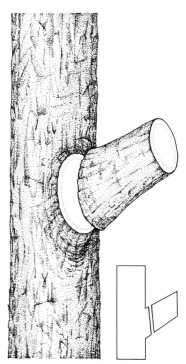

2 Cut the stump, beginning with an undercut, so that the collar at the junction of branch and trunk is left intact.

must be to cut out any dead, diseased and overcrowded branches in winter, leaving healthy, well-placed ones to form a balanced framework. Hard winter pruning stimulates vigorous growth and a carefully controlled pruning regime will need to be established to make the tree fruitful again. Shoots growing horizontally produce more flowers and fruits than those growing vertically and should be encouraged. Tying down vertical shoots can help stimulate fruit production. Summer pruning checks growth and unwanted laterals can be shortened in July to assist in forming fruit buds. For further details, see the *Pruning* and *Fruit* volumes in this series.

Shrubs

Many vigorous shrubs tend to become overgrown through neglect and may be rejuvenated by severe pruning in winter, or in late

spring in the case of evergreens. Some may react better to a less severe rejuvenation programme spread over two or three winters. With shrubs such as lilacs, in winter cut all weak branches back to ground level and the remaining branches to within 1ft (30cm) of the ground. Dig in generous amounts of manure. This treatment should stimulate new growth from the base of the plant. During the following winter thin these shoots, leaving enough to form the main branch framework.

If the plant is unhealthy, or if it is a species with twiggy growth such as *Deutzia* or *Philadelphus,* phase the renewal process over two seasons. In the first winter, cut out weak shoots and half the old main stems. Vigorous basal shoots will develop, enabling the remaining old wood to be removed during the second winter. Once again, make sure the plant has sufficient nutrients and water.

Pruning shrubs

The second year

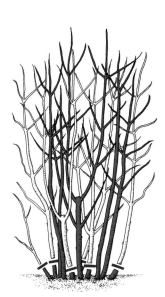

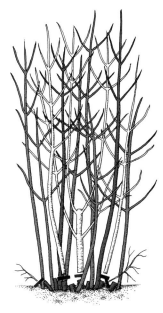

1 Winter Remove half of the old stems, cutting them close to the base.

2 June to July On remaining growth, blooms from laterals are sparse. Vigorous basal shoots develop.

3 Winter Cut out remaining old wood and weak new growths. Mulch with well-rotted compost.

Renovation: borders

Renovating a border requires patience. Allow a year to go by before undertaking any major work so that all the plants present can appear and can be noted. During this year, confine work on the border to the removal of large and obvious weeds. If renovation is begun too soon, plants such as bulbs which are dormant at the time may be missed. During the year make a plan of the border.

The first year

In early spring, or in autumn on light soils, clear the overgrown border. Carefully lift all clumps of plants. Discard those which are diseased, sickly or surplus to requirements. Split the plants to be saved into smaller sections, carefully removing all weeds and pieces of weed root or stem. Older herbaceous perennials may need their centres discarding as the young growth develops at the edges, leaving a dead area in the middle. Split up such plants into small, healthy sections. Store the plants on spare land for the growing season, watering well during dry periods in summer. Allow weed growth to take place unchecked on the fallow ground. In late spring, carefully apply a proprietary weed-killer containing glyphosate with a dribble bar or spray. Persistent perennial weeds such as field bindweed may grow again in late summer or early spring. If necessary, spray again before growth dies down in the autumn. If there is regrowth in spring, apply a paint-on formulation of glyphosate.

In late summer, single dig and manure the bed, adding garden compost if manure is not available. Carefully remove any remaining perennial weed roots.

In late autumn, or spring if autumn is not practicable, firm the soil by treading or with the head of a rake. Rake in a dressing of compound fertilizer at 4oz (110g) per square yard. Replant the border to a previously prepared plan. Lift the heeled-in plants, trim the roots and discard any weak portions. Replant spacing to allow plants to develop.

1 Early spring Clear the overgrown border and split plants to be saved into smaller sections, carefully removing all weeds.

4 Late summer Single dig and manure the bed, carefully removing any perennial weed roots.

2 Early spring Store the plants to be saved by moving them to spare land.

3 Late Spring When perennial weeds are growing strongly, apply glyphosate weedkiller with a dribble bar or sprayer.

5 Late autumn Lift stored plants, trim the roots and discard unwanted portions. Replant at appropriate spacings.

6 Early spring Hoe in a surface dressing of compound fertilizer at 4oz (110g) per square yard (metre).

Growing for competition

In many towns and villages throughout the United Kingdom there are local horticultural societies that organize shows and competitions. Amateur gardeners may be reluctant to enter produce for a show because of their lack of knowledge and experience. However, provided a few basic principles are observed, there is no reason why any gardener should not be successful. The complete novice should start by visiting shows, taking note of the quality of the crops and the way they are displayed, and talking to more experienced exhibitors. Far from being secretive about their methods, most exhibitors are willing to advise on the culture of a wide range of crops.

Do not expect to sweep the board at the first show attended. Start by entering only one or two classes in a local show and gradually progress to larger shows, entering a wider range of fruit and vegetables. It may be several years before all the hard work is rewarded by a prize, but the satisfaction gained from producing a well-staged, good-quality crop is a reward in itself.

The show schedule

The show schedule is a booklet issued by the organizers, usually in the autumn or early winter preceding the event. This enables the gardener to choose and plan his crops well in advance, so that they are in peak condition on the date of the show in late summer or autumn.

As well as details of the date and time, the entry fees and the closing date for the receipt of entry forms, the schedule also contains much vital information such as who is eligible to enter a particular class and the precise number and type of fruits or vegetables that constitute an exhibit. The exhibitor should pay close attention to these conditions since deviation from them in even the smallest detail will result in disqualification of the entry as "N.A.S." – not according to schedule.

Classes Most shows have various classes of competitor: "Open" classes may be entered by amateurs and professionals; "Amateur" classes are open to those who do not make a living from gardening or from selling their produce; "Members" classes are open to members of the organizing society, and "Novice" classes to those who have not previously won a prize.

Exhibits Make sure that the items in the exhibit fit the description in the schedule. Stump-rooted carrots, for example, should not be exhibited in a category for long-rooted varieties. Similarly, if six apples are specified, the judges will disqualify entries that consist of five or seven.

Cleaning

Carefully clean soil from root crops with a soft brush before it dries hard.

Selection

Choose healthy specimens with no bruises or blemishes and as uniform in size as possible.

All exhibits should be clean, but not polished, and fruits should have their stalks intact. Labels should be clearly written to show the name of the variety, and placed with the entry.

The judges will award points for freshness, tenderness, the absence of blemishes and the general health of the crop. Size is usually only of secondary importance to uniformity: a plate of potatoes that has six even-sized and well-shaped tubers will always be placed higher than a plate with five extra-large tubers and one smaller one.

Staging Make the exhibit as attractive as possible, while remaining within the constraints of the schedule. The produce can be displayed in baskets of various shapes and sizes, on boards or simply on plain white plates. Leaves from the plant, or fresh green parsley, can also be used for decoration.

The staging must be completed before judging begins and the fruits or vegetables may not be removed until a given time afterwards. This is to prevent possible cheating by competitors.

Further information on shows and competitions for organizers, exhibitors and judges can be obtained from "The Horticultural Show Handbook", published by the Royal Horticultural Society.

CULTIVATION

Keen exhibitors go to considerable lengths to grow plants likely to win competitions. Before adopting competition growing techniques, decide whether winning prizes takes precedence over size of crop or number of flowers, flavour and other qualities.

Special varieties of fruit and vegetables are sometimes recommended for showing. Consult seedsmen's catalogues. These varieties are known to produce larger specimens than those normally grown.

With flowers such as roses and chrysanthemums, the exhibitor's aim is to produce a single large bloom on each stem. Therefore varieties that tend to produce clusters of blooms must be stopped, or have side buds removed.

Competition quality vegetables are often raised in specially prepared beds and given lavish quantities of manure. Such beds, kept going year after year, are capable of growing massive onions and leeks, for example. There is a danger of build-ups of pests and diseases if normal rotation is not followed. Root crops need soil that has been especially deeply dug.

Staging

1 Display fruits such as apples and pears on plain white plates. Label each plate clearly with the name of the variety.

2 Carrots and other roots can be displayed in a fan basket, filling in the gaps with fresh green parsley.

Cut flowers

Although many keen gardeners prefer to see their flowers in the garden where they look most at home, it cannot be denied that even the most observant plantsman will become better acquainted with his blooms if he views them at close quarters. Picked and arranged in bowls or vases, flowers and leaves will bring brightness to the dullest room and will interest both arranger and observers.

Gathering the blooms
Flowers are best cut from the garden in the early morning or late evening when the air is relatively cool and the plant's stems are turgid. If picked in full sun the flower stems may not be able to take up water fast enough to stop them from wilting. They may also wilt if picked on mornings when a heavy dew has fallen.

Cut the stems with secateurs or special flower gatherers. Plunge the stems into water as soon as possible after picking so that the ends do not have a chance to dry out and impede the absorption of water.

Making cut flowers last
Cut flowers will last longer if a few sensible precautions are followed.
Leaf removal Whatever the plant, remove any leaves that arise from the portion of stem that will be under water in the vase. This prevents the water from being fouled too quickly, and it also allows room for more stems to be inserted.

Submerging Wilting flowers can often be revived if they are plunged up to their necks in warm water (use a wash basin or a bucket). Leave the flowers until they have revived completely and then arrange them without delay, keeping them out of water for as short a time as possible. This method is particularly useful for roses.

Wounding Many plants with woody stems have difficulty in taking up water when cut. Some arrangers use a hammer to crush the stem ends and allow them to take up water more easily; others prefer to split 1in (2.5cm) of the stem end with a knife.

Boiling water treatment The stems of certain plants will take up water more readily if the ends of the stems are stood in a vessel which contains 1in (2.5cm) of boiling water. After one minute, fill the container to the brim with warm water and let the flowers stand for a few hours. This method is particularly useful with roses, hollyhocks, tropical plant leaves, euphorbias, poppies and other plants that bleed.

Stem plugging Hollow-stemmed flowers such as lupins and delphiniums should be held

Making flowers last

1 Plug the hollow stems of flowers such as chrysanthemums with cotton wool or tissue after filling the stems with water.

2 Perforate the stems of hollow-stemmed flowers with a pin at 1in (2.5cm) intervals to prevent wilting.

upside down, their tube-like stems filled with water and then plugged with wet cotton wool or paper tissue. This prevents an air lock from forming and so obstructing the uptake of water.

Chemical aids Many arrangers find that an aspirin dropped into flower water helps the blooms to last longer, and it also keeps the water relatively clear. Charcoal can be used for the same purpose. Proprietary powders sold specifically for dissolving in the water to prolong cut flower life are sometimes effective and especially useful where rare or expensive blooms are being used.

Stem perforation Flowers that tend to wilt when cut and arranged, regardless of their freshness, often do so as a result of an air lock in the stem. Tulips are a common example. Overcome this by pricking the stem at 1in (2.5cm) intervals from top to bottom with a needle when the blooms are arranged.

Maintenance

Keep arrangements attractive by topping up the water frequently. Use tepid water. Instead of totally dismantling and rearranging the display when blooms fade, remove the faded stems and replace them with fresh ones.

SOME CUT FLOWERS TO PROVIDE YEAR-ROUND INTEREST

In many cases only certain species of the genera listed flower at the given times.

Consult a good nursery or seedsman's catalogue for specific recommendations.

January
Crocus, Eranthis, Hamamelis, Iris unguicularis, Jasminum nudiflorum, Prunus × subhirtella, Dianthus barbatus, Pulmonaria rubra, Viburnum.

February
Bergenia, Chaenomeles, Chionodoxa, Crocus, Eranthis, Erica, Erythronium dens-canis, Galanthus, Garrya elliptica, Hamamelis, Helleborus, Iris unguicularis, Jasminum nudiflorum, Narcissus, Prunus × subhirtella 'Autumnalis', Pulmonaria, Scilla, Viburnum.

March
Anemone, Bergenia, Camellia, Chaenomeles, Chionodoxa, Crocus, Doronicum, Eranthis, Erica, Erythronium dens-canis, Forsythia, Galanthus, Helleborus, Leucojum vernum, Narcissus, Pulmonaria, Scilla.

April
Amelanchier, Anemone, Bergenia, Camellia, Cheiranthus, Convallaria, Doronicum, Endymion, Erythronium, Forsythia, Fritillaria, Helleborus, Iberis, Magnolia, Muscari, Narcissus, Primula, Tulipa.

May
Allium, Aquilegia, Ceanothus, Cheiranthus, Convallaria, Cytisus, Dianthus barbatus, Doronicum, Endymion, Fritillaria, Genista, Geranium, Iris, Laburnum, Myosotis, Paeonia, Primula, Rosa.

June
Achillea, Allium, Aquilegia, Astrantia, Borago, Campanula, Ceanothus, Deutzia, Dianthus, Digitalis, Geranium, Hebe, Hemerocallis, Iris, Laburnum, Lathyrus, Phlomis fruticosa, Lupinus, Rosa, Syringa.

July
Alchemilla, Allium, Alstroemeria, Althaea, Buddleja,

Calendula, Campanula, Centranthus, Chrysanthemum (border perennials),Clarkia, Crocosmia, Eryngium, Eucryphia, Gaillardia, Galtonia, Gypsophila, Helenium, Hemerocallis, Hypericum, Iberis, Iris, Kniphofia, Lavandula, Lilium, Lysimachia, Monarda, Nicotiana, Physostegia, Rosa, Solidago.

August
Acanthus, Achillea, Agapanthus, Allium, Althaea, Aster, Campanula, Crocosmia, Dahlia, Dianthus, Echinops, Eucryphia, Gaillardia, Gladiolus, Helenium, Hemerocallis, Kniphofia, Lavandula, Liatris, Lilium, Monarda, Penstemon, Rosa, Rudbeckia, Scabiosa.

September
Achillea, Aconitum, Anemone, Aster (Michaelmas daisy), Chrysanthemum, Coreopsis, Cotoneaster, Crocus, Dahlia, Helenium, Hypericum, Kniphofia, Lilium, Nerine, Penstemon, Pyracantha, Rosa.

October
Aconitum, Anemone × hybrida, Aster (Michaelmas daisy), Calluna, Chrysanthemum, Crocus, Erica, Gaillardia, Hebe, Liriope, Nerine, Physalis, Rosa, Scabiosa, Schizostylis, Sedum spectabile.

November
Chrysanthemum, Cotoneaster, Crocus, Erica, Galanthus, Hebe, Iris unguicularis, Jasminum nudiflorum, Liriope, Physalis, Prunus × subhirtella 'Autumnalis', Pyracantha, Schizostylis, Viburnum.

December
Celastrus, Crocus, Erica, Galanthus, Hamamelis, Helleborus niger, Ilex, Iris unguicularis, Jasminum nudiflorum, Prunus × subhirtella 'Autumnalis', Pyracantha, Schizostylis, Viburnum.

Miniature gardens

Miniature gardens have two uses: to make the best of limited space or to display small plants. Use them to grow alpines, dwarf conifers, annuals and biennials and a wide range of miniature bulbs.

Sinks and troughs

Old stone sinks and troughs, though scarce and costly, make attractive miniature gardens. Place them on plinths made of bricks to improve drainage and make close observation easier.

If stone troughs cannot be found, old square porcelain sinks can be disguised to resemble natural stone. First, thoroughly scrub down the sink with detergent and water so that the surface is clean inside and out. Wipe dry with a clean cloth. Remove and discard the plug, leaving the plug hole clear to allow free drainage. Stand the sink on bricks to keep it clear of the ground, and coat the sink with a bonding agent such as Unibond or Polybond and allow this to dry.

Mix peat, sand and cement together in equal parts with water to form a stiff paste that can be easily moulded with the hands. Press the mixture on to the treated surface of the sink so that it sticks firmly to form a ¼ in (0.5cm) thick coating. If desired, a more liquid mix can be painted on with a brush, though this covering will be thinner and will wear off more quickly than the thicker mix.

Allow the treated sink to dry for at least seven days. The coating will take time to weather. Eventually it will become encrusted with mosses and lichens, giving it the appearance of weathered rock. Repeated frosts may cause some of the coating to break away, but bare patches can be retreated.

Compost When properly prepared and dried the sink should be filled with suitable compost. Do not use ordinary garden soil, which is likely to be deficient in nutrients and not free-draining. First place a 2in (5cm) layer of crocks, coarse gravel or washed ashes in the base of the sink to provide speedy drainage. Use proprietary compost or a mix consisting of 2 parts loam, 1 part leaf-mould, and 1 part sharp sand. Add a light dusting of bonemeal during mixing. No other fertilizers need be added.

Fill the sink to within 2in (5cm) of its rim with the compost, which should be well firmed. If desired, pieces of rock can be bedded into the compost.

Planting Carefully take out planting holes with a small trowel. Plant slightly high so that a 1-1¼in (2.5-3cm) layer of gravel or stone chippings can be spread over the surface of the compost afterwards without burying the plants. The gravel layer will prevent weed seeds from germinating in the compost, and it will help to retain moisture, and it safeguards the plants from rain splashing. Do not plant too densely. Allow the plants enough room to expand to their mature size.

Plants grown in sink gardens are subject to the same constraints as those grown in other containers. The compost must be kept moist but should not be allowed to become waterlogged. Usually the natural rainfall is sufficient except where the miniature garden is sheltered by a wall or roof overhang. In spells of very dry weather hand watering may be necessary. Feed with a light application of a slow-release fertilizer in March. Most sink and trough gardens will withstand normal temperate winter weather conditions if the plants are chosen with care.

Plants for miniature gardens

Dwarf shrubs and conifers can be used to add height to miniature garden planting. Many alpines, especially the low-growing mat-forming sorts, will look attractive in a miniature garden. Trailing plants can be positioned at the edges and allowed to cascade down the sides. Use annuals with care, as they can grow too large and spoil the miniature garden's scale. Dead-head and tidy all plants regularly.

Tufa

Tufa is a pitted, rock-like material which has been formed from calcium carbonate deposited round a spring or stream. It is very porous, and large pieces of it can be used to make miniature gardens. It can be obtained from garden suppliers.

Create plant pockets in the tufa by chiselling out cavities. Dwarf or cushion-forming plants can then be planted in these pockets using the soil mixture described above.

1 Clean an old sink thoroughly then cover with a bonding agent, applying a thin but even coating.

2 Mix peat, sand and cement together in equal parts with water to form a stiff paste that can be moulded with the hands.

3 Press the mixture onto the treated surface so that it sticks firmly, forming a ¼in (0.5cm) coating.

4 Place a 2in (5cm) layer of drainage material, crocks, gravel or weathered ashes, in the base of the sink.

5 Fill the sink to within 2in (5cm) of the rim with compost, adding a light dusting of bone-meal when mixing the compost.

6 After planting, sprinkle a 1in (2.5cm) layer of gravel or stone chippings on the surface of the compost.

Bedding 1

In private gardens and public parks all over the country "bedding out" is practised twice a year to keep flower beds and borders well filled and colourful. This system of flower growing produces two peak seasons of interest; one in spring and the other in summer. Plants used for summer display are half-hardy annuals and perennials while bulbs and biennials are used in the spring. Traditionally, bedding plants alone are used in a formal, regimented bedding scheme. A more flexible system is to add bedding plants to the herbaceous or mixed border. This allows the attractive plants used for bedding to be displayed in an informal setting.

Spring bedding

Spring bedding plants are usually planted in September or October, before the hard frosts of autumn, to allow the young plants to become firmly established. They replace the summer bedding plants which are dying down by this time. Biennials such as wallflowers, forget-me-nots, sweet williams, pansies and dwarf double daisies are planted to form a carpet, with bulbs such as hyacinths and tulips set among them to provide colour at a higher level. In May the spring-flowering plants are removed to make way for the summer bedding plants. The bulbs may be heeled in on a spare patch of ground, or else dried off straight away and stored. The other plants are usually discarded. Spring bedding must be planned a year ahead if the biennials are to be grown from seed. Sow seed in spring for planting out in the autumn. Alternatively, buy plants in the autumn.

Summer bedding

Summer bedding is planted in late May or early June when the spring flowers have finished and the severe frosts are over. Half-hardy annuals form the backbone of this display. They are raised under glass before being hardened off and planted out. Tender perennials such as fuchsias, pelargoniums and dahlias are also used in summer bedding schemes.

The half-hardy annuals, like the spring-flowering plants, are discarded at the end of the season, but right through the summer cuttings may be taken from the tender

perennials. These are rooted in a propagating case and used in place of their parents the following year.

Sub-tropical bedding

Large-leaved, sub-tropical plants, normally grown under glass, can be used in summer bedding schemes. They add height to beds and borders and when placed appropriately they will create a superb display. Any sub-tropical plant can be used that will withstand temperate summer conditions. However, many of these plants are tender and only suitable for standing out in the hottest of summer weather in a sheltered spot. Bedding with sub-tropical plants is easier if the plants are left in their pots, which can then be plunged in the flower bed for the summer and then lifted and brought in under cover from early to mid-September.

Cultivation

When beds and borders are first being prepared for bedding plants they should be thoroughly cultivated. Dig over in autumn or winter, incorporating well-rotted manure, compost, or leaf-mould at the rate of 10-15lb (4.5-6.8kg) per square yard (metre). This improves the texture and moisture retentive qualities of the soil.

In spring firm the soil by treading gently, finally raking the soil level. Do not produce too fine a tilth. Then rake a general fertilizer into the soil at the rate of 4oz (110g) per square yard (metre).

The edges of the bed or border should be well defined so that an adjoining lawn can be easily trimmed. A gulley around the perimeter will allow edging shears to be used comfortably.

When the soil is to be used for both spring and summer bedding it should be forked over and dressed with fertilizer at the rate of 2oz (55g) per square yard (metre) after the spring-flowering plants are lifted, then dug over and organically enriched immediately after the summer-flowering plants are removed.

Planting

If bedding plants are being purchased rather than raised at home, buy from a garden centre or nursery where the plants are known to be

Preparing the bed

1 Autumn or early winter Dig the border one spit deep, incorporating well-rotted manure, compost or leaf-mould at 10-15lb (4.5-6.8kg) per square yard (metre).

2 Spring Firm the soil by treading and rake level. Do not rake too much or an over-fine tilth will be produced.

3 Spring Rake a top dressing of general fertilizer into the soil at 4oz (110g) per square yard (metre).

4 Spring Tidy the edges of the bed, heaping the soil back from the adjoining lawn or path, forming a shallow gulley. This aids lawn mowing and weeding.

Bedding 2

fresh and of good quality. Do not buy summer bedding plants too far in advance of planting time unless a frame or greenhouse is available to protect them from frost. Look for bushy plants, avoiding those which are spindly and those which are in full flower. Bedding plants must be watered while still in their boxes or trays a few hours before planting. Stand wallflowers in a bucket of water for an hour or so prior to planting.

Planting distances and depths will vary with the plants used in the bedding scheme. The aim is to ensure that at flowering time a mass colour effect is achieved, covering the entire soil surface. This depends to a large extent on the use of good quality plants.

Always plant spring bedding plants before bulbs where the two are to be used together to avoid damage to the bulbs when taking out planting holes. This sequence also helps to avoid a patchy effect as if the bedding plants are put in last, they may inadvertently be placed on top of bulbs. The plants can be seen and the gaps between them chosen; while the bulbs if planted first will be invisible below ground.

Colour schemes

The choice of scheme depends entirely on the gardener. However, plant with a definite colour combination in mind. For instance, keep to a range of blue, white and red, or perhaps orange and yellow.

Bedding is frequently planted in a formal fashion. A strip of low-growing plants is used as an edging; robust, bushier plants as "dot" plants. This is the traditional approach but it is by no means obligatory.

Spring bedding which incorporates bulbs must be especially well planned so that the bulbs flower at the same time as the carpet. Study bulb and seed catalogues to discover flowering times and periods.

Maintenance

Both spring and summer bedding will need close attention in the early stages of growth. Irrigate the soil if it becomes excessively dry, and remove weeds by hand or carefully hoe until the plants have covered the soil. Use canes to support tall plants and tie in as growth is made. Remove faded flowerheads as necessary. This will keep the bed tidy as

Planting

1 If buying in plants, choose sturdy bushy plants, avoiding those already in flower. Buy from a reliable source such as a nursery or garden centre.

2 Water the trays or boxes of bedding plants a few hours prior to planting.

well as stimulating the plants to produce further blooms.

Carpet bedding

Carpet bedding is the most rigid form of bedding. Dwarf plants grown primarily for their foliage effect are planted closely together in geometrical form to create a crest, a coat of arms or a distinct picture. The display is almost always planted in spring for summer.

Carpet bedding must be planned on paper before planting is executed. Squared paper should be used, and a scale of 1in to 1ft (3cm to 30cm) will be found workable. The precise position and name of each plant should be indicated so that the scheme can be reproduced in the garden. Mark each square foot (0.1sq m) of the bed with string or a sand trail. The planter will find it most convenient to work from a plank supported on bricks so that the raked surface of the soil is not disturbed. Watering and weeding should be attended to throughout the summer, dead-heading and trimming as necessary. Suitable plants for carpet bedding include acaena, ajuga, alternanthera and alyssum.

PATTERN BEDDING

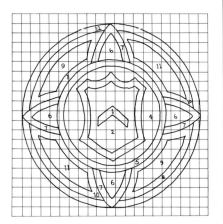

Bedding plants can be laid out in elaborate patterns in island beds or borders. Design the pattern on squared paper at a scale of 1in to 1ft (3cm to 30cm). Take care that all the plants will bloom at the same time, staggering planting times if necessary.

3 Plant to a pre-arranged plan, spacing the plants so that they will cover the bed completely when fully grown and in flower.

Bulbs

Plant spring bedding plants before bulbs when they are to be grown together. Fit the bulbs into the gaps between the bedding plants, keeping to a regular pattern.

Low effort gardening

Gardening is no pursuit for those who are lazy. However, when there is little time or the gardener is in some way disabled, the garden must be planned so that work is kept to a minimum. Many routine tasks can be avoided by careful planning and by the sensible use of the appropriate plants in the right places. For example, do not have intricately shaped beds in the lawn, for they will require edging and will complicate mowing. Do not grow plants that require too much pruning, staking and dead-heading. Instead, plan borders with a mixture of shrubs and those herbaceous perennials that can grow without support, or with shrubs alone. Shrubs will be easier to manage, particularly if those requiring little care, except occasional light pruning, are chosen. The most time-consuming, though necessary, tasks in most gardens are weeding, mowing and trimming hedges. The following techniques will be effective in reducing the workload in these areas.

Ground cover planting Spreading and creeping perennial plants, and some carpeting shrubs, can be used to cover the ground and thus suppress weed growth. Evergreens will be of interest all the year round, but herbaceous ground cover plants such as hostas, epimediums and some geraniums are useful, though are only effective in spring and summer when their foliage is present. It will be necessary to weed among the plants in the early stages until they are large and vigorous enough to smother the weeds, but after this they require relatively little maintenance.

Ground cover can also be used to save mowing. Plants such as ivy provide good cover on steep banks, which are very difficult to mow. For full details on suitable plants, planting distances and maintenance, see a companion volume in this series, *Lawns, Weeds and Ground Cover*.

Mulching A 3-4in (8-10cm) thick mulch applied in spring to moist soil around all garden plants will help to suppress weed growth and retain soil moisture in dry seasons. The mulch can be of well-rotted manure, compost, leaf-mould, spent hops, mushroom

Mulching

Weeds

Hedges

Spread a 3-4 in (8-10cm) layer of organic material on the soil around plants.

Use a paint-on formulation of glyphosate to control perennial weeds.

Spray a growth retardant chemical on hedges to slow growth of terminal shoots.

compost or pulverized bark. Fork the mulch into the soil the following autumn.

Weedkillers Where mulching is not practicable, material is difficult to obtain or not an effective weed control, dichlobenil, as a granular formulation, can be applied in late winter around well-established roses, bush fruits, most ornamental shrubs and most hedge plants. This will give residual control of annual weeds at germination stage for several months, kill existing annuals and suppress some established perennial weeds. Paint-on formulations of glyphosate can be used to control perennial weeds.

Hard surfaces Another solution to the problem of mowing is to choose a surface that needs no maintenance. Natural or reconstituted stone slabs, granite setts and concrete can be used to make patios and terraces; cobbles and raked gravel are less practical to walk on, but are nevertheless attractive alternatives. Plants can be grown in gaps between patio slabs.

All such surfaces need no more than a rake or a sweep to keep them tidy, and any weed growth through or between them can be prevented with a routine early-spring application of a weedkiller specially formulated for use on paths.

Hedges Much of the work involved in maintaining hedges can be avoided by growing informal hedges; these only need sufficient pruning to stop them becoming straggly and overgrown. However, if formal hedges are required, choose plants that only need trimming once or twice a year, such as yew, and avoid those such as *Lonerica nitida* that require clipping every 4-6 weeks during the summer to keep them tidy.

Alternatively, where the hedge is accessible and is not fronted by a dense display of border plants, it can be treated with a chemical growth retardant. This slows down the growth of terminal shoots, while at the same time encouraging the sideshoots to grow and thicken up the hedge. It is sprayed on after trimming in spring.

RAISED BEDS

Raised beds are particularly useful and labour-saving for the elderly and infirm who are unable to bend down, and for gardeners in wheelchairs.

Construct beds from brick, stone or wooden railway sleepers. The sides of each bed should be 18-24in (45-60cm) high, and it should be no wider than 3ft (90cm) if the bed has access on only one side; 6ft (1.8m) if it is accessible from both sides. Where wheelchairs are to be used ensure all paths are smooth and wide enough. Fill the bed with a 9in (23cm) layer of rubble for drainage, followed by a layer of old turves grass-side down. Fill the remainder of the bed with good garden soil or compost.

Living in the garden

Most gardeners nowadays look upon their plots as places of relaxation as well as hard work, with the result that more leisure time is spent outdoors. Purpose-made garden furniture, or built-in seats, can add to the enjoyment given by the garden.

Furniture

Choose furniture which is good to look at, comfortable, and designed for outdoor use. Chairs, tables and sun loungers are available in a variety of materials such as aluminium alloy, cast iron, reconstituted stone, teak, western red cedar and plastic. Plastic-coated metal furniture can stand outside in all weathers.

Choose a design that fits in with the garden and the house and which is not too large for the lawn or patio on which it is positioned.

Robust timber benches or seats can remain outdoors all the year round, provided they are treated with timber preservative every two or three years. Other furniture may have to be brought under cover during the winter months. Check that it can be easily stored and is light enough to carry easily. Folding tables and chairs are less of a problem to store than large sunloungers with padded cushions. Whatever design is chosen check that the legs of tables and chairs are simple and solid so that they neither wobble nor sink into the turf. When patios, terraces and other sitting areas are constructed, seats can be built into brick or stone walls surrounding them. The framework will be present all the year round and fitted cushions can be slotted into place when the seating is in use.

Good garden furniture may be expensive to purchase initially, but it will last far longer and be more comfortable than cheaper, flimsier designs.

Barbecues

Cooking food outdoors has a universal charm, and the advent of the charcoal-fuelled barbecue has made cooking in the garden easier and cleaner. Wood fires are rarely suitable for cooking except in the largest of gardens.

A barbecue at its simplest is merely a metal grid supported on bricks above a charcoal fire. Leave gaps between the bricks to allow a draught, and place a second layer of bricks

on the grid to act as a windshield. Site the barbecue where smoke will not cause annoyance, either to the garden's occupants or to neighbours. Study the garden's microclimate and the prevailing summer winds to find a location that allows smoke to blow away. Do not put the barbecue in a windy position. Take care to keep all barbecues away from trees, fences and buildings that could be damaged by heat and smoke. Pave the area around a permanent barbecue to minimize wear on the lawn.

The basic type of purpose-made barbecue is the hibachi or firebox design which consists of a heavy cast metal "dish" in which the fire lies, and over which is held a metal grid that supports the food. Hibachis are portable and may be equipped with simple legs or a wheeled stand. The height of the grid can be adjusted on some models.

The "kettle" design typifies the more sophisticated (and expensive) barbecues. A lidded bowl (which is normally constructed of porcelain enamelled steel) contains the fire, and there are usually facilities within the lid for a rotating spit. The lid provides shelter

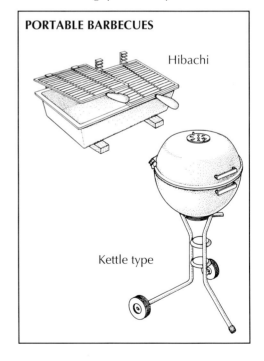

PORTABLE BARBECUES

Hibachi

Kettle type

from the wind and can be lowered to turn the barbecue into an oven.

Whichever design is chosen, make sure that the barbecue is stable and sited in a sheltered spot away from wooden buildings or furniture which could be ignited by flying sparks. Bear in mind the need to store barbecues during winter. Large models can be cumbersome and hard to store.

Permanent barbecues Permanent barbecues can, like seats, be built into patios and sitting areas, and cupboards built next to them make useful storage boxes for charcoal and other accessories. The design and materials of a built-in barbecue should blend with the garden surroundings. If patios and walls are of brick, build the sides and back of the barbecue in the same brick. If stone is the predominant material, use stone or concrete in a complementary colour.

If building a brick barbecue, it is worth adding bays beside it for charcoal and a hard surface at the same level for standing cooking utensils. Line the back and sides of the barbecue with firebricks if possible, and use a one-piece metal grid that can be lifted off the angle iron supports for easy cleaning.

Fuel Barbecues are fuelled with lumpwood charcoal or charcoal briquets. These can be obtained from hardware stores and garden centres. The charcoal is easily ignited with firelighters, though several types of liquid and solid "fire starters" are offered for sale. Do not use petrol, oil or grease, which are dangerous. When using firelighters allow them to burn away before cooking, or they will taint the food. Gas-fuelled barbecues are available, using bottled gas.

The firebox can be lined with aluminium foil to ease cleaning and reflect heat. Put out the fire by covering it with the extinguishing tray, if the barbecue has one, or by damping it with old charcoal, sand or with a mist spray. If the coals are dampened, dry them for reuse. Do not pour water on to the barbecue, for it may crack stone or concrete, or weaken metal parts.

Portable barbecues should be thoroughly cleaned and stored in a dry place when not in use. The metal parts of brick-built barbecues should be cleaned then brought under cover in winter to reduce corrosion.

Building a barbecue

  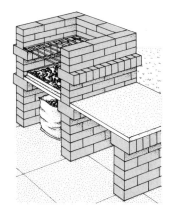

1 On an existing hard surface, lay five courses of fire-proof bricks and top with a layer of bricks on edge.

2 Add three further courses of bricks on one side of the 'E' shape only. Top with another course of bricks on edge to support the grill.

3 Lay three further courses of bricks to form a windbreak. Lay a metal grid on the shelf. Lay a slab on the other side.

Children in the garden

The gardener whose plot is used by children must take certain precautions to ensure their safety, and he may also wish to provide facilities and equipment for them.

Safety

A number of garden features which provide enjoyment for adults may be potentially lethal to children. Ponds, streams and swimming pools are all dangerous, for a small child can drown in just a few inches of water. Either fence off the water, do away with it altogether or be prepared to give constant close supervision to children in the garden. Even with supervision some kind of barrier is desirable to prevent them falling in. Ideally, surround a swimming pool area with a wall or fence and a gate that locks.

Greenhouses are another danger area. Children may break the glass, cutting themselves and of course damaging the greenhouse. The designs which use smaller panes of glass, while they are no safer where children are concerned, are certainly cheaper to repair than the Dutch light type of house which has larger panes. Polythene houses may be less satisfactory than the glass types when it comes to plant cultivation, but they are certainly much safer.

Check that garden walls, fences and hedges are sound and impenetrable so that children are kept in. Thorny shrubs planted in close rows will often deter small children from reaching parts of the garden from which they are best excluded, such as the vegetable patch and collections of prized pot plants.

Avoid constructing steep slopes in gardens used by children, and put gates at the top of steps to prevent accidents. Paths are best constructed in curves so that safe progress on tricycles and wheeled toys is possible.

Play equipment

The list of garden play equipment is long and varied. Climbing frames, see-saws, slides, paddling pools (closely supervised) and other constructions should all be sited on the lawn, rather than on hard surfaces, and firmly anchored to the ground to ensure stability.

Sandpits are popular with small children but they should be properly sited and constructed for convenience and enjoyment.

Build them within view of the house and away from trees that will shed their leaves on to the sand in autumn. The sides should be 12-18in (30-45cm) deep and made from flagstones to keep the sand firmly within the pit and free of soil. The base should be well drained. Ram a 6in (15cm) layer of hardcore into the bottom and top this with washed pea shingle before 6-9in (15-23cm) of sand is poured in. Use washed river sand (not builders' sand which contains impurities and stains clothing). Damp down the sand in dry weather and provide a netted frame for the top to keep out dogs and cats when the pit is not being used.

Swings may be purchased in one piece (consisting of a frame, ropes and a seat) or made at home and slung from a *sturdy* tree branch. Use synthetic nylon rope and a wooden disc, a plastic seat or an old car tyre. Earth or turf is safer than a concrete or flagged strip under the swing, even though turf may become badly worn.

Make it clear to children where they should and should not go in the garden and explain to them why. Co-operation will save both accidents and plants.

MAKING A SWING

For a timber seat use 1½in (3.75cm) thick board, 2ft (60cm) long and 9in (23cm) wide. Drill holes 1½in (3.75cm) from the ends. Pass strong, sound ropes through the holes, knotting them securely on the underside. Fix the other ends and check for level.

Constructing a sandpit

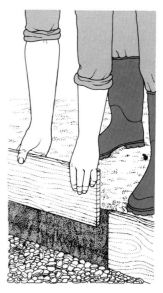

1 Dig a pit 12-18in (30-45cm) deep in view of the house and away from trees.

2 Ram a 6in (15cm) layer of hardcore into the bottom of the pit to allow drainage.

3 Line the sides of the pit, preferably with wooden boards, though flagstones or slabs may be used.

4 Cover the hardcore with a layer of washed pea shingle.

5 Pour in a 6-9in (15-23cm) layer of washed river sand and spread evenly. Do not use builders' sand.

6 Cover the pit when not in use with a netted frame which will keep out dogs and cats.

Games

Gardens which possess a good area of reasonably level lawn can be used for a variety of sports, and provided that the turf is kept in good condition, enjoyable games of croquet, badminton and putting are possible.

Croquet

A standard croquet lawn measures 35 yards by 28 yards (31.5 metres by 25.2 metres) and should be laid out as shown in the diagram right. Those who approach the game at a less than wholly dedicated level may arrange the pegs and hoops in the pattern shown but closer together if space is limited.

The finer lawn seed mixtures should be selected for croquet lawns so that the ball can move rapidly. The surface should be firm (though not rock hard) and as level as possible. Close mowing will be necessary to leave the grass at a height of around ⅜in (1cm) so that the game is fast.

During autumn and spring the full programme of scarification, aeration and top-dressing should be carried out to keep the turf in good condition, and regular mowing and irrigation will be needed through the summer.

Badminton

Although badminton should strictly be conducted on a wooden-floored indoor court, it is often played in the garden to more flexible rules than those which are laid down by official bodies. The quality of the turf is relatively unimportant for at no time is the shuttle played from its surface. A hard-wearing lawn seed mixture (possibly one containing ryegrass) should be used when sowing a lawn with outdoor badminton in mind. The surface should be level to provide a firm grip for the feet.

The diagram shows the official dimensions of doubles and singles badminton courts, though frequently in garden badminton the net is the only indication of the court's position. The net should be supported on posts 5ft 1in (1.5m) high and the top edge should be 5ft (1.5m) from the ground in the centre. The depth of the net should be 2ft 6in (75cm).

Putting

Even the smallest lawn can be used for putting, both as a practice ground for golfers anxious to improve their putting and for family amusement. A fine, firm, close-mown lawn is best and it should be mown and cared for in the same way as a croquet lawn.

The hole or holes may be taken out with a special auger. They should be 4¼in (10.5cm) in diameter and 10in (25cm) deep. Cylindrical steel linings (hole cups) and flags are available from sports accessory suppliers. If the game is to be played solely for family amusement then a 4in (10cm) plastic flower pot may be sunk into the lawn and used as the hole. Take care that the rim of the pot or the hole is 1in (2.5cm) below the surface to allow for safe mowing and minimum ball impedance.

Other games such as boules and quoits can easily be played on any reasonably level lawn; though where bowls and tennis are concerned it is advisable that a proper green or court be constructed and maintained.

FLOWER POT GOLF

Elementary practice in putting can be had if a 4in (10cm) plastic flower pot is sunk into the lawn as a golf hole. Choose a spot giving a 20ft (6m) "putt" but not too close to the edge of the lawn. Sink the pot in a hole cut with a sharp knife and excavated with a trowel. Place a 2in (5cm) layer of gravel in the bottom.

Badminton

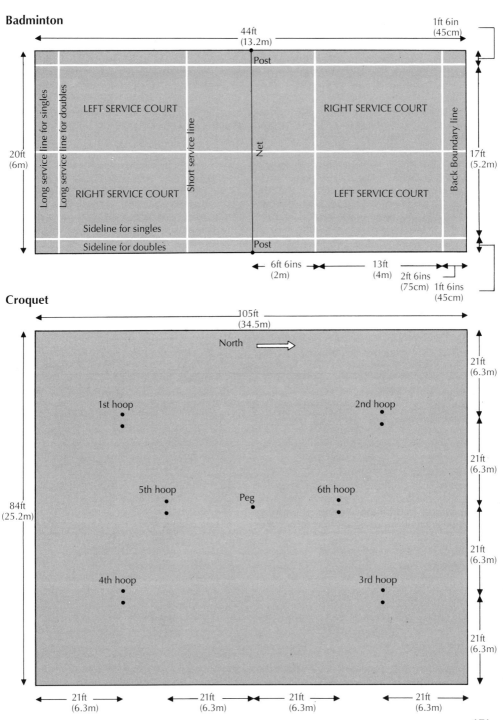

Croquet

Pets and wildlife

With the continued destruction of hedgerows and woodland the role of gardeners in providing habitats and food sources for a wide variety of wildlife becomes increasingly important. By growing the right plants and creating certain garden features they can attract the maximum number of species of birds, insects and animals to the garden.

Pond life
The smallest garden pool in rural or suburban areas will soon be colonized by insects such as pond skaters and water boatmen, damsel flies and dragonflies. Frogs, toads and newts will return year after year to spawn and increase their numbers. Do not underestimate the value of frogs and toads in keeping down slugs and other garden pests.

Ensure that any necessary pond clearing takes place before the spring spawning period of the amphibians, and that clumps of moisture-living flag irises and rushes are present to provide them and the dragonflies with cover and egg-laying sites. For full details of pond care see pages 100-107.

Birds
Bullfinches, sparrows, pigeons and occasionally blackbirds can be garden pests when they devour fruit tree buds, soft fruits, pea pods, and brassica leaves, but by far the majority of birds in the garden are beneficial and delight-

---

PLANTS THAT ATTRACT WILDLIFE

Some plants visited by bees

Acer	Daphne	Malus
Aesculus	Delphinium	Malva
Allium	Deutzia	Nemophila
Althaea	Doronicum	Nepeta
Alyssum	Echinacea	Oenothera
Anchusa	Echinops	Phacelia
Anemone	Erica	Polygonum
Arabis	Eryngium	Reseda
Aster	Eschscholzia	Rosa
Borago	Fuchsia	Rosmarinus
Buddleja	Galtonia	Rubus
Campanula	Godetia	Rudbeckia
Caryopteris	Helenium	Salix
Ceanothus	Helianthus	Salvia
Centaurea	Heliopsis	Scabiosa
Clarkia	Hyssopus	Sedum
Clematis	Inula	Senecio
Coreopsis	Lavandula	Sidalcea
Cosmos	Limnanthes	Thymus
Crataegus	Lobularia	Tilia
Crocus	Lupinus	Verbascum
Dahlia	Lythrum	Wisteria

Some plants enjoyed by birds
For food

		For cover	
Berberis	Pinus	Berberis	
Cotoneaster	Pyracantha	Crataegus	
Hedera	Rosa	Hedera	
Ilex	Sambucus	Ilex	
Mahonia	Sorbus	Lonicera	
Malus	Taxus	Wisteria	

Some food plants for butterfly larvae
Brassicas
Cirsium (spear thistle)
Humulus (hop)
Lonicera (honeysuckle)
Rhamnus (buckthorn)
Rumex (dock)
Salix (willow)
Ulmus (elm)
Uncut grasses
Urtica (stinging nettle)

Some plants which attract butterflies

Agrostemma	Hesperis
Alyssum	Iberis
Anthemis	Lavandula
Armeria	Lavatera
Aster	Liatris
Aubrieta	Lobularia
Buddleja	Lonicera
Caryopteris	Lunaria
Centranthus	Melissa
Chrysanthemum	Mentha
Coreopsis	Nepeta
Dianthus	Phlox
Echinacea	Reseda
Echinops	Scabiosa
Erigeron	Sedum
Eryngium	Senecio
Hebe	Solidago
Helenium	Syringa
Heliopsis	Tagetes

ful to watch. Starlings can help rid lawns of leatherjackets and worms, and bluetits will help to keep down aphids on roses and fruit trees.

Hang fat, suet and nut feeders among fruit trees and bushes and roses to encourage the tits, and provide other garden birds with wild bird food or kitchen scraps from December to February – longer if there is snow on the ground. Place food where cats, dogs and other animals cannot reach either it or the birds which come to feed. A bird table, which can be simply made from a piece of plywood and a post, is the best solution. Site the table in an open area away from places where cats may hide, but in view of the house windows.

Specially designed boxes fastened to trees, fences and house walls will provide nesting sites. The Royal Society for the Protection of Birds, at The Lodge, Sandy, Beds. SG19 2DL, will offer advice on the correct size and siting of nest boxes for different species.

The lists opposite show plants which will provide birds either with cover or food.

Butterflies and bees

Colourful butterflies can be encouraged to visit the garden if plenty of nectar-rich plants are cultivated. Bear in mind that the plants which the adults frequent are not the plants on which the eggs are laid and which support the larvae. The lists show plants that may be cultivated for both purposes.

Bees visit every garden, but beekeepers anxious to provide ample supplies of pollen and nectar right through the year may wish to increase their stocks of major food plants. The list shows suitable genera. It should be remembered that double flowers are often useless to bees, the stamens usually having been replaced with extra petals.

Animal pests

Moles can cause severe damage to lawns. They can be controlled by the use of traps or chemicals. For full details, see the companion volume in this series, *Lawns, Weeds and Ground Cover*. In rural districts, strong, efficient fences will be necessary to keep farm animals out. Wild animals such as deer may cause trouble in some areas, grazing and stripping bark from trees and shrubs.

PETS IN THE GARDEN

Most pets cause few problems in the garden and there are ways in which damage can be minimized if dogs and cats are particularly and repeatedly destructive. Dogs can be disciplined to keep off the garden, or confined to the house if they are correctly exercised during the day. Thorny barriers will effectively discourage their entry into forbidden parts of the garden. Cats, especially other people's cats, are more difficult to control. Fruit cages constructed of nylon netting will usually exclude them, but few other barriers are effective, and disciplining is usually impossible. Dogs, cats, birds and rabbits can sometimes be kept away from plants by the use of chemical deterrents containing aluminium ammonium sulphate. The powder is mixed with water and the solution applied to the plants or the ground. It will last for up to six weeks, though for a shorter time in rainy weather. On lawns bitch urine may cause severe scorching. Avoid letting the animal loose on the grass (especially when she is in season) and if accidents do happen soak the area immediately with a hose pipe.

Soak any areas vulnerable to damage by pets with a diluted solution of a chemical animal deterrent.

Storing and preserving 1

Storing the harvest surplus of fruits and vegetables for the winter months can be a source of great satisfaction to the gardener. The success of the operation depends basically on selecting produce in the best possible condition and using the method of storing or preserving most suitable to the crop. Where natural storage methods are not suitable, produce can be safely processed at home by bottling, freezing, drying or pickling.

Traditional fruit storage
Hard fruit, such as apples, pears and quinces, store well provided that they are picked and handled with care. Pick the fruit by hand on a dry day. The fruit is ripe when it comes away from the spur easily and with the stalk intact. Avoid bruising which allows rot fungi to enter the fruit. Mid-season varieties will keep for one to two months; late varieties, which ripen from September onwards, will keep for three to eight months. Never store mid-season and late varieties together.

Preparing fruit for storage Keep the fruit cool in a cellar or similar storehouse for one or two weeks after picking. This helps to cut down condensation and susceptibility to disease. Wrap apples in oiled or waxed paper to extend their storage life. Or, in the case of cooking apples, use squares of newspaper. Place an apple with the stalk upwards in the centre of the paper square, fold the bottom point to the middle, then fold in the two side points, and finally fold down the fourth point. Place with the folded side down in the storage box or tray. Store pears unwrapped, in single layers on trays with the stalk uppermost. Store different types of fruit separately.

Storage containers Wooden orchard boxes with slatted sides and corner posts are the traditional storage containers, and can be stacked without harming the fruit. Many gardeners now use fibre or polystyrene moulded trays. Fruit should not be wrapped when stored in this type of tray. Instead, lay a thin sheet of polythene over the fruit to delay shrivelling. Another successful method uses clear polythene bags in which no more than 4-5lb (1.8-2.3kg) of fruit should be stored. Ensure that air can circulate by cutting off the bottom

Apples and pears should be picked when the fruit leaves the spur readily. Leave the stalks on the fruit.

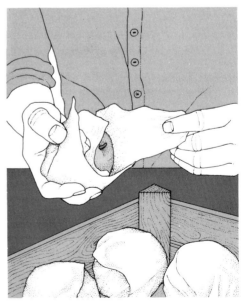

Wrap apples in oiled or waxed paper. Fold one point to the middle, fold the two side points in, then fold in the final point.

two corners of the bag. Store at the coolest temperature possible but not below 3°C (37°F).

Storehouse Gardeners who expect a regular surplus each year may find it worth while to build a special storehouse. To store small amounts of produce, however, all that is needed is a cool cellar, attic, garden shed, garage, or a space under the stairs. Aim for an airy place, away from light. An even temperature of 3°-4°C (37°-40°F) is ideal, but this cannot be achieved without refrigeration equipment. Next best is a temperature of about 4°-7° (40°-45°F) during the winter months.

Storehouse hygiene

Storage shelves should be scrubbed each season before they are used, to prevent fungus spores from decaying the new fruit. The floor of the storehouse should also be cleaned each year. If there is a soil floor, lay down fine-mesh wire netting about 1ft (30cm) below soil level to protect from rats and mice. Ventilation and humidity are important to prevent fruit from rotting or shrivelling. Fit ventilators covered with wire mesh at each end of the storehouse. Damp down the floor from time to time to maintain a humid atmosphere.

Storing vegetables

The simplest way to store hardy vegetables such as the root crops is in the ground for use as needed. Obvious dangers of this method are frost and pests. To protect against these, store about half the crop in a clamp.

Making a clamp Spread a 1-2in (2.5-5cm) layer of straw on the ground, ideally as near to the kitchen as possible, and on it carefully pile the vegetables to be stored, which should be dry, in the shape of a pyramid. Cover the pyramid with a further 2in (5cm) layer of straw and seal this in with a 1-2in (2.5-5cm) layer of earth top and sides. Carefully tamp down the earth with the back of a spade. Let some air into the clamp by inserting a few hollow canes into the earth layer. Store only undamaged vegetables in this way, as damaged vegetables spread rot.

Some gardeners make sure that the vegetables are kept from touching each other in the clamp because with this method one

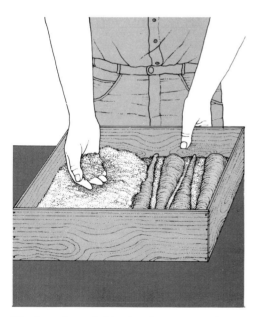

Stack root vegetables in a box or barrel with sand, peat or vermiculite between each one.

Before freezing vegetables, lower them into boiling water to blanch them. Cool them in ice-cold water.

Storing and preserving 2

diseased vegetable would soon cause the rest to rot. An improved kind of clamp involves storing the vegetables in layers, with straw between the layers, so that a layer at a time may be extracted. Alternatively, the whole crop may be stored in a container such as a box or barrel in which the vegetables are stacked individually with sand, peat or vermiculite between each one. The stored vegetables will keep so long as they are dry and in the dark.

Freezing fruit and vegetables
Freezing is one of the best methods to store foods and keep their fresh taste and nutritional value. Freeze only firm, ripe fruit and fresh, young vegetables. Fruit is usually frozen either in dry sugar or in a syrup. Pears are not suitable for freezing and strawberries tend to lose flavour when preserved in this manner. Some vegetables must be blanched before freezing. Lower them into boiling water and leave for the required time (this will vary for each vegetable). Remove and cool the vegetables in ice-cold water. Pat dry with a cloth and either open-freeze by spreading

the vegetables on trays, or pack in special air- and moisture-tight bags or boxes. Label with a description of contents and the date. Keep an inventory of the freezer store. Each kind of food has its own freezer "life". Freezing should take place as rapidly as possible. Ideally, the freezer should run at −21°C (−6°F).

Bottling and preserving
Bottling was the most common method of preserving before the advent of the home freezer. Fruit is packed into special bottling jars, a syrup is added, the jars are sterilized in a large saucepan or pressure-cooker, and then sealed. Vegetables, however, are non-acid foods and as such do not contain enough acid to stop bacterial action. Instructions for processing must be carefully carried out because badly preserved non-acid foods may be dangerous. To bottle vegetables, clean them thoroughly and pack in jars with a 2 per cent salt solution. A temperature of at least 115°C (240°F) is essential for safe processing. This can only be achieved with a pressure

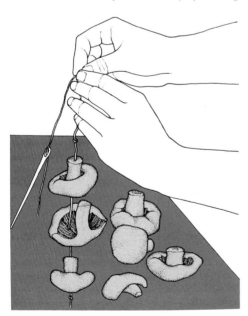

Dry mushrooms by threading them on to a string or twig. Place them in a cool oven, in an airing cupboard or the sun until crisp.

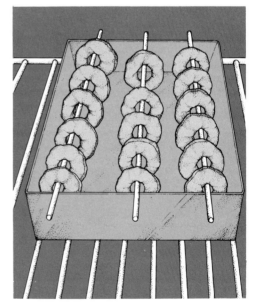

Cut apples, plums and pears into rings, suspend them on sticks or place them on a rack, and dry them in a cool oven.

cooker using a medium (10lb [4.5kg]) pressure. Small bottle jars should be used. Blanch all vegetables before packing them into jars. Jars of fruit and vegetables should be left to cool overnight. Check that a vacuum has formed by removing the screw rings and lifting up each bottle by its lid. If the lid stays on, the seal is good and the food can be stored. Fruit may be re-processed if the seal fails the first time but do not re-process vegetables. Examine each jar of bottled vegetables before serving and discard without tasting any whose quality appears suspicious.

Fruit preserves Fruit can also be turned into jams, jellies, fruit butters, cheeses and curds, juices and syrups, or may be crystallized.

Pickling Fruits and vegetables are also preserved in vinegar as pickles. Vinegar and salt corrode certain metals so make sure that none of the pickling equipment is made from iron, copper or brass. If possible, use a stainless steel saucepan and a plastic or earthenware bowl. Jars should have plastic tops. For best results use block salt for the brine and high strength pickling vinegar.

Drying fruit, vegetables and herbs

Drying is one of the oldest and simplest ways of preserving food. The best fruits for drying are apples, plums and pears, all cut into rings. They can be dried in the sun but an oven with its heat set to not more than gas ¼ or 70°C (150°F) is more reliable. Drying will take up to six hours in the oven and the fruit will take 12 hours to cool at room temperature. Pack in layers between waxed paper and store in a cardboard box in a cool, dry place.

Mushrooms are excellent for drying. Thread them on a fine string or on a twig and dry them in a cool oven (gas ¼ or 70°C [150°F]) in an airing cupboard or in the sun until they are crisp. When they are cool, pack them tightly in jars with cork stoppers.

Herbs that are to be dried should be picked just before they flower and preferably on a dry day. Tie them in bundles and hang to dry in a garden shed or a ventilated cupboard.

Onions, garlic and shallots should be dried off in the sun. Leave enough stem so that they may be strung. Hang the strings in a cool but frost-free place.

Pack dried fruit in layers between waxed paper and store in a cardboard box in a cool, dry place.

String onions by pleating them on to a length of cord or rope. Leave adequate stem on the onions to allow plaiting.

The year in the garden 1

Vegetables

Fruit

JANUARY

Sow early radishes under cloches and cold frames until early February. Order seeds, plan and clear vegetable garden. Inspect stored crops and remove any decaying vegetables. Sow peas in sheltered districts. Sow broad beans for an early crop.

Spray trees and bushes with tar-oil if not done in December. Begin regular checks for canker on apple and pear trees, treat if necessary. Plant new trees, bushes and vines in suitable conditions. Check stakes and ties. Check fruit in store and remove any that are diseased or rotten. Apply sulphate of potash to strawberries, raspberries, apples and pears; nitro-chalk to apricots; balanced fertilizer to cobnuts and filberts. Cover strawberry plants with cloches or polythene tunnels at any time until mid-March for early crop. Take black currant cuttings. Spray peaches and nectarines against leaf curl.

FEBRUARY

Sow borage; red cabbage (until March); broad beans (until April); summer cabbage (until May); salad onions (until June). Sow early bunching turnips; carrots, parsnips and early beetroot (until March); bulb onions (until April) under cloches and frames.
Plant rhubarb crowns; shallots, garlic and Jerusalem artichokes (until March).
Top-dress over-wintered crops such as onions, broad beans, spring cabbage and asparagus when growth begins. Chit seed potatoes and rub the sprouts off stored potatoes. Rake in a balanced, general fertilizer two weeks before sowing early crops.

In suitable conditions continue planting trees and bushes or store in frost-free places. Treat canker on apples and pears. Protect blossom on fan-trained trees from frost with hessian or bird netting. Mulch sweet and Duke cherries and figs. Spray peaches and nectarines against leaf curl two weeks after January application. Cover early fruiting strawberries with cloches. Feed trees and bushes.

MARCH

Sow chives, thyme, onions; Brussels sprouts (until early April); summer cauliflower, leeks, early beetroot, asparagus, summer corn salad (until April); summer spinach (until May); peas (until June); autumn and summer lettuce successively (until early August); endive and carrots (until August), celery under cloches and cold frames. Plant seakale, horseradish, onion sets (until early April); watercress, globe artichokes and early potatoes (until April). Hoe between over-wintered and perennial crops. Harvest seakale (late March to early April); turnip tops (until April); rhubarb (until July); radishes (until October).

Finish planting when soil conditions permit, especially trees and bushes lifted by frost. Feed trees and bushes established in cultivated soil. Spray apples, cherries, peaches, nectarines, pears, plums and damsons where pests and diseases are known to be troublesome. Train new shoots of blackberries and loganberries on to wires. Protect flowers on wall-trained peaches and nectarines and pollinate artificially if insects are scarce. Plant raspberries and strawberries. Mulch blackberries, raspberries, black currants, vines and newly planted apple and pear trees.

Timing
The timings given in the chart below are for a reasonably sheltered garden in the southern half of England.
Further north, or in the favoured areas of the south-west, timings can be earlier or later. Altitude will also affect the start and finish of the growing season.

Greenhouse
The plants mentioned are suitable for a cold greenhouse. Information on heated greenhouses can be found in *Growing under Glass* in this series.
Pruning
The category "General maintenance" includes pruning.

Lawns

Remove any accumulations of leaves from the lawn.
Check drains if water is standing on the surface for any length of time after rain, and drain persistently wet sites. Overhaul the mower and other lawn tools before the start of the new season.
Continue aeration treatment. Lay turves in favourable weather.

Greenhouse

Plan the year's crops and order seeds and seedlings. Ventilate the greenhouse on sunny days.
Sow onions for transplanting. Sow early radishes in soil borders or peat pots.
Bring in plunged bulbs to flower in the greenhouse (*Babiana, Chionodoxa, Crocus, Narcissus, Fritillaria, Iris, Leucojum, Ornithogalum.*
Bulbs which have finished flowering can be planted out into frames. Sow lily seed. Begin sequence of chrysanthemum cuttings later in the month.

General maintenance

Clean garden machinery and arrange for servicing and sharpening of mowers and other tools. Knock snow from trees and shrubs and garden structures if necessary. Clean and disinfect greenhouse equipment such as pots and seed trays. Clear fallen leaves from rock gardens and borders. Do remaining digging. Prune newly planted cane fruits, bush fruits, vines and apples and pears (until March). Cut back summer-pruned laterals on red and white currants and gooseberry cordons (until March). Inspect stored crops and remove anything that is decaying.

From February check regularly for signs of worm activity or unhealthy turf following mild spells. Disperse worm casts regularly on dry days. Complete all major turfing work by the end of the month. Apply a mosskiller in late February if weather is settled; if still cold leave until March. Top-dress lightly if necessary. Towards the end of the month begin preparations for spring sowing if soil conditions and weather are suitable.
On established lawns continue aeration and scarify in dry conditions.

Ventilate as necessary. Water sparingly.
Sow lettuce, early bunching turnips, carrots, parsnips and early beetroot (until March), bulb onions (until April). Sow tomatoes in heat later in the month.
Bring potted strawberries in to crop in late spring.
Bring in remaining plunged bulbs. Pot on and divide ferns if necessary. Pot on over-wintered coleus, fuchsias and pelargoniums.
Sow and place in a propagating case: abutilons, tuberous and fibrous begonias, celosias, coleus, gloxinias, *Streptocarpus*.
Pot on annuals sown in autumn. Re-pot evergreen azaleas.

Prune hedges, especially if overgrown, towards the end of the month. Continue to plant ornamental and fruit trees, shrubs and bushes during mild, dry weather. Order seeds and plan vegetable plots and flower borders. Prune bush, standard and half-standard plums, gages and damsons and figs (until early March); young fan-trained sweet and Duke cherries, peaches and nectarines, apricots, plums and figs (until March); brutted laterals on established cobnuts and filberts, passion fruit. Cut back the tips of summer-fruiting raspberries. Cut down newly planted raspberry canes if not pruned on planting.

On established lawns re-seed worn areas, and realign ragged edges. Continue aeration. In southern Britain apply spring fertilizer, in late March if the weather is mild and settled. Cut new lawns when the grass is 2in (5cm) high with blade set high. Begin to mow established lawns. Roll before mowing if turf has been lifted by frost.
Treat against worms if necessary. Apply selective weedkillers when grass is growing actively.
Rake and treat seedbeds for new lawns, apply pre-seeding fertilizer. Choose seed mixture, and sow at 1-2oz (28-55g) per square yard (metre). Give the first mowing when the grass is 2in (5cm) high.

Sow lettuce, celery, carrots, mustard and cress.
Sow in heat: aubergines, sweet peppers, dwarf French beans, tomatoes if not sown in February. Prick out lettuce seedlings. Pot out late in month.
Sow for transplanting: broad beans, runner beans, brassicas, leeks, celery, peas, sweetcorn, chives, thyme.
Continue to bring in pot strawberries.
Sow half-hardy annuals and alpines. Pot on over-wintered annuals. Take pelargonium and dahlia cuttings. Plant out rooted cuttings taken in winter. Pot up hippeastrum bulbs.

Begin weed control measures by the use of path-weed killers to kill annual weeds and control perennial weeds in paved areas, paths and gravel drives. Check trees and bushes for constricting ties. Combat slugs by scattering slug pellets containing methiocarb or metaldehyde among bulbs and vegetables. Prune newly planted pyramid plums and acid cherries; established bush and pyramid acid cherries and apricots. Continue to weed. Inspect over-wintered herbs regularly.

The year in the garden 2

Vegetables

Fruit

APRIL

Sow spinach beet and seakale beet, cardoons, broccoli, cauliflower and winter cabbage (including savoys); leaf lettuce successively (until mid-May); kale (until May).
Sow dwarf French beans, sweetcorn and celeriac under cloches and cold frames. Plant second early and main crop potatoes, asparagus crowns; red cabbage and summer cabbage (until May).
Stake peas. Thin spinach. Clear winter brassica debris. Thin summer lettuce (until mid-August). Apply fertilizer to potatoes. Prepare celery trenches at the end of the month. Harvest early turnips, spring lettuce, asparagus and spring cabbage (until June) salad onions (until July).

Prepare the planting site for Cape gooseberries. De-blossom summer-fruiting strawberries in their first year if planted in late autumn or early spring. Apply a balanced fertilizer to citrus fruits. Begin regular liquid feeding of plants in containers. Ventilate strawberries and uncover plants in flower on sunny days to allow access for pollinating insects. Control any pests on leaves and fruitlets. Protect wall trees and soft fruit bushes against frost when in bloom. Plant late-flowering strawberries. Check tree ties and stakes for stability. Spray as necessary.

MAY

Sow sweetcorn, asparagus peas, basil, sweet marjoram, chicory, soya beans, marrows, courgettes, pumpkins and squashes; ridge cucumbers (until early June); runner beans, swedes, main crop beetroot (until June). Plant Florence fennel, sweetcorn, New Zealand spinach, Brussels sprouts, leeks, celery, celeriac (until June). Earth up early potatoes (until June) and Jerusalem artichokes. Prepare the ground for leeks. Stake broad beans. Harvest lettuce sown previous August/September; leaf lettuce (late May onwards); early carrots and bunching turnips (May onwards); early beetroot (until July); summer spinach.

Plant out alpine strawberry seedlings by the end of May. Also plant out Cape gooseberry seedlings and protect with cloches. De-blossom newly planted two- and three-year-old trees, spring-planted runners of summer-fruiting strawberries and perpetual strawberries.
Apply liquid fertilizer to vines throughout the growing season. Water plants as necessary. Scatter slug pellets around strawberries before strawing down. Protect strawberries from birds and frosts; ventilate on sunny days. Pick early strawberries and gooseberries from late May. Spray as necessary.

JUNE

Plant marrows, courgettes, pumpkins and squashes raised in heated greenhouses (early June onwards); winter cabbage, autumn, winter and summer cauliflowers, broccoli, tomatoes, okra, sweet peppers and basil; kale (late June until August).
Pinch out the growing points of runner beans if bushy plants are required. Support climbing runner beans. Pinch out broad beans when in full flower. Earth up potatoes. Spray celery against celery fly. Stop cucumbers after 5-6 leaves. Support tomatoes. Remove the flowering shoots on rhubarb (June onwards). Hoe, water and mulch growing crops.

Plant out melon seedlings in cold frames and Cape gooseberry seedlings, outside. Watch for pests and diseases. Harvest strawberries, summer-fruiting raspberries, dessert gooseberries, sweet and Duke cherries. Water all fruits and protect from birds. Ventilate protected strawberries on sunny days. Remove protection when fruiting is finished. Peg down strawberry runners and remove those not wanted for propagation. Destroy apple and plum fruits attacked by sawfly. Train new shoots of blackberries and outdoor grapes. Spray as necessary.

Lawns

Increase the frequency of mowing according to the weather and grass growth. Continue checking at intervals for signs of unhealthy turf. Apply a spring feed in early to mid-April if not already done; a few days after feeding apply a weedkiller if necessary. Remove patches of coarse grass and re-seed. Scarify and seed in any sparsely grassed areas. Check newly turfed areas and top-dress lightly if necessary to fill joints. Apply selective weedkillers and moss compounds. Mow new lawns twice a week if necessary. Roll to firm seedlings if required.

In early May adjust the mower to the summer cutting height. Continue weedkilling; if very mossy apply a mosskiller. From May onwards irrigation may be needed in drier periods. During mid- to late May apply a light dressing of nitrogenous fertilizer. Cultivate sites for new lawns and leave rough during the summer for autumn sowing.

Continue mowing, raising blades during very dry weather. If patches of creeping weeds are troublesome lightly scarify before mowing. Continue weedkilling and irrigation as necessary. Spike the lawn to allow water to penetrate. Lightly top-dress and irrigate areas that are subjected to heavy wear. Mow regularly; scarify patches of creeping weeds and unwanted grasses before mowing. Feed lightly early in July. Apply weedkillers as necessary and water copiously in dry weather.

Greenhouse

Sow according to needs: lettuce, radish, mustard and cress, beetroot, endive, parsley. Sow sweetcorn, celeriac, dwarf French beans, cucumbers. Plant out tomatoes late in month/ early May. Harvest early radishes and lettuce, chicory, seakale and rhubarb. Complete sowing half-hardy annuals. Sow biennials for spring flowering under glass. Prick out March-sown seedlings. Begin to harden off bedding plant seedlings. Take fuchsia cuttings, pot rooted dahlias and other cuttings. Pot up tuberoses for flowering. Start feeding camellias.

Plant aubergines, sweet peppers, okra and cucumber, melons. Harvest early carrots, early bunching turnips, beetroot. Harden off bedding plants and plant out after frosts have ended. Take cuttings from regal pelargoniums. Sow *Calceolaria, Freesia, Schizanthus* for winter flowering.

Harvest lettuce, radish, endive, mustard and cress, French beans, parsley. Tie in cucumber plants. Continue to sow biennials. Pot on cyclamen seedlings. Take cuttings of pinks. Plunge azaleas outside and feed every 14 days.

General maintenance

Order seedlings for the vegetable and ornamental beds. Weed and hoe beneath hedges. Check trees and shrubs planted in autumn and winter and firm in if necessary. Hoe beds and borders. Control weeds among perennial vegetables. Prepare ground for sowing early, leave for two weeks, and hoe to control annual weed seedlings. Mulch beds with organics. Prune young pyramid plums and fan-trained mulberries. De-blossom summer-fruiting strawberries in their first year if planted in late autumn or early spring. Apply a balanced fertilizer to citrus fruits. Begin regular liquid feeding of plants in containers.

Remove suckers as necessary from roses, shrubs and fruit trees. Control pests such as aphids as they appear. Water seedlings, and water and liquid-feed established plants as necessary. Pull out any unwanted raspberry canes. Thin shoots of established fan-trained peaches and nectarines and remove misplaced shoots of wall-trained plums, damsons and cherries (until early summer). Cut back the leaders of mature apples and pears grown as cordons, espaliers and dwarf pyramids and established pyramid plums. Begin thinning gooseberries. Apply liquid fertilizer to vines.

Guard against and combat pests and diseases. Stake, pinch out and tidy herbaceous plants. Hoe beds and borders to control weeds and mulch where necessary. Water the garden in dry spells. Cut back laterals on red and white currant and gooseberry cordons and bushes (from late June to early July). Pinch out the growing points of selected shoots on established fan-trained plums and apricots (until late July). Pinch out selected growing points on cropping fan-trained figs. Cut down old canes on newly planted raspberries when new shoots appear. Hoe, water and mulch crops.

The year in the garden 3

Vegetables

Sow Chinese cabbage, red cabbage for over-wintering, leaf lettuce, rape kale, spinach beet and seakale beet; spring cabbage, main crop turnips and winter radishes (until August). Plant winter cabbage (including Savoys). Earth up Brussels sprouts if necessary. Protect cauliflower from the sun by breaking leaves over the curds. Pinch out the growing points of runner beans when they reach the top of the support system. Tie up celery plants when they are 12in (30cm) tall, then begin to earth up (repeat every three weeks). Watch for aphids, cabbage caterpillars, pea moth and slugs. Hoe regularly and water in dry weather.

Fruit

Support trees with heavy cropping branches. Check ties on trained trees are not too tight. Train in new blackberry and loganberry shoots. Pick black currants and raspberries. Tie in replacement shoots on peaches and nectarines. Protect peaches and other fruits against birds, wasps and earwigs. Tidy up strawberry beds and discard plants which have given three crops. Ventilate protected fruit on hot days. Spray as necessary.

Sow onions for over-wintering; angelica, onions for spring salads, spring lettuce, winter spinach and winter corn salad (until September). Propagate sweet bay from cuttings of ripe shoots (until September). Earth up kale and winter cauliflower. Bend down the tops of onions. Blanch cardoons (until September). Stop tomato plants when 4-5 trusses have set. Hoe between vegetable rows regularly and water the crops in dry weather.

Pick early apples and pears while under-ripe. Pick loganberries. Plant rooted strawberry runners. Protect ripening grapes with glass. Support heavily laden plum branches. Protect ripening fruit from birds. Begin regular checks of apples, pears, plums and quinces for brown rot and remove and burn infected fruits. Ventilate protected fruit on hot days. Spray stone fruits against bacterial canker in mid-August if necessary, repeating one and two months later.

Sow turnips for turnip tops, and lettuce in cloches and cold frames. Plant out spring cabbage and spring greens (mid-September to mid-October). Bend down the tops of spring-sown onions. At the end of the month cut down asparagus foliage. Remove yellowing leaves and any "blossom" sprouts from Brussels sprouts. Clear away the debris from all harvested crops. Earth up kale (until November). Cover watercress, land cress and lettuce with cloches from mid-September onwards. Store marrows, pumpkins and squashes for winter use.

Plant runners of summer-fruiting and perpetual strawberries by mid-September if possible. Plan new planting season, and order trees. Choose late-flowering varieties for frosty areas. Remove trees infected by honey fungus. Ventilate protected fruit on hot days. Check and clean storage trays and boxes and the storehouse floor. Harvest blackberries, raspberries and loganberries, plums and damsons. Spray cherries. Protect autumn-fruiting strawberries against birds and slugs and cover with cloches in cold weather.

Lawns

Mow regularly. Give final summer feed in mid- to late August, followed by a final application of weedkiller. Inspect for areas that need renovation.
Apply fertilizer dressings to sites for new lawns well into August. Sow grass seed in late August/early September during mild, damp weather.

Greenhouse

Harvest sweet peppers, lettuce, radishes, mustard and cress, parsley, tomatoes (late in month). Pinch out cucumbers, stop laterals, remove male flowers.
Take hydrangea cuttings.
Take half-ripe cuttings.

General maintenance

Take advantage of warm weather to remove plants and repair and paint greenhouses. Construct paths, steps, plant supports and erect buildings. Continue watering and feeding. Ensure that crops are picked regularly. Prune cordon, espalier and dwarf pyramid apples, pears and mulberries and pyramid plums (until September). Cut back unwanted laterals on fan-trained sweet and Duke cherries. Pinch out laterals on young fan-trained apricots. Cut out old raspberry canes after fruiting, tie in new ones and remove unwanted suckers. Watch for and control aphids, cabbage caterpillars, pea moth and slugs. Hoe and water regularly.

Raise the cutting height of the mower towards the end of the month, since the rate of growth will slow. Carry out renovation where necessary: scarify to remove matted growth or thatch, spike and top-dress, and seed-in sparse patches. Apply a lawn sand to control moss. Do not use mosskillers containing sulphate of ammonia at this time of year. With the onset of cooler, moister conditions check regularly for signs of unhealthy turf and worm activity. Continue to seed-in new lawn sites.

Sow lettuce, radishes, mustard and cress, winter endive.
Harvest lettuce, radishes, mustard and cress, tomatoes, sweet peppers, aubergines, okra, melons, cucumbers.
Sow cyclamen seeds. Take fuchsia cuttings, pot on half-ripe cuttings.

Spray as necessary against pests and diseases. Water freely when weather is dry. Take cuttings of hardy plants as required. Continue to harvest crops and plan winter storage. Cut back the pinched-out shoots on fan-trained plums (until mid-September). Cut out old fruiting laterals on established fan-trained acid cherries. After harvesting cut back old fruiting laterals on peaches and nectarines in the greenhouse. Break (brut) laterals on cobnuts and filberts and leave them hanging. Thin out congested shoots on established sweet chestnuts and walnuts. Hoe between vegetable rows regularly.

Raise the mower blades to the winter height and mow as needed. Brush to remove early morning dew and encourage rapid drying in fine weather. Spike and top-dress if not done in September. Prevent accumulation of fallen leaves because this can create conditions in which diseases may establish themselves.

Sow lettuce, radishes, mustard and cress, alpine strawberries. Plant late in month: apricots, peaches, grape vines. Harvest lettuces, parsley, radishes, mustard and cress, tomatoes, peppers, aubergines, okra, cucumber, melon.
Lift seakale roots late in month, pot up and blanch.
Sow hardy annuals for spring flowering under glass.
Pot on hardy biennials for spring flowering.
Bring in evergreen azaleas, pot-grown chrysanthemums. Plant bulbous irises and hyacinths in pots.

Before winter, check electrical installations, the condition of fences, buildings, paths and structures, and complete construction jobs. Begin to clear leaves as necessary. Do not neglect watering and pest control. Cut back pinched-out laterals on fan-trained sweet and Duke cherries. Order new bushes and trees for winter planting. Check and clean storage trays and boxes and the storehouse floor. Store marrows, pumpkins and squashes for winter use.

The year in the garden 4

Vegetables

Fruit

OCTOBER

Sow spring lettuce in cloches and cold frames. Plant rhubarb (until November). Cut down asparagus and mound up the soil in the rows. Lift chicory and rhubarb for forcing (until November). Cover winter spinach and winter corn salad with cloches for winter protection. Protect parsley with a cloche or take it indoors as a potted plant along with sweet bay, rosemary and other less hardy herbs. Clean and store canes, stakes and other supports. Examine all stored crops regularly from October onwards and remove any decaying vegetables.

Sow alpine strawberries in a cold frame or cold greenhouse. Prepare the ground for autumn planting. Order fruit trees and bushes for autumn delivery. Remove unripened figs on outdoor trees but leave embryo fruits. Re-pot or pot on fruit plants grown in containers. Tidy perpetual strawberry beds after fruiting by removing and burning old leaves and straw. Cover perpetual strawberries with cloches or polythene tunnels. Pick autumn-fruiting strawberries. Pick and store apples and pears as they mature. Spray cherries, peaches and nectarines.

NOVEMBER

Sow broad beans for over-wintering. Protect late cauliflowers from frost. In sheltered districts, complete sowings of lettuces. Trim the outer growths of globe artichokes, detach suckers from the plants, and grow on in pots in a cold frame or cold greenhouse until planting out in the following April.

Bury pots in which hardy fruit trees are growing up to their rims in an ash or sand bed. Protect tender plants such as figs (outdoors) against frost. Check supports and vines. Check that the fruit cage is closed and check its condition. Inspect stored fruit, and ripen pears at room temperature.

DECEMBER

Continue to inspect stored produce and remove any that is decaying. Protect celery and globe artichokes with straw or bracken against frost. Lift and trim swede roots for packing in boxes to produce shoots as spring greens. Clean, oil and repair garden tools. Winter digging can start now (until February). Protect bay, rosemary and marjoram from severe winter weather.

Take strawberries in pots into the greenhouse for fruit in early spring. Control weeds. Check fruit in store and remove any that are diseased or rotten. Spray all fruit trees and bushes with tar-oil winter wash when dormant. Continue planting in suitable conditions. Apply nitrogenous fertilizer to trees grown in grass.

Lawns

Remedy defective drainage and lay new drains if necessary. Treat against worms and leatherjackets if necessary. Lay turf lawns from this month onwards. Mow when 1½-2in (3.75-5cm) high. Roll seed-beds to firm seedlings if they appear loose.

Greenhouse

Sow lettuce for crops in spring.
Plant fruit trees.
Harvest lettuce, tomatoes, peppers, aubergine, okra, melon.
Continue to pot up and blanch seakale.
Bring in tender bedding perennials for over-wintering.
Repeat sowings of annuals. Prick out annuals sown in September.
Pot on biennials. Sow sweet peas.
Over-winter chrysanthemum stools and dahlia tubers.

General maintenance

Clear fallen leaves from rock gardens, lawns, beds and borders. Protect pools from leaves with a net. Check gutters and drains for blockages. Plant trees and shrubs, including hedges. After leaf-fall, if secondary growth occurs prune cordon apples and pears. Cut out old canes from blackberries and related hybrids after fruiting and tie in new ones. Greaseband apple and cherry trees against winter moth.
Examine all stored crops regularly from October onwards and remove any that are decaying.

A final mow may be necessary if the weather is mild. Do not mow in wet or frosty weather. Apply autumn fertilizer. Continue treatment against earthworms and clearing up fallen leaves. Continue laying turfs when conditions are suitable. Prepare sites for sowing new lawns next spring.

Take tender plants in containers inside the greenhouse for the winter.
Sow onions for transplanting. Box up rhubarb crowns, chicory and remaining seakale. Insulate boxes if necessary.
Bring in pots of herbs for winter supply.
Plant grape vines.
Cut back chrysanthemums to 6in (15cm) after flowering to encourage growth for cuttings.
Prick out October-sown sweet peas. Pot on annuals. Bring plunged bulbs into the greenhouse as shoots appear.

Begin to dig beds and borders. Dress with lime if required. Clear up fallen leaves. Finish planting of trees and shrubs. Continue to cut back summer-pruned laterals on red and white currant and gooseberry cordons (until March). Shorten leaders on red and white currant and gooseberry bushes (until March). Prune apple and pear espaliers and dwarf pyramids; fan-trained figs; elderberries and mulberries; quinces and medlars; established Chinese gooseberries.

Apply lime if soil tests show that it is needed. Complete leaf clearance. Continue turfing. Dig over areas to be seeded in the spring. Clean and overhaul machines and equipment.

Harvest chicory.
Bring in remaining plunged bulbs for spring flowering.
Take advantage of quiet period to do cleaning and maintenance jobs on greenhouse and equipment.

Check stored crops and remove any that are diseased or rotten. Clean, oil and repair garden tools. Protect container plants left outdoors with wrappings of straw, polythene or sacking to prevent the rootball freezing.

Information sources

Most gardeners soon find a need to consult reference sources such as books and catalogues. The very wide range of plants available, and the many different specializations into which gardening is increasingly divided, make it essential to turn to books and experts. The sources of information listed here, books, magazines and organizations, are only a start. There are thousands of books on gardening in print, and many more are published each year. They vary from the general to the extremely specialized, and from the good to the useless. New gardening books are selectively reviewed in *The Garden*, the journal of the Royal Horticultural Society, and in other periodicals.

The Encyclopaedia of which this book forms one volume is designed to cover the practical techniques of gardening. The other volumes are listed on the back page.

Other books are listed (right) in three categories: General, Plants, and Fruit and Vegetables. Many of these books contain bibliographies which cover specialist subjects in more detail. Specialist societies can recommend books on particular areas of gardening to their members.

Apart from books, the gardener can tap the experience of others by joining national and local gardening organizations. Local groups are invaluable sources of knowledge on microclimate, soils and locally successful plant varieties. Many groups operate bulk-buying systems which can save members money on the purchase of seed, compost and fertilizers.

The premier national gardening organization is the Royal Horticultural Society. The Society owns a 200-acre (80-hectare) garden at Wisley, Surrey, where trials of flowers, fruits and vegetables are carried out and where examples of many kinds of garden, such as rock, water and woodland gardens, can be seen. The RHS also organizes the annual Chelsea Flower Show, where the latest products of the horticultural industry can be viewed. Members of the RHS receive the Society's Journal, *The Garden*, which lists Society events, publishes the results of trials at Wisley, and carries articles by the RHS staff and other experts on matters of horticultural interest. Many other societies exist. Most cater for specialists in particular plants. The Northern Horticultural Society has built up a great deal of experience on gardening in the conditions in the northern part of the UK. Other national societies are listed below.

Many gardeners gain both pleasure and instruction from visits to other gardens. Many gardens are open to the public at set times during the year. They range from the great classical landscapes preserved by the National Trust and private owners to cottage gardens opened for a few hours in aid of charity.

Nurseries and garden centres often display mature plants and garden fixtures, such as fences and seats, so that potential buyers can compare varieties and types. Local authority gardens and parks often have fine examples of bedding, roses and shrubs, and those in charge of them may be able to pass on to local people knowledge of prevailing weather, soils and planting dates.

Horticultural Societies
Alpine Garden Society, E. M. Upward, The Alpine Garden Society Centre, Avonbank, Pershore, Worcs WR10 3JP

British Cactus and Succulent Society, Mr T. E. Jenkins, St Catherine's Lodge, Cranesgate Road, Whaplode St Catherine, Lincs PE12 6SR

British Fuchsia Society, R. Williams, 20 Brodawel, Llannon, Llanelli, Dyfed SA14 6BJ

Garden History Society, 5 The Knoll, Hereford HR1 1RU

Hardy Plant Society, Mrs T. King, Bank Cottage, Great Comberton, Pershore, Worcs WR10 3DP

National Chrysanthemum Society, H. B. Locke, 2 Lucas House, Craven Road, Rugby, Warwicks CV21 3HY

National Dahlia Society, Mr E. H. Collins, 19 Sunnybank, Marlow, Bucks SL7 3BL

Northern Horticultural Society, The Administrator, Harlow Carr Botanical Gardens, Crag Lane, Harrogate HG3 1QB

Royal National Rose Society, K. J. Grapes, Chiswell Green, St Albans, Herts AL2 3NR

Bibliography

General

Hawker, M. F. J. and Keenlyside, J. F., *Horticultural Machinery*, Longman, Harlow, 3rd edn, 1985

Hellyer, Arthur, *Collingridge Encyclopaedia of Gardening*, Hamlyn, London, 1982

-, *Your Garden Week by Week*, Bounty, London, 1992

Johnson, Hugh, *The Principles of Gardening*, Mitchell Beazley, London, 1979

The New Royal Horticultural Society Dictionary of Gardening, Macmillan, London, 4 vols, 1992

Reader's Digest New Illustrated Guide to Gardening, Reader's Digest, London, reprint with amendments, 1992

Reader's Digest Gardening Year, Reader's Digest, London, reprint with amendments, 1992

Plants

Beales, Peter, *Classic Roses: An Illustrated Encyclopaedia and Grower's Manual of Old Roses, Shrub Roses and Climbers*, Collins Harvill, London, 1985

-, *Twentieth-century Roses: An Illustrated Encyclopaedia and Grower's Manual of Classic Roses from the Twentieth Century*, Collins Harvill, London, 1988

Bean, W. J., *Trees and Shrubs Hardy in the British Isles*, John Murray, London, 5 vols, 8th edn, 1970-80

Brown, George A., *The Pruning of Trees, Shrubs and Conifers*, Faber, London, 1972

Evans, Alfred, *The Peat Garden and its Plants*, Dent, London, 1974

Hillier's Manual of Trees and Shrubs, David & Charles, Newton Abbot, 6th edn, 1991

Ingwersen, Will, *Alpines*, John Murray, London, 1991

Joyce, David, *Pruning and Training Plants*, Mitchell Beazley, London, 1992

Lancaster, Roy, *Trees for Your Garden*, Floraprint, Wisbech, 1980

Malins, John, *The Essential Pruning Companion*, David & Charles, Newton Abbot, 1992

Mathew, Brian, *The Larger Bulbs*, Batsford, London, 1978

-, *The Smaller Bulbs*, Batsford, revised edn, 1990

Mitchell, Alan, *Field Guide to the Trees of Britain and Northern Europe*, Collins, London, revised edn, 1992

Reader's Digest Encyclopaedia of Garden Plants and Flowers, Reader's Digest, London, reprint with amendments, 1992

The Royal Horticultural Society Gardeners' Encyclopedia of Plants and Flowers (ed. C. Brickell), Dorling Kindersley, London, 1989

Thomas, Graham Stuart, *Climbing Roses Old and New*, Dent, London, 1978

-, *The Old Shrub Roses*, Dent, London, 1979

-, *Ornamental Shrubs, Climbers and Bamboos: Excluding Roses and Rhododendrons,* John Murray, London, 1992

-, *Perennial Garden Plants*, Dent, London, 3rd edn, 1990

-, *Plants for Ground Cover*, Dent, London, revised edn, 1990

-, *Shrub Roses of Today,* Dent, London, revised edn, 1980

Titchmarsh, Alan, *Climbers and Wall Plants*, Ward Lock, London, 2nd edn, 1987

Fruit and Vegetables

Baker, Harry, *Fruit*, Mitchell Beazley, London, revised edn, 1992

Biggs, Tony, *Vegetables*, Mitchell Beazley, London, revised edn, 1992

Larkcom, Joy, *Oriental Vegetables: The Complete Guide for Garden and Kitchen,* John Murray, London, 1991

-, *Vegetables for Small Gardens,* Faber, London, 2nd edn, 1986

The Fruit Garden Displayed, Royal Horticultural Society, London, revised edn (H. Baker), 1991

The Vegetable Garden Displayed, Royal Horticultural Society, London, revised edn (Joy Larkcom), 1992

Salter, P. J. and Bleasdale, J. K. A., *Know and Grow Vegetables,* OUP, Oxford, 1982

Index 1

Index 2/Acknowledgements

The Royal Horticultural Society and the Publishers can accept no liability either for failure to control pests, diseases or weeds by any crop protection methods or for any consequences of their use. We specifically draw our readers' attention to the necessity of carefully reading and accurately following the manufacturer's instructions on any product.

Acknowledgements
Artists: Arka Cartographics Ltd, Lindsay Blow, Pamela Dowson, Will Giles, Edwina Keene, Roman Kowalczyk, Sandra Pond, Ed Roberts, Ann Savage, Lorna Turpin, John Woodcock.
The garden designs on pages 75 and 76 are by David Stevens.

Typesetting by SX Composing Ltd, Rayleigh, Essex
Origination by M&E Reproductions, North Fambridge, Essex
Printed and bound in Great Britain by
Butler & Tanner Ltd, Frome, Somerset

THE R.H.S ENCYCLOPEDIA OF PRACTICAL GARDENING

EDITOR-IN-CHIEF: CHRISTOPHER BRICKELL

Mitchell Beazley and the Royal Horticultural Society have joined forces to produce this practical, clear and fully comprehensive library of gardening.

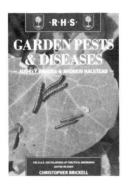

"hard to fault" *Stephen Lacey*

MITCHELL BEAZLEY